Students' Essential Guide to .NET

Tony Grimer

ELSEVIER
BUTTERWORTH
HEINEMANN

AMSTERDAM • BOSTON • HEIDELBERG • LONDON • NEW YORK • OXFORD
PARIS • SAN DIEGO • SAN FRANCISO • SINGAPORE SYDNEY • TOKYO

Elsevier Butterworth-Heinemann
Linacre House, Jordan Hill, Oxford OX2 8DP
200 Wheeler Road, Burlington MA 01803

First published 2004

British Library Cataloguing in Publication Data
A catalogue record for this book is available from the British Library

ISBN 0 7506 61313

For information on all Elsevier Butterworth-Heinemann publications
visit our website at http://books.elsevier.com

Trademarks
Many of the designations used by manufacturers and sellers to distinguish their
products are claimed as trademarks and regisitered trademarks. All product
names mentioned within this text remain trademarks of their respected owners.

Java and all Java-based marks are trademarks or registered trademarks of Sun
Microsystems Inc.

.NET and all .NET-based marks are trademarks or registered trademarks of
Microsoft Corporation.

©2000 is a trademark or registered trademark of Microsoft Corporation.

Every effort has been made to trace owners of copyright material. The author
would be glad to hear from any copyright owners for material produced in this
book whose copyright has unwittingly been infringed.

Typeset at Neuadd Bwll, Llanwrtyd Wells
Printed and bound in Great Britain

Contents

Contents

Preface

There are many excellent textbooks available dealing with various aspects of .NET. The range of topics covered includes the .NET supported languages Managed C++, C#, and VB.NET as well as those that deal with specific technologies including ADO.NET and ASP.NET.

All such textbooks have a specific goal, to identify the associated technology in the context of the .NET architecture and to provide suitable examples that allow the reader to investigate the technologies in specific instances.

All such textbooks are therefore excellent reference material for students studying modules that investigate specific topics such as operating systems and programming in the .NET environment. However, many of these books do not always put the material being investigated into the wider overall context of the .NET architecture.

Microsoft have always promoted the .NET Framework as just that, a solutions framework offering an architecture which scales from simple desktop applications to multi-tier enterprise level systems.

The key wording here is architecture, the .NET Framework is not one technology it is the integration of separate technologies to provide a prefabricated framework or environment providing a common foundation layer for any solution.

This concept of a foundation layer allows the technologies to interact with each other and equally with the end users. The discussion and investigation in this book is aimed specifically at looking behind the detail of how to use or how to program the technologies.

The premise is that to utilise the .NET Framework effectively requires a broad understanding of the overall concepts of the architecture itself. As an analogy, if a student is studying computer science you would expect them to be aware of the Von Neumann machine architecture, they would not have the specialist knowledge to be able to design and build the electronics of the architecture, but they should be aware of the goals and possibly the constraints this hardware architecture may impose on software design and development.

Carrying this analogy forward therefore, a computer science student studying Visual Basic programming in the .NET environment should be aware of the constraints that may be imposed by the .NET architecture.

The detail presented in specialist textbooks means that they normally run to greater than 500 pages with a price that is in proportion to size. In which case students can rarely afford to purchase more than one specialist text; it is therefore not always possible for students to comprehend how the use of a standardised framework impacts programming language independence in for instance an ASP.NET solution.

Solution-based architecture, whether .NET or any other technology, can be viewed as having a major impact on the computer science syllabus. Such architectures mean we should not simply be looking at teaching, systems analysis, systems design, programming or the principles of operating systems in isolation. The availability of these new prefabricated structures integrates key aspects of both system design and software engineering, requiring students to gain an appreciation that, in the correct environment, relatively simple designs can be scaled to large enterprise-level solutions with only minor modifications.

The important factor is that the student has a clear understanding of the structure of such frameworks and the constraints and advantages these frameworks impose on the design process.

I have felt for a considerable time that a book was required that looks at filling in this void, providing a general overview of solutions frameworks and in particular the .NET architecture. In this book we will be looking at the underlying programming language structure, the platform independence of the virtual machine abstraction that is called the .NET Framework, the relevance and usage of 'metadata', XML definitions and many other concepts that form the basis of solution-based architectures.

In taking the approach of looking at how the key technologies are built into the overall architecture will naturally lead to a better understanding of each of the technologies and their role in the framework.

Obviously, it will not be possible to cover all the key aspects of the .NET technologies and framework within a single reasonably sized book. Some of the more advanced topics would require a complete book to put them into context within the framework, the choice of material to include was not simple. I hope I will by the end of the book stimulate your interest sufficiently for you to do further research.

Approach to the subject

My aim from the start of this project has been to produce a text that is easy to read. Initially from the comments above, it may seem that the breadth of the material is too large; however, most of the underlying principles associated with the topics are straightforward. Following the description or theory on a particular topic, I have tried to support further investigations with simple games-based software development examples. I do stress simple games, this is not intended as a text to teach any aspect of games programming and the implementations are only skeleton solutions.

At Wolverhampton, we have for a number of years run a module looking at Personal Computer Operating Systems, within this module we have encouraged students to experiment with C/C++ development, based in the main on solving problems associated with simple games development (drawing a games board, moving aliens around the screen). This was to encourage the investigation of basic operating system principles in a traditional Windows programming environment. The results of using the approach have been very positive with some excellent student implementations of simple games such as Pac-man and Space Invaders.

Features

Throughout the book I have adopted the following chapter structure:

■ Each chapter has an identification of its objectives.

■ The examples within a chapter relate primarily to the topic under discussion. I have avoided looking in detail at the GUI of the examples, this would have detracted from the solutions and the prime objective of the examples is to demonstrate how a particular technology fits into the .NET Framework.
  ❑ Within the examples there are clear solution objectives identified.
  ❑ A brief requirement specification is presented.
  ❑ Specific design considerations related to the .NET framework are also discussed.

❑ Some suggestions for self-assessment extensions the reader could make to the example are given.

■ The summary at the end of each chapter briefly reviews the content, and as appropriate review questions or suggestions for further study are presented.

■ References in Appendix B offer a starting point for further study material on many of the topics.

Required background

This book could be used to complement a level one programming module, you may find it useful to have some background in the framework when learning to program for the first time, but it is not directly aimed at level one students. To be able to study topics associated with the .NET architecture it is assumed that a student will have some knowledge and skills within the following areas:

■ Computer organization or architecture

■ Introductory programming either procedural or object oriented

■ Protocols and networking.

To look at the more advanced topics at the end of the book related to ADO.NET, ASP.NET and web services we should add to this list:

■ Multi-user database technologies

■ Some appreciation of HTML and associated WWW material.

So more probably you are a level two or level three student studying advanced programming techniques, networking or operating systems.

Further reading

While this text broadly covers most of the fundamental aspects of the .NET solution-based architecture, because of the breadth of the topic, the detailed coverage of each of the technologies is naturally quite limited. Dependent on the individual students; needs, the references in the appendix and on the support web site are mainly to specific material looking at aspects of the technologies in far more depth.

Using the example

All the example code has been developed on an old and fairly low-powered portable. To run the examples you are going to need to have as a minimum the .NET Framework installed on a machine. Your choice of development environment is either the .NET SDK kit or the Microsoft Visual Studio .NET environment. The .NET SDK kit can be downloaded from http://www.microsoft.com. This provides a complete set of command line tools; you may find it a little difficult to use in places but every example in the book has been built and executed using the SDK tools. The alternative Microsoft Visual Studio .NET environment offers all the facilities you will require and of course has the visual programming interface making it ideal for the Windows Forms-based applications. The environment I used on my portable comprised:

- Windows 2000 professional.
  - ❏ With the Internet Information Server (IIS) loaded and installed as an option following the basic Windows 2000 setup.

- The Front Page extensions are required for IIS, if you want to debug server-side applications successfully.

- Initially I was going to use SQL server for the ADO.NET examples but since SQL server is difficult to set up and the portable was starting to run out of steam at this point, I have used instead 'Access 2000' as the RDMS in the examples.

- Visual Studio .NET professional was used for the initial development of all the examples. VS.NET includes all of the tools for the SDK kit; some of these are used in the chapter dealing with interoperability to demonstrate type library import and export. All the examples have also been built and run using only the SDK tools.

■ I used a full help installation with VS.NET since there are many thousands of pages of useful information especially on XML and component design.

Basic overview

The arrangement of the material in the book is fairly traditional: I start with a review of how the .NET Framework and its technologies have been derived based on the need for and the evolution of solution-based architectures.

Then I look at specific aspects of the underlying framework, with a view to identifying design goals that lead to language and platform independence. This allows the discussion to progress towards an investigation of the basic technologies that support language and platform independence.

The chapter covering the two programming languages C# and VB.NET is quite brief; this book is not intended to teach programming. The chapters on the Windows forms application development and .NET component development by their very nature require programming examples to illustrate the technique, these chapters provide further insight into both VB.NET and C#.

The overall theme of the examples in the book is to take some very simple ideas, dealing in the main with problems on simple games play, and produce .NET Framework solutions using various technologies. As an indication of the philosophy adopted in deriving the examples to use in the chapters. If we consider the problem of creating, shuffling, dealing and monitoring a hand of playing cards, within the book this is addressed by using an incremental approach.

■ The initial solution is a simple console application implemented in C# and VB.NET to demonstrate how the two languages create a similar overall solution when developed using the .NET prefabricated framework.

■ The solution then progresses using the .NET class libraries and the Windows forms environment to include GUI components.

■ This solution then evolves into a .NET component, which extends the original design and creates a .NET game of cards control.

■ Finally the .NET component is used as a template in web-based solutions including a web service offering the client the ability to engage in a multi-player game of 'Pontoon'.

I hope this approach of showing how such a simple initial concept can be taken forward in incremental steps identifies the flexibility of the .NET Framework. This approach also means that if you are already familiar with some of the earlier concepts, i.e. creation of a stand-alone application, you can if you wish skip forward to the later topics safe in the knowledge that if any aspect of the earlier topic requires review the earlier solution is reflected within the later sections.

.NET new versions

As the initial drafts of the material for this book were finalised, Microsoft announced the probable release date for .NET version 2.0 as early 2005. This obviously raises the question 'will the material in this book become obsolete?' The answer is most definitely no.

As the technologies of .NET are refined there will of course be new features added within the architecture. This can be seen by the fact that VS.NET 2002 had no direct support for mobile devices whereas VS.NET 2003 offers comprehensive support for the .NET compact framework. The new version of .NET 2.0 is another natural progression, the VS.NET to support this is codenamed 'Whidby' and it is the starting point for an environment to support the 64-bit operating system codenamed 'Longhorn'.

A possible analogy we can draw being that the original motorcar had a basic set of concepts and rules; internal combustion engine, wheels, brakes, etc. Modern motorcars still use these concepts but the manner of implementation is totally different. The underlying theory for these technologies has not changed, the basic principles remain the same today as they have always been.

The underlying technologies and architecture of .NET are not being changed. The aim of this book is to look at the derivation of these two topics not at the detail of what functionality is directly available now and how future releases may enhance specific class libraries etc.

Support material

The source files for the examples along with other reference material for this book are available at the support website:

■ http://essentialguideto.net

The author of this book has used his best efforts in preparing the support material for the book. These efforts include the development and testing of the example programs. However, the material at the support site is used at your own risk, the publishers and the author of this book cannot accept any liability for software malfunction or for any problem whatsoever caused by use of the software either from listings published in this book or downloading source files and other material from the above support website.

It should also be noted that due to printing restrictions on line lengths some of the code listings in this book may not be syntactically correct. However, any listings downloaded from the support site should be correct.

Acknowledgements

Throughout the early research for this book and during what seemed to be a very long slow process of drawing together the material for the chapters, thanks must go to many of my colleagues and students at Wolverhampton University. I must have been quite a bore, questioning their understanding of words and topics both within the scope of this text and in other fields.

I owe a very big thank you to Simon Steel of Leeds Metropolitan University, for his help in the later stages of the book; his comments on some of the chapters made me re-evaluate some of the key material.

I would like to dedicate this book to my wife Jan who has been supportive during the whole process and who has also patiently done a great deal of the initial draft proof reading even though she knows very little about computer science. Thanks must also go to Dave Hatter who encouraged me to start on the project and who in a few dark days during some very lean times on the first draft was very supportive via email.

1

An overview of .NET

Objective

Considered on its own the desktop PC is a very powerful environment, from its humble beginnings it has grown to be a tool that most modern businesses cannot do without.

However, technology has moved forward, the evolution of new design ideas has created an environment running on the PC that is far removed from the early single user applications that every one loved, on the humble basic desktop machine.

The development of these large modern applications has become very big business, but this growth has naturally brought with it the age-old problems associated with complex software design and development, among which are the initial cost of the implementation, the ongoing maintenance, and compatibility problems caused by the ever changing hardware and operating systems.

Some investigations carried out by leading business experts still maintain that the economic benefits of having a machine on every desk in a large organisation are yet to be satisfied or proven. Yet it is still the case that many large organisations spend thousands of pounds developing sophisticated systems that only solve very specific problems associated with their own business practices.

The advent of networked systems and more specifically the Internet has allowed single desktop machines to be linked to each other creating the potential for the design of even larger solutions. In addition, machines on a corporate or even a home network can be linked to non-PC devices such as palm tops, microwave ovens and even refrigerators. This interconnection usually comes at effectively no additional cost, as the extra hardware components in the specialist devices are usually available, this is because the integration cost of the hardware has reached the bottom of the cost/benefit curve. It can be, and will probably continue to be, argued that the potential for the transfer of information when such devices are linked together via the Internet has yet to be exploited fully.

Within the very brief history of the Internet, its overall usage has changed from simply browsing and transferring mainly text information, to the modern idiom that any data that can be encoded electronically can be accessed.

This change of emphasis and increase in information availability coupled with the lowering of the complexity for interconnection, guarantees for the foreseeable future a continual expansion of the Internet and the need to design and develop complex distributed systems. The initial hardware and connectivity costs associated with a connection to the Internet are low. Dependent on your own viewpoint, bandwidth may or may not require consideration, available bandwidth is always a very mute point.

A home user on a 56 Kbit modem tends to argue that 56 Kbits is far too slow for effective surfing but equally a graphics designer with a 100 Mbit link when working on a complex problem puts forward a similar argument.

However, given all these points and considering all the arguments, the only conclusion that can be drawn is that the Internet user population is increasing and will probably continue to increase. This fact alone leads to the overwhelming conclusion that to satisfy this new user population, new cost-effective and reliable software development techniques will be required for the foreseeable future.

The common structure

Analysis of the development cost for a particular application always leads to the same conclusion; it is more expensive to develop for a distributed environment such as the Internet, than for a stand-alone desktop machine. The problem is that distributed applications although trying to create a similar solution to the real world problem using the same basic algorithms (the actual problem generally will not have changed between a stand-alone and a distributed system) has other resource constraints that need to be considered.

New software development techniques are proposed quite regularly. The science of software engineering is quite turbulent as new concepts or techniques are proposed, such new ideas then lead to so-called new technologies; sometimes these new technologies lead to new techniques while at other times they are simply absorbed incrementally into existing methodologies.

At other times the changes proposed are too radical and lead to a total rethink and re-evaluation of the fundamental nature of the software development problem under consideration. This appears to be the path that .NET is following.

Welcome to the world of .NET

What you are about to embark on is a learning experience like no other. Unlike many books with .NET in the title we are not simply going to look at the details of programming within the .NET environment.

The overall objective of this book is to answer the question:

**As a student what do I need to understand
about the .NET architecture?**

Obviously there are other books written that look at .NET in this manner, not simply as a vehicle to support the programming languages such as VB.NET but as a total environment. Unfortunately, most of these other books assume the reader has the previously acquired skills and knowledge of commercial software development, allowing them to draw upon experience and make informed judgements on the suitability of .NET For a specific task.

Students of course do not have this background; the aim of this book is therefore to explain the technologies used within the .NET environment and the relevance of these to modern software engineering techniques. Each chapter of this book will investigate specific technologies encompassed within the overall .NET architecture and place these into context.

Basic introductory texts on software engineering topics have little interest to a student without real world examples. In this book the aim is to go beyond the traditional approach of using trivial solutions to emphasise a particular topic:

■ A program to print out the times tables, to investigate programming language loop control.

The examples presented within this book identify and solve some of the fundamental requirements of simple games development. It must be pointed out that this book is not a games programming text, the examples, although solving non-trivial problems are not constructed in such a manner that by the end of the book you are a games programmer. Each example looks at some aspect of the .NET architecture and places it into the overall context.

In the later chapters of the book ASP.NET and web services are investigated, when we look at the associated examples they do become more comprehensive but again they only illustrate technologies. When looking at technologies such as ASP.NET and web services they have many complex features and wide-ranging implications on the future direction of distributed solutions design.

In these later chapters I could have taken the approach of explaining the impact on for instance e-commerce solutions and the role of such technologies in shaping e-commerce in the future. However, it is rarely possible for a student to fully investigate an e-commerce distributed example, such examples require far more physical resources than a student will have available. To try to let you the student experiment with such technologies I have chosen to use instead a case study on a multi-player game. The case study presented in the final chapter requires the use of some of the more advanced topics, it has been designed to use previously developed examples of .NET components for the card game 'Pontoon'. The result is an outlined design of a fully multi-tiered enterprise-level solution.

Many modern books investigating software development environments, programming languages, and operating systems use the classic approach of first selecting a suitable programming language to use throughout the book. The selected language is then explained in terms of its structure and semantics, this is followed by an overview of the operating system structure and then specific topics are introduced.

Such books, once the overall theoretical aspects have been covered, investigate the integration of operating system features into system-level or application-level development. This overall structure aims to promote an understanding of the applications programmers interface (API) and programming considerations first, followed by suitable examples of applying such technologies to the solution of various real world problems.

Obviously this book must cover the same ground; however, rather than starting with any theory I have chosen to start with a question.

What is .NET?

My reason for taking this as the starting point is quite simple. While investigating the answer to the question, the reader should be able to appreciate how the .NET architecture creates a common framework on which developers can build system solutions.

Once the rational for this common framework has been established, each of the various technologies that come under the umbrella title of .NET can be more fully investigated and these technologies positioned into the common framework architecture. Once we have this stable structure in which technologies can coexist our investigation can progress towards the interaction between technologies. Finally this will highlight the key aspect of an architecture such as .NET, its ability to provide a solutions platform spanning from a simple application on a desktop machine, to a distributed multi-tier system running across the Internet.

Solutions platforms and frameworks

Solutions frameworks should offer the most cost effective alternative to the development of a particular application. Any solutions framework should offer a prefabricated structure onto which a particular real world application can be built.

The idea of a solution framework is not new; software engineering has strived to develop reusable common base code techniques, enabling the simplification of the design and implementation of new applications for many years.

Probably the most obvious example is 'object orientation'. Many books have been written that promote the ideals; however, one phrase I heard a number of years ago that always sticks in my memory is 'by using "OO" techniques we are building islands of software in an ocean where no bridges or tunnels are yet planned to be built'.

The true goals of 'OO' technology have never actually happened. The three basic premises for 'OO' – encapsulation, inheritance and polymorphism – are of course the foundation for most software development today. However, the question that a new development needs to address is how much of the implementation in this development would be 'new' against how much would come from 'reuse' of existing 'OO' designs?

In a total in-house situation where the reuse code belonged to the company, then we would expect a high reuse percentage. However, if the reuse code was from a third party source, the accuracy of the design documentation required is really quite staggering, meaning that in many cases it is cheaper to develop new code than it is to experiment with 'reuse' proven code that is badly documented.

However, in both scenarios any reuse will require some 'glue code' to make the objects talk to each other. If on the other hand such objects conform to some standard framework specification then the amount of 'glue code' reduces significantly.

Componentware concepts

The obvious answer to our problem is to adopt an implementation approach that uses a standard object model. Use of a standard design model ensures compatibility and removes the uncertainty regarding integrating third party supplied reusable code into any new application. Using such a model offers the potential for hundreds, perhaps thousands, of third party componentware objects available for evaluation when any new software development is being considered. New applications can be built by integrating componentware objects into the final solution and since these third party supplied componentware objects have been fully designed, developed and tested for conformity to a standard model, this instils a high overall confidence factor in the final solution.

Various standard models for componentware objects have been developed; in fact we will be investigating the interoperability problems they pose in the .NET Framework in a later chapter. Componentware models such as COM (Common Object Model), allow specific software functionality to be packaged and reused in a relatively simple manner. If you are familiar with the Visual Basic 5 or 6 development system, then you may have used the option to import a third party ActiveX control into the application under development. The ActiveX control model is in fact a derivation of basic COM, you only need to search the Internet to realise that you can find ActiveX controls that perform virtually every function you could ever imagine you might need in a Visual Basic program.

However, as with any seemingly perfect solution to a problem, there have been major drawbacks to the currently used componentware models. Each has worked within the limitations originally specified. In the Microsoft world, OLE (Object Linking and Embedding) led to the development of COM; this model was expanded to encompass DCOM and COM+, but the problem with these models is that they work well on the Microsoft operating system platform but they need a great deal of persuasion in terms of man hours of additional coding to function on other operating systems.

The CORBA (Common Object Request Brokerage) initiative attempts to eliminate such platform dependence using similar object modelling techniques to COM. However, this was a joint venture by a number of commercial software developers and obviously such a venture will always suffer from commercial pressures and the withholding of information from the public domain, these factors alone make it very unlikely that such a model can ever become truly internationally agreed and supported.

Does the .NET Framework kill the concepts of componentware?

The answer is most definitely no, in fact .NET enhances the whole concept of a componentware model; the design of the .NET Framework reviews the overall structure of the previous componentware models and adds to it:

- The realisation of the ideal of software development language independence.

- Probably more importantly as it evolves, the .NET Framework should also offer operating system and hardware platform independence as well.

Such a framework that is now development language and platform independent could form the basis of truly scalable solutions architectures, from a palm top machine to a full multi-tiered distributed solution.

In this brief review of componentware solutions frameworks, I have avoided any of the more proprietary ideas created by some manufacturers; these involved development wizards, foundation class libraries and so-called visual objects libraries. Each of these offered techniques aimed at selling specific development environments; any form of interoperability from one to another is very difficult to achieve and the scalability of the solutions produced is very limited. The most obvious omission is the Java Virtual Machine; we will in fact be looking at the JVM in Chapter 2.

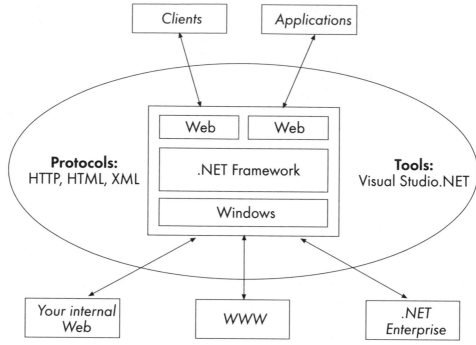

Figure 1.1   *A possible answer to 'What is .NET?'*

What is .NET?

In Figure 1.1 we can see that the .NET Framework plays a central role in the overall .NET architecture. The framework coupled with the foundation classes and the key technologies allow the development of solutions that range from a simple desktop application through to web enabled distributed applications.

However, have we answered the fundamental question 'What is .NET?' Indirectly we probably have, Figure 1.1 shows that .NET covers aspects of many topics: programming language derivation operating system independence, application design methodology and large-scale distributed system solutions. The .NET architecture allows a new and exciting updated approach to creating all kinds of applications in the Windows environment. In order to appreciate how this is possible we are going to need to identify the key component parts, review how these have either been designed to fit into the overall architecture or how older established technologies have been revised to satisfy the need for the new architecture.

Probably the most visible of the technologies within the .NET architecture are the web-based services and web-based applications.

This is simply because of the name the .NET Framework. In most people's minds the word .NET relates to the Internet and the World Wide Web (WWW), but in order to appreciate the significance of these web-based features we will need to gain an understanding of the underlying framework and development methodologies intrinsically built into the whole architecture.

This book is structured to allow the reader to gain this level of knowledge, allowing the reader to comprehend the full impact of web services and web-based distributed applications. The first chapters will review some of the theoretical aspects that were considered during the requirement analysis for an environment and the impact this analysis had on the overall design of the architecture including the derivation of the new programming language C#. (Pronounced C sharp as in the musical note). The investigation will then proceed to the more specialist areas; the modifications of the information services available using ADO.NET (access to relational database management systems) and finally look at ASP.NET (Active Server Pages), the .NET Framework version of ASP technology.

If we start with Figure 1.2 and Table 1.1 we can gain an understanding of the component parts of the .NET architecture. To understand .NET architecture requires a basic understanding of all of these technologies. In the remainder of this chapter we will overview each one leading to the more detailed investigation of specific topics in subsequent chapters.

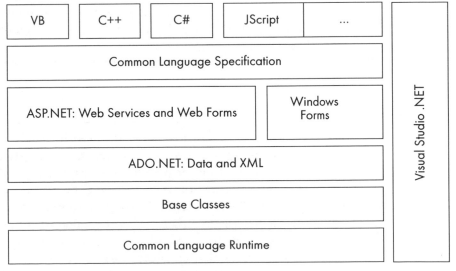

Figure 1.2   The .NET components

Table 1.1   *The component parts of .NET*

Item	Contains
The .NET Framework	The CLR (Common Language Runtime) The .NET Framework Class Library
ASP.NET	Part of the Class Library dealing with Active Server Pages and derived from the older ASP technology
ADO.NET	New and completely revised from the older ActiveX Controls (ADO) techniques to interface information services such as RDMS
.NET SDK & Visual Studio .NET	Support for software development within the .NET Framework VB.NET – New generation of Visual Basic specifically for the .NET environment C# .NET – Totally new language designed specifically for .NET C++ .NET – enhanced C++ allowing migration of C++ applications into the .NET architecture
My Services	This topic is beyond the scope of this introductory book, but you should be aware that these services allow personal information to be stored and recovered by other web services in a highly controlled manner
Enterprise Services	Another advanced topic that is beyond the scope of this introductory book. Includes the integration of B2B servers such as Exchange Server within the overall .NET architecture. Offering the potential for the design of very large scalable enterprise solutions.

The web services

We have already identified that the World Wide Web is radically changing the way people access information, buy products etc. It is usual for people to interact with the WWW using a graphical user interface; it could be argued that the success of the WWW today is directly attributable to the GUI. However, we must be realistic, GUI will probably not drive the WWW into its next major phase of expansion. It is quite difficult to perceive that all future distributed system designs will utilise the WWW browser interface, common today. For instance a business to business (B2B) system connecting two dissimilar computer systems using the Internet as the transport medium requires programmatic access to applications on each system; it just is not feasible to have a person sitting at a terminal at each end.

Such a requirement makes it impossible to limit WWW access to using the HTTP protocol (discussed in Chapter 10) and the information encoded and transferred using the WWW to be limited by such technologies as HTML (discussed in Chapter 10), rather we will need to encode information in a machine readable form such as XML (discussed in Chapter 9). In other words, the applications' functions are accessed programmatically as web services.

To be able to use a web service the client application must first be able to find it on the WWW and then interrogate the service to determine how to use it. To find the service we have to look to the UDDI (Universal Description, Discovery and Integration) standard. This allows clients to browse and locate web services from a central database. Once found the service must be able to describe its functionality, this is accomplished using the WSDL (Web Service Descriptive Language). In order to avoid any additional overheads the information from a UDDI source and the WSDL description is sent via SOAP protocol packets in XML formatted documents. The current specification for UDDI version 3 can be found at http://uddi.org/pubs/uddi-v3.0.1-20031014.htm In a later chapter we will investigate web services in far more detail.

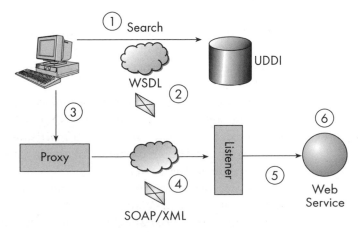

Figure 1.3   The web service process (derived from a Microsoft diagram on MSDN)

As an introduction Figure 1.3 identifies a typical client web service interaction.

1   **Discovery** – Search UDDI site(s) for the proper web service.

2   **Description** – A description of the selected web service is returned to the client application as a Web Services Description Language (WSDL) file.

3   **Proxy creation** – A local proxy to the remote service is created.

4   **Soap Message Creation** – A SOAP/XML message is created and sent to the URL specified in the WSDL file.

5   **Listener** – A Soap listener at the host site receives the call and interprets it for the web service.

6   **The web service** performs its function, and returns the result to the client, via the listener and the proxy.

The .NET Framework

Having identified the overall components of the .NET architecture in Figure 1.2 we can return to the question of a solutions framework. Within the previous section we saw that the HTTP protocol and the SOAP standard are vital components in offering a web service.

The software requirements for a web service application to be HTTP aware and have the ability to transfer information using SOAP can be fully satisfied if this functionality is part of a prefabricated software structure onto which a particular requirement is built. Such is the nature of the .NET Framework, it provides a common structure offering not only the prefabricated base structure for all applications but also specialist technologies.

In the most recent past, developers of Windows applications, both stand-alone and within the DNA (Distributed Network Architecture), have had to rely on a multitude of development technologies that became flavour of the month and then were revised to something better.

Currently probably the most commonly used programming languages have been Visual Basic for the more commercial applications and Visual C/C++ for the more technical applications. Hundreds of thousands of applications have

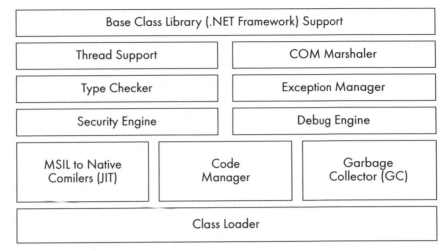

Base Class Library (.NET Framework) Support	
Thread Support	COM Marshaler
Type Checker	Exception Manager
Security Engine	Debug Engine

MSIL to Native Comilers (JIT)	Code Manager	Garbage Collector (GC)

Class Loader

Figure 1.4   *The .NET Framework structure*

been developed using these languages and the associated technologies and many are still used today.

The .NET Framework is a major move away from the traditional software development techniques that have not significantly changed in decades. The framework encompasses changes that should they all be a success will certainly have a significant impact on the development of distributed solutions, with a knock-on effect to the development of stand-alone desktop applications.

Although the .NET architecture contains many very important changes to the overall philosophy of software design and development, when it comes to actual implementation of a solution, the most important aspect that needs to be understood is the framework definition itself.

.NET componentware

By its very name .NET, the most startling changes in the design and development of software are reserved for people developing in the distributed systems market. In a previous section we have identified that componentware is probably the major contributory factor to cost reduction on large system development. The technology of the COM model revolutionised the development of component functionality but as indicated it does have major drawbacks. The overall integration of this componentware technology into the Windows environment was incomplete, it required additional effort to fully integrate the components when developing a distributed system.

In some cases it has been sited that having the ability to develop a complete solution using a variety of programming languages would be an advantage. Key technical aspects of the implementation could be developed in one programming language while others, probably in the area of the graphical user interface in a different language. Prior to the .NET Framework, such an option although theoretically possible presented a huge technical problem and hence was rarely exploited. The major stumbling block was making data available from one part of the application to another.

Another major hurdle to having flexibility in the development language selection stems from the fact that programming languages accessed operating system functionality in many different ways. For instance, C/C++ application makes direct calls to the operating system through the Win32 interface (the Win32 interface was designed specifically for C/C++ calling conventions), whilst on the other hand Visual Basic typically makes such calls indirectly through a run-time library.

With such significant incompatibilities attempting such a cross language development it is very challenging for a development team; the extra work involved in the past has usually outweighed any potential development benefits. From this we can produce a very concise definition of the .NET Framework.

An environment in which there is a common transparent foundation layer through which any programming language can access either data or operating system functionality.

We can identify two key components within the framework.

1   A layer called the Common Language Runtime (CLR), which offers the major services that allow a .NET application to execute.

2   The .NET base class library which is a large set of classes and types that can be used freely in any supported language within an application running in the CLR.

These two components and the knowledge that the base class library offers such a wealth of classes available to any application irrespective of the implementation language removes the previous problems of componentware incompatibility forever.

The .NET class library

The class library categorises the functionally available to any application into five important sections.

- ASP.NET – The new generation of support for Active Server Pages. This allows the construction of web accessible applications with the major additional component being the web services interface.

- ADO.NET – The new generation of Data Access Objects, replacing the older ActiveX controls, these new objects offer total freedom to the developer to store, update and retrieve information from database systems.

- Windows Forms – A standard set of building blocks for the GUI aspects of any application. You can think of these as the unbundling of the GUI design function previously found only in Visual Basic and making the functionality available for all .NET Framework supported languages.

- Web Forms – These building blocks extend the Windows Forms components into the WWW arena. Once again they allow the simple development of the GUI for web-based applications and of course web services. They also seamlessly integrate with the functionality of ASP.NET making a complex distributed system design much less difficult.

- Interoperability and Enterprise – These classes allow .NET applications to make use of older technologies such as COM and COM+ services allowing options such as transactions and object pooling.

The .NET class library contains far more than these highlighted items. In Chapter 3 we will look more extensively at some of the classes available, to identify the overall organisation and structure of the library.

My Services

Another import technology within the .NET architecture is the My Services technology. It is far beyond the scope of this essential guide to .NET to look at the .NET My Services in any detail. My Services is a group of .NET technologies created using web services. In essence it is a mechanism that allows users to store as much, or as little, of their private or personnel details on a web server. Access to this information being controlled by security protocols, the Microsoft implementation most commonly seen being '.NET Passport' used to authenticate users on the WWW at various web sites.

There are obviously huge issues to consider when talking about storage of personal information on a web server on the Internet. The .NET architecture has within both the CLR and the class library, prefabricated solutions to assist with such security issues. In this introductory text my aim is to make you aware of the technology. The ethical, moral and security issues need a debate elsewhere.

Enterprise services and servers

The final piece in the .NET architecture jigsaw is the Enterprise Services and Servers. Once again this topic is far beyond the scope of this introductory text. It is worth noting that during .NET initial release the question was asked, 'Why is .NET Enterprise Services and Servers actually part of .NET?'

The reason for inclusion is clear, many of the Enterprise Servers had been recently rewritten in a distributed form. By making them integrate directly into the framework and utilising the prefabricated nature of the framework these powerful server products are now part of the foundation layer for any distributed systems. There are now more than eight Enterprise Servers in the family including Exchange and SQL; these two alone clearly show the integration potential. A book aimed as an essential guide to students cannot hope to look at enterprise-level applications that require such servers.

Possibly in the future someone will write a student guide looking at how to make use of the .NET Framework in conjunction with an enterprise-level solution.

Summary

There is a great deal to absorb the first time you are faced with the .NET architecture. If you have previously studied or read a book on VB.NET or C# .NET you may have felt that all there is to .NET is an object-oriented language environment, with a comprehensive set of class libraries (far more than any one person could ever fully memorise), and a very clever common run-time system that seems to be the same no matter what the application.

These are all very valid observations but I am afraid you have only just scratched at the surface. One analogy I read likened the changes to software engineering brought about by the release of .NET to an earthquake. Whether this Microsoft solutions architecture called '.NET' is a success long term or whether the wind of change will take componentware-based solutions in another direction, the debate on the right mechanisms and methodologies for software development will continue to run.

The .NET architecture and its basic framework components have opened yet another thread to the debate on the future of both software development and operating system structure. Some people will feel we are not moving forward, certain technical aspects of the .NET Framework reflect back to ideas from the late 1980s. The C# language has been called in the press Java without SUN.

My objective in this chapter was to identify the key components in the .NET architecture and then to look for the lowest common denominator within the technologies leading to a basic definition for the .NET Framework. I hope you feel I have met these and that you can now progress into the subsequent chapters in the knowledge that the .NET Framework can be described as 'an environment in which there is a common transparent foundation layer through which any programming language can access either data or operating system functionality'.

The remainder of this book is aimed at giving you some technical feel for the technologies involved whether your interest is software development, web-based applications and services or simply a more general interest in componentware models.

The examples are presented in both C# and VB.NET, the extracts in the text will be in one or other of the languages, the source files of the examples available on the support web site offer the opportunity to compare the sample implementations since both options are available.

Review questions

1 Investigate and compare the Common Object Model (COM) with CORBA. What in your opinion are the strengths and weaknesses of each?

2 HTTP and SOAP are fully defined by a document called an RFC. What is an RFC?

3 If you have Visual Studio .NET installed, take a look at the help topics on the class libraries and identify how many top-level library entries exist for the system namespace.

2 The Common Language Runtime

Objective

In the previous chapter we identified that the .NET Framework comprises two key elements:

- The Common Language Runtime (CLR)

- The .NET base class library.

These two main components form the basis of the .NET architecture and an understanding of the design of each will greatly enhance your understanding of the overall philosophy of .NET. Within this chapter we will be looking at the derivation of the CLR, such a discussion cannot be attempted without reviewing:

- The Common Type System (CTS) and its influence on the design of the CLR

- The change of emphasis on programming language design for both VB.NET and C#.

Introduction

As a starting point for our initial look at the CLR we can focus on one simple basic assumption that:

any piece of application software has the purpose of solving a real world problem.

From such an assumption we have to assume that some form of algorithmic approach is possible to solve a given problem and

Figure 2.1   *The simplest application model*

that we can derive a very simplistic graphical representation of the solution.

The diagram in Figure 2.1 identifies that by combining just three elements we can form an algorithmic solution. The solution to any problem begins by having some means of collecting suitable input, the actual mechanism for the collection is unimportant, and the form of that data can also be ignored for the moment. Once collected the input data is passed to the algorithmic process itself; this will have been derived from the real world problem and will manipulate the data in a given manner. The degree of manipulation is dependant on the problem itself. Once such manipulation is completed, the result will need to be produced and delivered to the output; again the mechanism and the form of the data at this stage is unimportant.

Most algorithmic solutions to even the most complex real world problems can be reduced to these three steps. In practice of course the problem is generally decomposed, and reduced into smaller sub-problems; all of these smaller solutions are recombined to allow the actual final result to emerge. Using Figure 2.1 to illustrate such decomposition requires that we view the boxes marked input and output in a slightly different manner. In a large problem once the decomposition of the solution has been completed the output from one sub-solution will form the input to another.

Although Figure 2.1 looks simple, and it does identify the basic structure of an algorithmic solution to a problem, it suffers from a major flaw. It does not highlight the fact that to be effective the data input and output from the process must be in some standard form.

Hardware model

The Von Neumann architecture, the most commonly used generalisation of the physical implementation of a computer system, identifies that the binary patterns stored in the memory represent both the data to be manipulated and the program steps to be used for such manipulations.

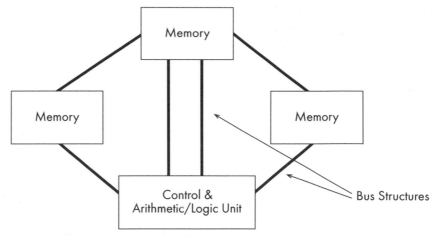

Figure 2.2   *A view of the stored program model*

From Figure 2.2 we can identify the basic process model from Figure 2.1 but in this case we have the data transferred by an internal processor bus structure.

This internal bus structure enables the transfer of information in the architecture between any of the relevant items. The Von Neumann architecture model also makes some key assumptions:

■ The Instruction format is standardised.

■ The Data format is standardised.

■ The Instructions run sequentially in Memory.

■ The Control unit maintains a position indicator of the next instruction to execute.

The most important of these in the context of the CLR is the standardisation of the data format. This standardisation must exist not only within the process itself but also to the data received from the input devices and the data transmitted to the output devices.

The Von Neumann assumptions create some additional questions when the conceptual model is extended to encompass an operating system/hardware platform combination. How, when a real world problem has been translated to an algorithmic solution, is it possible to obtain the required input and then display the relevant output?

Run-time support libraries

In general terms the answer lies in a run-time support package. Such packages offer pre-written library software that is operating system and platform dependent. The software in the libraries has the functionality to read input from a keyboard or display output to a screen while maintaining a common data format when the data is being manipulated by the actual application.

These run-time support packages are supplied by the programming languages' development environments, so if you are implementing a 'C' program it will need to access the 'C' run-time libraries to perform any I/O functionality.

It therefore becomes vital that software developers are aware of the format and limitations of the data manipulation available within such run-time support libraries. A problem arises when developers attempt to use more than one programming language within a particular system.

Adding this ability to utilise a particular run-time support library allows our simple process diagram without modification to represent the final application. The support for data manipulation and I/O on a particular programming language is not the only purpose of a run-time support library. Modern operating systems offer a variety of services to the application, a comprehensive file system (allowing creation, updating and deletion of structured information), process management (allocation of resources etc.) and of course memory management allowing the application to dynamically create and destroy storage areas for data as required. The interface to the particular operating system services is therefore another key aspect of the run-time library.

Source code portability

Source code portability is a major goal of any modern high-level programming language; the objective is to allow any application source-file to be compiled and built on any platform. Such a requirement means that a run-time library package must be available for every version of a particular high-level language compiler and these must have, as a minimum, support for:

■ Specific programming language syntax and semantics dependence

■ Programmatic access to operating system services.

Programming language syntax

Programming languages express the same functionality in different ways. Suppose we want to display on the output device a string:

Hello the results have been calculated

followed by a carriage return and a line feed.

■ In the 'C' programming language we could find source of the form:

```
printf ("Hello the results have been calculated /r/n");
```

■ In Visual Basic on the other hand we might find the source:

```
print "Hello the results have been calculated"
```

Although it could argue that the language syntax rules are a function of the compilation process, to perform the above operation both the 'C' and Visual Basic programs will require some run-time support library function that is able to actually display the data on the output device.

Programmatic access to operating system services

An application may require that a file on the disk storage be opened for read access. This required functionality is always programming language/operating system specific.

■ In the 'C' programming language we could find source of the form:

```
stream = fopen( "data.text", "r" );
```

In Visual Basic on the other hand we might find the source:

```
Open "data.text" for input as file #1
```

Again there are syntax differences, but in addition, in this case, the run-time support will need to convert the request for the file 'data.txt' to be opened in a read only manner and make the resultant data retrieved available to the application. This will involve a translation via the run-time support to a suitable API (Application Programming Interface), call to the underlying file system built into the specific operating system.

The standard run-time support package

We can generalise the definition of a run time support library package as:

a set of library functions that allow applications written in a programming language to interact with the operating system services.

Modern high-level programming languages as we have already noted, promote source code portability of applications across operating systems and hardware platforms as a major advantage for use.

Although in essence this is obviously correct, such a statement must be treated with a little scepticism. Any application designed and implemented in a high-level language theoretically has no inbuilt dependence on the hardware platform or operating system on which it will be executed.

There is an implied dependence that suitable and compatible run-time support libraries are available for the different operating system/hardware platforms. This dependence puts a great deal of emphasis on the high-level language compiler suppliers to ensure that high-level languages are mapped to all modern operating systems, and each of the run-time support packages offers 100% compatibility. Having identified the role of the run time support library we can turn our attention to software development models.

The traditional software development model

Figure 2.3 models a traditional software development scenario and shows where the platform-dependent run-time support enters the process. The platform-specific run-time is linked with the object code during the latter stages of the development cycle. The final executable created is 100% specific to just one operating system/hardware platform combination (it can be argued that for operating systems such as Windows, this is not strictly true since many applications will execute across a broad spectrum of Windows variants).

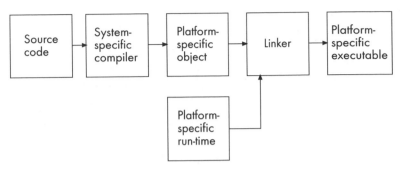

Figure 2.3 *The classic software development model*

An alternative model

In order to remove the platform and operating system specifics from any high-level language run-time environment would require the definition of an unambiguous generalised execution model. Such a model needs to be specifically designed to support the execution of applications, without reference to any operating system platform.

The design of such an environment must also ensure that the Application Programming Interface (API) is generalised. With such a design model, application software interacts with the execution environment only; the interaction with the underlying operating system platform is transparent.

Using this basic definition for the development of an execution model, it becomes possible to generate the programming language and platform independent specification for the CLR. Such a specification for the execution environment is not unique to the .NET architecture. One of the other most common modern run-time environments is the JVM, (Java Virtual Machine), specified by Sun Microsystems. An alternative definition for the .NET Framework could be the .NET virtual machine.

Virtual machines

Using the term Virtual Machine (VM) in this context can be very confusing. To a student studying operating system design and architecture the term VM has a subtly different meaning. The operating system VM solution provides each application with a unique environment; this environment simulates the physical resources, and provides an executing application with apparent unrestricted access to the system-wide resources.

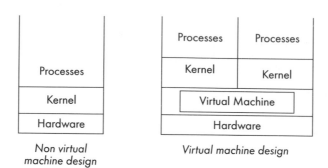

Non virtual
machine design

Virtual machine design

Figure 2.4   *The traditional virtual machine concept*

In order to provide this type of VM structure in a modern operating system a Virtual Machine Manager (VMM) process is required; this is a system-level process that controls and schedules how the physical resources are allocated between the various virtual machines. We can identify that in this context the term virtual machine produces a solution in which the application executes in an environment that is comparable in form and function with the underlying native operating system. The model of a traditional VM in Figure 2.4 must not be confused with the model used within the JVM or the .NET Framework. In the JVM and the .NET Framework the virtual machine defines an environment for the execution of an application that is not comparable in form and function to the underlying native operating system.

This alternative type of VM can be considered as using an emulation of some other system structure and is sometimes identified as a VME (Virtual Machine Emulator). Other examples of VMEs are found in the overall architecture of Windows 2000. Figure 2.5 shows how Windows 2000 has a number of VMEs one of which is the 'Unix' VM, allowing 'Unix' applications to seamlessly execute in the native Windows environment.

The unambiguous general environment

In order to achieve the design goal for the .NET Framework and in particular the CLR component the design of the VME must offer:

■ Platform independence for the run-time support package

■ Application programming language independence.

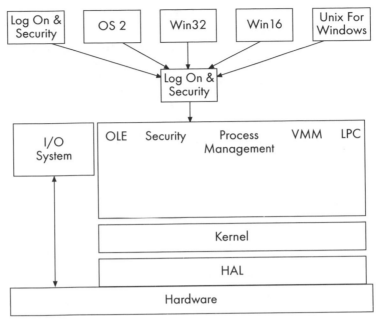

Figure 2.5
The Win32 basic operating system components

In order to meet these goals we must first ensure that the VME promotes an unambiguous generalised environment. Using a VME environment removes many of the previously identified constraints that have influenced the specification of programming language and their run-time support needs:

■ Syntax and semantics of instructions

■ Runtime support platform dependence

■ Run-time support operating system dependence.

Virtual machine environments also have the benefit of eliminating any considerations of the physical characteristics of the operating system and hardware platforms. It is possible for the architecture of the VM to be deriveded from any traditional design models both physical or conceptual, since a virtual machine is an emulation of the platform and any restrictions normally associated with such architectures are removed.

The .NET Framework is a generalised VM and embodies the Common Language Run-time (CLR) which offers this platform/language independence. In the remainder of this chapter we will investigate how the design of the .NET Framework was selected.

With an understanding of this specific VM design our ability to review the structure of the .NET architecture will be greatly enhanced and place into context the later investigations of the technologies that are encapsulated within the whole .NET architecture.

The design of the .NET Framework VM

What is an abstraction?

To demonstrate the concept of creating an abstract solution let us consider a real world example. How do we communicate with another person? The basic process for communication is:

1 Formulating the content of the message

2 Transmitting the message

3 Interpretation of the message by the recipient.

Taking as our required abstraction a mechanism for communicating messages over a long distance, when written communication was not feasible. History shows the use of semaphore flags or in the case of Native American Indians a mirror reflecting sunlight as methods that were successfully employed. Two people carried out the process, one as a transmitter and one as the receiver (in fact multiple receivers were possible provided they could all see the person transmitting). These two people could be quite a distance from each other, the only system constraint was they had clear line of sight. The rules within this abstraction were to define a simple set of flag shapes to represent letters or words. The process required the translation of the written words by one party, the flag was waved in sequence and at the receiving end another person watched the flag sequence, and wrote down the message.

Although this is an abstraction of a communications problem it certainly is not unambiguous, it relies on the sender and receiver having the same perception of flag shapes (if the rule said right arm at 90 degrees do both parties 100% agree how this shape should appear). Such a process relied on human perception of the validity of the letters and words in the message.

Rules to make an unambiguous abstraction

To design our .NET Framework VM one on the kcy factors must be that its execution rules make it 100% unambiguous. The key factors that need to be considered for unambiguous operation are:

■ Simple set of unique rules – equates to a limited set of operations.

■ Simple data – equates to precise definition for data types.

The first of these factors identifies that if we have a complex set of rules, there is a higher possibility of ambiguity. We must also ensure that we do not define a large set of even simple rules since the more rules we have the greater the chance of one rule partially conflicting with another and resulting in an ambiguity.

The second factor to consider is the definition of data types and formats, we will in the next sections be looking closely at the Common Type System.

The VM design chosen

The .NET Framework VM is defined as a stack-oriented execution engine. A stack-oriented execution design model is relatively simple to understand. In Figure 2.6 we see that the sequence of events to perform a simple addition of two values is:

■ Load the two values (operands) onto the stack

■ Load the request to perform an operation (operator) onto the stack

■ Request execution of the operation

■ On completion the result is left on the top of the stack and the operands and operators have been removed from the stack.

The form of defining the operation to perform is generally termed Reverse Polish Notation and in the 1970s was quite common on some calculators.

Stack before execution of
Result = Value 1 + Value 2

Stack after execution of
Result = Value 1 + Value 2

Figure 2.6   *A typical operation on a stack-oriented execution engine*

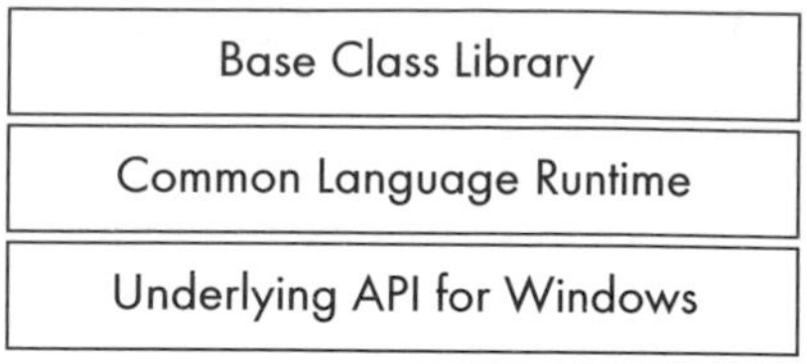

```
┌─────────────────────────────────────┐
│          Base Class Library          │
├─────────────────────────────────────┤
│        Common Language Runtime        │
├─────────────────────────────────────┤
│       Underlying API for Windows      │
└─────────────────────────────────────┘
```

Figure 2.7   *The bare minimum for a solutions framework*

This stack-oriented execution engine clearly defines function, add to this the use of the Reverse Polish data presentation technique, and we have defined a limit to possible data manipulation at each execution step. The .NET VM design further reduces the possibility of ambiguity by limiting the number of operations the engine is capable of performing. In a later section we will briefly review a subset of the operations available.

Obviously there has to be a further layer in the CLR (the .NET VM) itself, since once any application is executing within this engine, a mechanism has to exist to perform a translation to the underlying native code of the operating system and hardware platform. In Figure 2.7 we have identified the three basic components of the .NET VM design.

■ The CLR layer represents the main stack-oriented execution engine

■ The layer below the CLR interfaces with the underlying operating system and hardware platform

■ The layer above is the base set of class libraries that support the overall execution of any application.

Referring back to our generalised requirement, the overall .NET Framework specification called for the ability of the CLR to execute code developed in any compliant language, thereby offering full programming language independence.

This final feature of the .NET Framework offers an environment for application execution that has:

■ Standard Data Structure

■ Platform Independence

■ Operating System Independence

■ Programming Language Independence.

To design application language independence into the framework comes at a cost! The ability of the CLR to execute an application developed using any compliant language required some radical re-evaluation of the issues that need to be considered on any programming languages design.

The history of programming language design can be traced from its humble beginnings, when programming languages were no more than a human readable form of machine code, through to modern, sophisticated third and fourth generation languages that give the user the ability to create large complex solutions. Modern high-level programming languages can be viewed as a tool that allows developers the ability to specify real world problems in such a manner that the detail of the computer architecture or physical resources of the final system is of no consequence.

Modern programming language design has developed from the philosophy that any programming language fundamentally defines a set of syntax and semantics to manipulate data.

What is programming language syntax?

Grammatical syntax defines rules associated with expressing ideas in a consistent manner. Programming language syntax follows this general idea using a specific set of rules associated with a particular language:

```
int a,b;        // define the variables
a = 3;          // assign a value to the variable
b = a+4;        // arithmetic operation and assignment
```

In the above we have a set of programming statements, each statement represents an operation within the problem solution. A statement can represent either single or multiple steps. The semicolon identifies the end of a statement and is the syntax delimiter. Within any statement there can be additional syntax rules.

In the above case the first statement defines two variables, the comma delimits each variable's name. The action of defining variables (in simple terms somewhere for data values to be stored) reserves memory locations for that variable, in this case the variables are defined by a type (int) identifying that the storage will contain signed whole numbers.

The second statement is an assignment (allocate a value to the variable), the equals symbol being the syntax. The final statement performs the arithmetic operation addition with the plus symbol used for this syntax. Since the grammatical rules are clearly defined for specific programming languages, syntax checking has always been automatically performed on source code during the compilation process and any errors found clearly identified.

What does programming language semantics mean?

The semantics of a programming language define the validity of the operation on the data. Any sentence in English can be semantically investigated for validity of information.

**I rode from junction 9 to junction 7 of the M6
on horseback.**

This sentence is in fact syntactically correct (one could argue it is not grammatically correct), the sentence starts with a capital letter and ends with a full stop. Performing a semantics check on the information content highlights several errors, riding on the M6 and horses on a motorway, something must be wrong with the information that is being conveyed. In a programming language the compiler can in many cases detect semantic errors since most of the basic semantic rules associated with, for instance, manipulating a whole number can be defined:

```
int a,b;         // define the variables
a = 3;           // assign a value to the variable
b = a + "Hello"; // arithmetic operation and assignment
```

The syntax is correct, but the third statement is attempting to add an integer value to a character string, this must be an error since it makes no sense from a data structure viewpoint, an obvious semantics error. In the case of logical data errors, checking for semantic rules does not help. In the following example (again a simple variation of the previous), it is obvious that the semantics of the solution is wrong, there is an obvious mathematical error but this code would pass the basic semantic rules of most compilers:

```
int a,b;     // define the variables
a = 0;       // assign a value to the variable
b = 4/a;     // arithmetic operation and assignment
```

The second statement assigns the variable to zero, while the third statement now attempts to divide by zero, which is invalid. Running this program would result in a run-time error (the run-time support would detect from the hardware that an invalid arithmetic operation was being carried out).

If we trace the history of programming language development, nearly all such developments have followed the above stated design philosophy of defining syntax and semantics rules that enable programming statements to manipulate data.

One further argument for a change in the design philosophy, to satisfy the language independence requirement of the CLR, is the realisation that as new programming languages have evolved, they have identified different techniques for the storage and manipulation of common data structures. Although such different techniques may not seem a major problem in isolation (any one application in a particular language has consistency in the manner the data is stored), in a broader context such inconsistencies when considering a large system design can create a great deal of development overhead.

As a simple example, if we compare the storage of a character string within the 'C/C++' and Visual Basic languages we find that in each case the string is stored using ASCII coding. However, in 'C' the string 'ABCD' would be stored as a series of 8-bit values with a null terminator:

$$41_{16} \quad 42_{16} \quad 43_{16} \quad 44_{16} \quad 0_{16}$$

While in Visual Basic, using its most common storage mechanism for the string 'ABCD', it would be stored as a series of 8-bit values but this time the first value stored is the length of the string:

$$4_{16} \quad 41_{16} \quad 42_{16} \quad 43_{16} \quad 44_{16}$$

It would be ridiculous for the design of the Common Language Run-time, (CLR) to attempt to proceed further without reviewing the basic concepts of program language design, specifically in terms of data storage, syntax and semantics.

Figure 2.8 has now added a further layer to the previously defined .NET Framework we had in Figure 2.7. This further layer makes Figure 2.8 a far more realistic model of the true design goals of the .NET Framework.

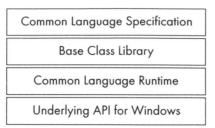

| Common Language Specification |
| Base Class Library |
| Common Language Runtime |
| Underlying API for Windows |

Figure 2.8   *The more realistic solutions framework model*

This new layer requires that in addition to designing the .NET Framework as a VM the overall architecture of .NET must specify a unique common base language specification enabling development language transparency.

Before we can look any further at the specification requirements of this common language we must first review what is meant by the term data type.

Data types

If we quickly review the topic we can state that within a programming language any variable declared and used must be defined as a specific data type. This declaration assists in the interpretation of the information that is stored in the variable, as well as limiting to some extent, the manner in which the data stored can be manipulated.

Some typical types are shown in the Table 2.1. This table can be viewed as a core set of data types that need to be available if we are looking at a common language specification.

Expanding on this core set of definitions we can further define that for any programming language to be compliant, within the CLR the language must offer support for a core set of semantic rules for each of the data types.

Supported languages must be able to manipulate these core data types using the data type semantic rules without specific reference to any syntactical rules that may be required by the language itself. Using this definition of semantics the mapping of any number of programming languages to the CLR becomes possible.

This approach allows for a significant simplification of the inextricably linked semantics and syntax of previous programming language definitions. These new design rules ensure that the syntax and semantics are being kept totally

Table 2.1   Core data types

Data type	Meaning
Byte	8-bit values 8-bit range 0 to 2^8-1
Integer	Signed whole number values 16-bit range -2^{16-1} to 0 to $2^{16-1}-1$ 32-bit range -2^{32-1} to 0 to $2^{32-1}-1$
Unsigned integers	Whole number values 16-bit range 0 to $2^{16}-1$ 32-bit range 0 to $2^{32}-1$
Character	Pattern of bits representing either the ASCII or Unicode for the characters
Float	Single precision IEE 32-bit floating point
Double	Double precision floating point

separate, allowing different programming languages the use of a common base set of data types without reference to any language specific constraints.

The common core set of data types have now become objects and in Figure 2.8 the object definition for these core types is moved out of the Common Language into the base class library. Within the development of the .NET Framework this base set of data types as used by the CLR has been published as the Common Type System (CTS) set and forms part of the ECMA-335 specifications.

In a later section the characteristics of some of these basic data types will be reviewed, as will the definitions of a 'value' type as against a 'reference' type. The use of the CTS standard therefore naturally allows any programming language, flexibility of its syntax provided that all variables are derived from the basic CTS data types. Equally a specific programming language may wish to either not implement a particular basic CTS data type or add a new data type. If a language requires a new data type then the specification states that this must be derived from one of the basic CTS data types. Alternatively if a language does not implement a particular data type, the language itself must offer, to the developer, flexibility in its syntax to avoid creating any ambiguous situations in the CLR environment.

The Common Type System

Every type supported by CTS is derived from System.Object basic type, the System.Object type being the foundation object within the CLR specification. Given this inheritance from System.Object every type supports the following methods:

Public methods

■ Boolean Equals(Object)
Used to test equality with another object. Reference types should return true if the Object parameter references the same object and for Value types when the values are equal

■ Int 32 Get Hash Code( )
Generates a number corresponding to the value of an object. If two objects of the same type are equal, then they must return the same hash code

■ Type GetType( )
Gets a Type Object that can be used to access metadata associated with the type and as a starting point for navigating the object hierarchy

■ String ToString( )
The default implementation returns the fully qualified name of the class of the object. This method is often overridden to output data that is more meaningful to the application.

Protected methods

■ void finalize( )
This method is called by the run time to allow for cleanup prior to garbage collection.

This CTS requirement defines the specification of all objects within the CLR. Having these inherent methods within all data objects greatly simplifies the previously attempted mechanisms, in several other programming language models, of allowing any object to be assigned any value.

The previous attempts to offer this level of flexibility to generalised objects has required the ideas of a variant type (one that can contain any value). The complexity of the syntax which was required to manipulate variant types generally left students in a flat spin. The specification that the root object can contain any value also removes the need for specific programming language syntax to explicitly type cast a variable from one type to another; once again students who have previously studied C/ C++ should breathe a sigh of relief.

Table 2.2   *Basic type definitions within CLR*

Storage size (in bits)	C# declaration	VB.NET declaration	
8	bool	Bool	
8	byte	Byte	
16	Short	Short	16-bit integer
32	int	Integer	32-bit integer
64	long	Long	64-bit integer
32	float	Single	Single IEEE
48	double	Double	Double IEEE
16	char	Char	Unicode
128	decimal	Decimal	

The CTS basic type definition

Table 2.2 highlights some of the basic type definitions within the CLR and the associated name in VB.NET and C#. The use of the CTS allowed the designers of the CLR to complete the basic design specification of the .NET Framework, it also highlighted a potential problem, since the CTS defines all data types as an object. The question this raises is how could the CLR be efficient when handling for instance an integer?

The solution was to separate the CTS types into two categories:

■ Value types (assigning actual values to the variables)

■ Reference types (referencing to point to the address of the object).

Value types in the CTS

The requirement for having value types can best be visualised by considering that in any object-based programming an instance of data will have the structure shown in Figure 2.9.

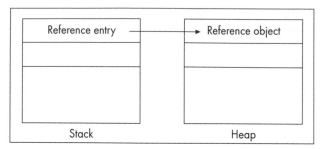

Figure 2.9   *The generalised instance of an object*

In Figure 2.9 we see that for any data object within an application we have two entries, the first is a reference to the object on the applications stack, which in turn points to the dynamically created object instance that contains the actual data and this is stored on the applications heap. Such a structure creates far too much overhead in terms of complexity for simple value data types such as an integer.

The alternative is to store simple data type objects on the applications stack. In taking this approach there is added complexity in terms of requiring two distinct data type definitions; however, the reduction in overhead for processing simple value types greatly outweighs this disadvantage. We can define a value type as one in which the data value is stored on the applications stack.

We will review later the problem created by this design choice; this data type is not subject to any automatic garbage collection (see Chapter 3). In being stored on the stack the object will only have a scope (or lifetime) defined by the method in which it was created. The types in the table in the previous section are the most common of these value types.

There is only one slight anomaly to this definition of a value type. The CTS specification defines a structure type which has similar characteristics to a class (class types are discussed when we look at reference types) in the next section. This is not unique to the CTS definition, structure types can contain elements of other types and may also contain methods, interfaces etc. Languages such as C++ have defined structures as value types so there is some historic precedent for this decision. We could spend the next ten pages debating the advantages of having structures as value types but it is left to the reader to consider these.

Value type declarations in C#

```
int First = 3333;
int Second = First;
First = 55;
```

Reference types in the CTS

Referring back to Figure 2.9 since reference types are far more complex than value types this generalised structure is well suited. In the main, reference types are classes. Within a class we have elements, sometimes called type members. The actual instance of reference types is stored on the heap, they are generally created and destroyed dynamically as the application executes, the final tidy up of the heap within .NET is handled by an automatic garbage collection system, this is more fully described in a later chapter. As you should be aware a class can contain:

■ Methods – Executable code that performs some operation. As with all 'OO' structure we can see overloaded methods, methods with the same name but a variant parameter list allowing the correct version to be called, based on the calling parameters

■ Fields – A value of some CTS type

■ Events – A mechanism used to communicate with another CTS type

■ Properties – These are no more than private values with a get and set method

■ Nested types – The ability to declare one class wholly within another.

It is beyond the scope of this book to look any further at class definitions etc., as you would expect attributes can be associated with a class element within the CTS. Among the most import reference types that are fully defined are:

Class   A CTS class can have all of the standard elements. The class itself can be public or private. The class can inherit from one or more other classes, it can be the direct parent for, at the most, one inherited child.

             Classes can be sealed, this stops any other class using it for inheritance. An abstract class cannot directly be used by a variable, it can only be used as the parent of another class

Interface	An interface can only contain methods, properties and events
Array	A group of variables of the same type
String	A group of Unicode or ASCII characters
Delegates	A delegate is effectively a pointer to a method

Reference type declarations in C#

```
Book objBook1 = new Book ();
ObjBook1.Name = "Blue Book";
Book objBook2 = objBook1;
objBook2.Name = "Red Book";
```

With this split between value and reference type definitions in the CTS and since the CLR will be required to deal with both, a mechanism is required to convert value to reference and vice versa. This is quite an advanced topic in respect of this overview of the .NET Framework. Therefore I have structured this chapter so that you can skip the next section without losing any continuity of the overall objective. The following section looks at the mechanism for conversion and allows an interested student to consider the implications of conversion, for instance on application execution efficiency.

Converting value types to reference types

There are situations when we want to treat an instance of one category of type, as the other (value as a reference or vice versa). The CLR design provides a mechanism to do this through Boxing and UnBoxing. Boxing occurs when an instance of a value type is converted to an instance of a reference type. While UnBoxing occurs when the reverse process takes place. Let's look at some C# code below to see how this is done:

```
int Red = 200;
Object RedRef;
RedRef = Value;
```

Here we assign an integer Red, a value. Then we declare a variable RedRef of type object and assign the integer Red to it. This is an example of implicit Boxing. The integer is said to be boxed in and converted to type System.Object. When Red is assigned to RedRef the following steps take place.

1 Memory is allocated on the managed heap to store the value of Red.

2 The value of Red is then copied to the managed heap.

3 Finally the reference to the data copied on the managed heap is stored in the memory previously allocated on the stack for RedRef.

```
int Blue
Blue =(int)BlueRef;
```

In the above two lines we are explicitly UnBoxing the data stored on the managed heap referenced by BlueRef. If you are familiar with C/C++, this syntax looks similar to casting. But here it has an entirely different meaning. We are converting a boxed variable back into a value type. Now Blue is set equal to the data referenced by BlueRef. All the data referenced by BlueRef on the managed heap is now copied into the memory location previously reserved on the stack for Blue.

Boxing will always take place implicitly when you pass a value type to a function that expects a reference type. From the above discussion a question comes to mind.

Why do we need Boxing and UnBoxing?

Actually the unification of the common type system, with the help of Boxing and UnBoxing, provides value types with the benefits of objectness without introducing unnecessary overhead. We cannot treat everything as a value type. But if we always treat every data type, even the primitive ones, as reference type then this causes a great deal of time overhead on the system. Therefore having this ability to treat value types as objects bridges the gap between value types and reference types that existed in previous languages. The above description is quite difficult, perhaps the following diagrams will help to explain value, reference and boxing. Figure 2.10 shows the stack/heap at

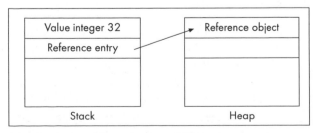

Figure 2.10   *A typical stack/heap without boxing*

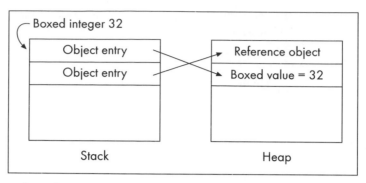

Figure 2.11   *A boxed integer stack/heap*

a point in time for a CLR application. We have a value type (Integer) on the stack currently with a value of 32; there is also a reference to an object on the stack pointing at a reference type on the heap. In Figure 2.11 we have boxed the integer value:

■ The integer value entry on the stack has been replaced by an object reference

■ A new object has been created on the heap containing the integer value.

Probably the only occasion when a developer may be faced with performing manual boxing is when dealing with legacy code in the managed 'C++' environment. However, Boxing and UnBoxing may significantly affect the performance of a particular application. When you are writing methods in an application you have the option when to specify if parameters are to be passed by reference or by value, it is left to you to investigate if particular strategies on parameter passing could adversely affect application performance.

Using the CLR environment

Having now investigated the structure of the framework and the specification of the design we will now look at the manner in which the CLR handles the execution of an application.

The two most common languages supported in the CLR are Visual Basic (VB.NET) and C# a derivation from the popular C/C++ language; other compliant languages either from Microsoft or other third parties are now becoming more popular.

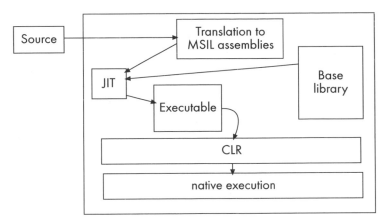

Figure 2.12   *The execution model for the .NET architecture*

VB.NET offers traditional Visual Basic, enhanced to conform to the CLR specification, to the developers who are looking to use their previous skills within the new environment. While C# offers existing C/C++ developers the increased flexibility of a language derived from the 'C/C++' stable.

I have deliberately ignored the third initially supported language, generally called managed C++. This is a set of managed code extensions for standard 'C/C++', it is certainly not for the faint hearted since the syntax to fit the 'C/C++' into the framework is quite complex.

No matter which language is used for an application development, the executable will be handled in the managed code environment of the CLR. In order to execute within this environment we no longer have native object code, the application is executed from an intermediate language that conforms to the virtual machine design of the .NET Framework. This intermediate language is called MSIL (Microsoft Intermediate Language).

The instruction set of MSIL is totally defined by the virtual machine and has no relationship to the actual native code environment. Figure 2.12 identifies the compiling and execution process associated with running an application within the managed code space.

The initial transformation takes a high-level language source file and creates a MSIL form that describes the execution required. It is during this transformation that syntax and semantics errors are identified. As the MSIL form of the code must finally be executed on a native processor, the final stage is to compile it through to the native object code for the system running the framework.

This final compilation is accomplished by a JIT (Just In Time compilation suite) by default JIT takes place on each method within the final application, as it is required. The performance degradation argument often associated with using JIT techniques needs careful consideration. In more traditional development scenarios where applications were always compiled to a native executable during the development process, there was a marked performance difference between for instance a 'C/C++' application and the same application written in VB.

Within the .NET Framework since all the languages are transformed into MSIL and it is this transformed code that is finally run through the JIT process, the difference in performance should be far less noticeable. Within this book all of the examples have been written in both VB.NET and C#, the reader is invited to make comparison on the performance of each of the solutions.

MSIL Microsoft Intermediate Language

We saw earlier in the chapter that the .NET Framework virtual machine is stack based, as you would expect therefore many of the MSIL instructions are defined in terms of stack operations. A few examples of MSIL are given below:

Add	Add the top two values of the stack and push result back onto the stack
Box	Convert a value type on the stack to a reference type and box the value for future use
Br	Branch execution to a specified location (often the top address stored on the stack)
Call	Call a specified method
Ldfld	Load the specified field of an object onto the stack
Ldobj	Load the whole object onto the stack
Newobj	Create a new object
Stfld	Store a value from the stack to a specified field in an object
Stobj	Store a value on the stack into a specified value type
Unbox	Convert back a boxed reference

The MSIL could be likened to an assembler language for the CLR. The above table only looks at a tiny portion of the MSIL instruction set, however, if this subset is compared to the previously identified design criteria for the .NET Framework:

■ Standard Data Structure

■ Platform Independence

■ Operating System Independence

■ Programming Language Independence.

The MSIL meets all four of these basic criteria.

Metadata

When the supported CLR language is transformed into MSIL, within the output file, in addition to the MSIL instructions there is also a metadata description stored using XML (we will be looking at XML as a mechanism for describing information in a later chapter). The metadata can be viewed as important in many aspects of the .NET architecture.

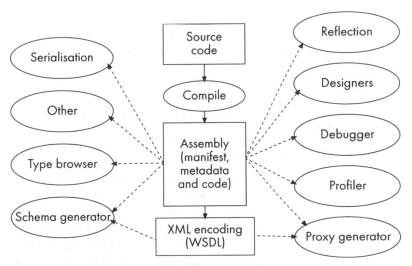

Figure 2.13   *How the metadata in the assembly is used within the .NET architecture, each of the dotted lines represent some interaction using metadata*

In Figure 2.13 we can see that this metadata is used, not only by the various intelligent development facilities, for example Visual Studio .NET for building development aids such as debug facilities and object browsers, it is also used by the CLR itself to assist in both security and code integrity etc. Typically the metadata for a particular type will include:

- The type name

- The base type that this type inherits from

- Any names interfaces that are implemented within this application

- Methods implemented within this application

- Properties exposed

- Events provided.

In addition for security of execution the metadata contains other details including parameter lists and return types for methods etc. Attributes specific to the application can also be created and stored within the metadata; in a later chapter we will review this with respect to the interaction of a piece of application code and its interface with the .NET class libraries themselves.

Some very advanced techniques on defining application specific attributes to the code can be added to the metadata, but such techniques are not relevant to the scope of this book.

Managed code organisation into assemblies

The .NET Framework does not manage its executables using the same overall structure as standard Windows applications. Any .NET application could be made up of a number of files with the standard extensions of DLL or EXE. Within the .NET Framework we have a new concept, the idea of an assembly; this is a grouping of files by functionality within a given application.

An assembly is a fundamental building block when considering developing, deploying and running a .NET Framework application. Within any assembly there is a metadata manifest, such a manifest indicates all the objects, files etc., which are required to execute that assembly. The manifest will always be contained in one of the files that make up the assembly. Visual Studio .NET, if used as the development environment, creates the assembly manifest file, it will have the extension of 'cs' if you are currently developing in C# or 'vb' if you are using VB.NET, the developer can make specific entries into the manifest and these will always be built into the final assembly.

The assembly structure

Any assembly can contain a .NET component rather than a complete application. Since we have yet to investigate componentware development techniques within .NET, in this chapter the only comment about the metadata is that it removes the need for registry entries related to components (do I hear a cheer from any student in the room who has tried to build COM components in C/C++ and has then attempted to register them on a system).

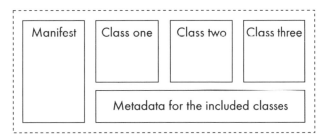

Figure 2.14   A typical assembly

Assemblies are also grouped into categories; the most basic grouping is a static assembly as opposed to a dynamic assembly.

■ Static assemblies are the simplest to understand, a static assembly is generated by a development facility such as Visual Studio .NET and the resultant assembly file is stored on the hard disk of the machine

■ Dynamic assemblies are created and executed directly from memory, the most common dynamic assemblies are those created by ASP.NET (a whole chapter later in the book is devoted to the technology of ASP.NET). These ASP.NET dynamic assemblies are created by the mechanism employed by ASP.NET. When an ASP.NET page is loaded from a server it has to dynamically create executable code that controls user events on the ASP page. Such code must be dynamically created as ASP pages and can be reloaded following some server side validation or event handling, so the requirement on the reload may be different to the handling on the initial load.

A final grouping that can be attributed to an assembly is to adopt a referencing technique using the assembly's name.

- The basic name grouping uses the simple text name assigned in the assembly manifest itself

- As an alternative the assembly can be referenced using a strong name. If this strong name reference is used, the CLR has the ability to compare the strong name to the assembly versioning information. With such an approach multiple assemblies can exist with the same basic name but different strong names, this eliminates the so-called DLL from hell problem from which Windows has always suffered. Using the strong name allows any application to be tied by reference to a particular assembly. This is a vast improvement over the DLL problem inherent with all older technologies where a new application would update an existing DLL and then some older application on the system would stop functioning.

How does the CLR manage execution?

The goal of any development is to finally run the application. Within this section we will briefly look at the manner in which the CLR finds all aspects of the application, manages the loading of the correct assemblies and finally executes the code. The first point to note is that unlike a fully linked native code application, the .NET Framework only loads the required assembly for the current state of the application. However, the first problem is finding the first assembly. The CLR search process is very complex, but the basic assumptions are first, identify the exact version number of the assembly trying to be located, then the currently loaded assemblies are checked to ensure it is not already in memory, if it is not in memory the CLR will search the GAC (Global Assembly Cache), this is the primary repository for all assemblies on a given machine (developers have a utility to deposit new assemblies into the GAC). If the assembly is not found here, then the CLR will search within the current users working directory, and finally if it is not found then the search will be broadened to encompass the whole file system, obviously this final search can take a great deal of time.

Creating the JIT compilation

Since all assemblies are held in MSIL, before any element in the assembly can run it will need to go through the JIT compilation. These compilations are accomplished, as indicated before, on a method-by-method basis, as each new method is required. Once a method has been compiled it is held in memory so if it is needed again the compiled version is available and duplicate JIT compilations of a method are not necessary. During the JIT process the metadata for the method is checked for type safety, this is the so-called managed code verification process, it is attempting to ensure that this latest compilation is not trying to perform any illegal operations within the managed code environment.

There is only one further basic feature of the assembly load and run that is important at this stage. Within the assembly the developer can set security attributes, this facility allows the developer to limit the use of the assembly either to who can use it or alternatively what the assembly can do when being used by a particular user. The exact detail of such concepts is beyond the scope of this introductory book but it is important to understand that features such as this are an intrinsic part of the .NET architecture. Once the application terminates then all the assemblies associated with the application are unloaded unless any of the common framework library assemblies are also being used by another application.

Summary

There is a great deal of information in this chapter, it is important to understand that the .NET Framework is the very heart and soul of the .NET architecture.

The objective of the chapter was to derive a basic specification for the .NET Framework. In doing this we have identified the basic structure of the framework and shown that it comprises four main elements:

1   Common Language Specification – derived from the CTS

2   Base class library components

3 Common Language Runtime

4 Interface to the underlying API for the operating system.

The descriptions given for the actual manipulation and execution of code in this chapter are very generic, the detail regarding the organisation of the CLR and its manipulation of actual code execution is extremely complex and far beyond a basic introduction into the .NET architecture.

However, what is important is for you to accept that the .NET Framework is not simply another software development language gimmick. There is an enormous shift in software engineering terms when one compares the philosophies of .NET to older technologies. In addition, in making this shift in development technique, the repercussions in the areas of operating system control of the execution of a particular application are also fairly revolutionary.

Once again it is important not to be trapped in the belief that the .NET architecture is the only viable solution to such ideas. At present .NET offers a meaningful environment in which these techniques are being employed. The history of software science is littered with such good ideas, which have been subsequently enhanced and improved upon both in the academic and commercial fields.

There are other aspects that need to be considered regarding the CLR and its place within the .NET Framework. Over the course of the next three chapters the investigation which was started here will broaden and key topics of memory management, the .NET class library structure, the supported languages of VB.NET and C# will be considered more fully.

Review questions

1 In order to more fully understand stack-oriented execution engines, you should attempt to define a simple calculator in terms of functionality as a stack-based machine.

2 One of the most basic programming languages defined as stack based was 'Forth'. In order to gain more insight into mapping a stack-based system onto a modern processor try to find details of the various implementations of 'Forth' on an Intel x86 processor.

3 Using the tools available in VS.NET investigate the metadata in any .NET assembly.

a. Can you identify the class name?

b. Can you identify the various data types used within the class?

c. Can you find the definition of the methods and the attributes such as parameters and return value?

4 Using the results from question 3 describe how these can be used both by intelligent development systems and also by the CLR itself to maintain managed code and security.

3 The framework class library and other support functionality

Objective

The efficient use of a class library is a difficult concept. Class libraries by their very nature are normally large and complex and are perceived by students as being very difficult to understand.

The aim of a class library is to reduce the complexity of developing applications for a particular environment. The Microsoft Foundation Class (MFC, which was the original Windows class library) was created to give developers a quick start into basic application development. Class libraries such as MFC aim to reduce the need to understand the intricacy of the overall windows software architecture.

Creating a software solution based on MFC was promoted as being quick and effortless once you understood the MFC structure. Although such an ideal was well founded, many years of experience have shown that teaching MFC to students is very difficult; in order to understand the MFC structure requires the student to have an adequate understanding of the design constraints inherent in the libraries' design, reducing its effectiveness as a teaching aid. Obviously as a development tool for experienced programmers with a good fundamental understanding of the Windows API structure, the number of large commercial applications that are MFC based is a good measure of its success.

This observation leads to the conclusion that understanding how to effectively use a class library requires an awareness of the underlying system structure. It is the objective of this chapter to give you some indication of how the .NET class library fits into the overall .NET architecture. To accomplish this objective we will need to identify the relevance of certain key topics within the .NET class library.

When you can appreciate that in a similar manner to the MFC library augmenting standard Windows application development, the .NET class library creates and augments the basic foundation layer of the CLR then you should be in a position to start to appreciate the overall .NET architecture.

In essence the basis of the .NET class library is to construct a prefabricated framework for any CLR compliant application. Even the simplest .NET application requires a substantial amount of the class library and relating this to our discussion in the last chapter, this software overhead although seemingly large is in fact quite manageable as we are working within MSIL, and using JIT execution techniques on a method-by-method strategy.

This chapter introduces the basic class library structure. The choice of what to include and what to leave out of this chapter was not easy. The .NET class library structure is large, it is organised into a fairly logical hierarchy but the problem was to choose which aspects of the hierarchy to examine in detail. Given that you will probably learn more by actually exploring examples, this introductory chapter on the class library concentrates on the uppermost levels, which offer the major support to an application. In the later chapters when specific technologies are discussed the example software used should enable the reader to investigate the more detailed levels within any particular .NET class.

Other topics

When planning the contents of this book some of the topics related to the .NET Framework did fit not well into the overall scheme; these topics are automatic garbage collection, the .NET process management mechanism and the subject of direct file IO support. These topics are important for an overall understanding of the .NET architecture but they do not directly relate to any one of the key technologies identified in Chapter 1. I therefore decided to include them at the end of this chapter where they could be considered as .NET Framework support functionality.

Introduction

The .NET class library is large. Microsoft published a claim that the vast majority of the development effort on the .NET architecture was taken up by the creation of the class library. Learning to navigate around the class library structure constitutes the steepest part of the learning curve for anyone looking at the overall .NET architecture.

The first two chapters have already equipped you with a significant portion of the overview of the .NET Framework. However, you will need to be prepared to spend time investigating the class library hierarchy before you will feel confident enough to tackle specific technological aspects of, for instance, ADO.NET.

At an introductory level it is difficult to give an exact estimate but you probably need to be familiar with about 10% of the total library to be able to effectively use the library to create applications for the framework. The most important part of the learning curve is to be able to identify where, in this vast volume of functionality, the relevant .NET objects you are looking for are likely to reside.

The .NET class library is organised into a fairly rigid hierarchical structure, in order to classify the hierarchy each element at the top level is called a namespace. As you traverse either sideways through the hierarchy or down into more detailed aspects you will enter new namespaces that are subordinates of the top level.

The absolute root of the whole hierarchical tree is called System, no application running in the .NET Framework could exist if it did not make use of the functionality offered by the root namespace System. Within System many of the core data type objects are to be found, along with most other vital components that enable an application to exist, execute, and be terminated within the framework.

There are more than twenty subordinate namespaces below System, some are far more important than others in the context of the examples in this book. To give you at least a basic overview I have constructed the table below showing the major namespaces that will be used in the examples. Many will only be used in one or two of the examples since they are specific to a particular technology, others will appear in most.

The table is only intended to indicate the breadth of the hierarchy; it is beyond anyone, unless you are an insomniac with nothing better to do, to study and comprehend the functionality and detail of the total library.

Table 3.1   *Major name spaces*

Root	First evel	Second level
System		
	Collections	
	Components	
		Design
	Data	
		OleDB
	Directory Services	
	Drawing	
		Drawing2D
		Text
	IO	
	Net	
		Sockets
	Runtime	
		InteropServices
	Text	
		Format
	Threading	
	Timers	
	Web	
		Services
		UI
	Windows	
		Forms
		Controls
	Xml	
		XPath
		Xsl

Even this short list looks large; however, as we look at the functionality within each subordinate group we will only be scratching at the surface of the vast amount of detail that each contains. The objective is to make use of these class library items to demonstrate in the examples how the total .NET architecture offers a standard set of techniques to solve real world problems Such solutions can span from a simple stand-alone implementation to a multi-tiered distributed system.

It could be argued that it would have been an advantage to include some code examples at this point to augment these descriptions. However, we have not yet considered the topic of the .NET Framework programming language support, this appears in the next chapter. So rather than trying to produce code samples, I have limited this overview to a basic written description.

The System namespace is the ultimate parent of all other namespaces, the most important functionality for the purposes of the examples within this book include:

System

- **Core types** – value types include Int32, Int16, Char, Boolean, and the basic reference types such as arrays and delegates. Obviously the basic reference type object is also defined here

- **Console** – This is the class we will initially use in Chapter 4 when we start to look at some applications that communicate with a command window

- **Maths** – This class contains most of the standard mathematical functions used in many of the examples in the book

- **Random** – This class is used in some of the examples when pseudorandom number generation is required.

System.Collection

This namespace includes the functions used in some of the examples to create array lists. Collections extend the ability of the supported languages. Each language now supports a syntax that allows iteration through a collection list. All controls placed and accessed on any .NET Form are generally held in a collection.

System. ComponentModel

This namespace includes the classes that a user designing .NET components will inherit. In Chapter 6 we will be developing .NET components and will make use of some of the functionality from this namespace. In Chapter 7, when we look at issues dealing with the interoperability of older technologies such as COM in the .NET Framework, this namespace in conjunction with System.Runtime.InteropServices allows these other technologies the ability to reside and function correctly within the .NET architecture.

System.Data

This namespace is one of the most important, when dealing with any form of structured data. This namespace contains the revised controls that constitute ADO.NET. In Chapter 9 we will be investigating the technology of creation, updating and deletion of structured information from data servers.

System. DirectoryServices

Although not directly used by many of the examples in the book, the importance of this namespace cannot be overemphasised. In the previous chapter when managing assemblies were discussed we saw that they had assembly manifests that include security information. It is within the DirectoryServices namespace that access to the X500 Active Directory Service Interface (ADSI) is available. These services allow .NET applications access to user and resource information on a system-wide basis. This is a topic that is a little too advanced for this introductory text but which would prove a very suitable self-study topic for any student who is looking to expand their knowledge into the security aspects of the .NET architecture.

System.Drawing

As its name suggests this provides the standard drawing types that are needed by an application if graphical information is to be provided to the user. Several of the examples in later chapters, such as the client–server game of battleships in Chapter 10, use the drawing namespace.

System.IO

This provides an extensive set of types for reading and writing files, directories etc. Although we have seen that the System.Data namespace offers access to structure information from data servers, it is still important in many applications to have direct access to locally stored files.

System.Net

This provides the ability to connect not only to standard web protocols such as HTTP, but also to build specialist sockets-based communication systems. Once again in the client–server game of battleships developed in Chapter 10, this basic socket communication technique is used.

System.RunTime

This in fact is actually a parent name space for several quite advanced topics. In the description of System.ComponentModel above, reference was made to the subordinate namespace System.RunTime.InteropSevices. In a later chapter when we look at interoperability issues we will review the run-time namespace in more detail.

System.Text

This is one of the smallest namespaces, within the examples the only functionality we will use is the ability to transform string variables normally encoded using Unicode, or ASCII, into byte streams for transmission on a standard socket connection.

System.Threading Although this namespace is not covered as a unique topic in this book some of the examples and explanations refer to thread design models and the use of multi-threading in the .NET Framework. This namespace provides the consistent interface to the CLR for all aspects of a multi-threaded design.

System.Timers Some of the examples make use of periodic timers to provide elapse event control. This namespace provides the timer functionality.

System.Web Two full chapters later in the book consider how the .NET architecture can be used in the distributed environment of the WWW. The first, Chapter 10 is specifically concerned with web forms and the technology of ASP.NET, while the second, Chapter 11 is looking at the topic of web services. The System.Web namespace provides all of the support functionality for these topics.

System.Windows For this book this namespace should really be referred to as System.Windows.Forms. It contains all the data types required to construct any Windows application GUIs. As applications have started to become more distributed it could be argued that a local GUI is less important than the creation of a reasonable HCI within an Internet browser. However, as will be discussed in Chapter 11, with the availability of web services, it is probable that dedicated clients may become the normal clients for such specific services. If this becomes the case the whole subject of local GUI design will once again become more prominent.

System.XML This namespace contains useful types for dealing with XML documents. The .NET architecture as we have already seen when we investigated the idea of metadata in assemblies, uses XML to describe aspects of both the development environment itself as well as descriptive information about the assembly. In Chapter 8 we will investigate the topic of XML and use this namespace.

What about the other subordinate namespaces?

As indicated in the introduction this brief overview has been limited to the major namespaces used by the examples in the book. If you investigate the hierarchical tree of the class library these namespaces represent about half of the direct subordinates below System.

Those not identified are of course important, but they represent specialist areas that at the level of this book can be safely ignored. If you are interested in investigating these other namespaces simple overviews are available in the Visual Studio .NET help system. The overviews give an insight into the functionality of each namespace, for instance look at the namespace System.Security and its subordinates, the description provided for the cryptography objects is adequate, and the overall functionality within the namespace is quite extensive.

Garbage collection

Although within the class library there is a subordinate namespace called System.gc that deals with garbage collection, it is not intended here to look at the use of this in an application.

The .NET Framework has an inbuilt automatic garbage collection facility, which, when any application is executing in the .NET Framework, takes care of the clearing and tidying up of all used and discarded dynamic memory allocation (garbage) objects.

In order to clarify what is meant by automatic garbage collection it is important we review how dynamic memory allocation and tidyup has been handled in the previous execution environments.

The traditional memory map for an application

Any application executing on a standard Windows platform when started is allocated a chunk of memory by the operating system. This allocation can conceptually be viewed as four regions., shown in Figure 3.1.

1   Code – Contains the executable binary.

2   Data – Contains the static or compile time variable declaration space.

3   Stack – An area that can be used to create call stacks etc., as methods are accessed and used.

4   Heap – A free area in which dynamic data variables can be created and subsequently destroyed.

Figure 3.1   *Traditionally the memory map can be viewed as four regions*

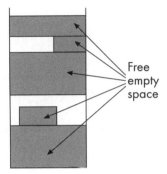

Figure 3.2   *A snapshot of a heap starting to get fragmented*

This is a very simplistic overview of a complicated topic but for the purposes of this explanation it will suffice. The area we are most concerned with is the heap.

In most applications, classes or large data structures need to be created dynamically; the use or lifetime of these classes or data structure is defined by the term scope. A variable is in scope when the process is using it. It is said to be out of scope when the executing code that created it terminates, it is at this time that the application must dispose of the allocation freeing up heap space for future use.

Although we would like to believe that all application developers performed the necessary tidyup of the heap, in reality and from bitter experience allocations from the heap can get lost.

Losing track of these allocations means the memory left allocated became unavailable and this is termed a memory leak. In the worst case an application could have a large leak, and eventually all of the heap space allocated to this application is lost, the application runs out of free memory and generally crashes.

There is another problem with this mechanism, even if the application disposes of its dynamic memory allocations correctly, during the life of the application this continual allocation and release of the heap space causes fragmentation.

Once fragmentation becomes too great, allocation requests become slow. Modern operating systems have a background process that will compact the heap (reorganise the used and freed space into a contiguous block for future use), thereby making larger contiguous blocks available for allocation. Although this may seem a reasonable solution, there are two drawbacks:

■ The time it takes for the compaction to take place

■ Any allocation pointers held within an application may now point to invalid memory addresses.

The first of these, the time to perform the compaction, simply puts a delay into all processes on the system during the heap reorganisation, the second, however, is far more dangerous, if allocation pointers were to become corrupted the application could overwrite any portion of its or any other memory space.

The .NET Framework addresses these two points by first monitoring for objects stored on the heap to go out of scope and marking them as garbage and collecting this garbage in an orderly fashion in a given time frame. The second problem of random pointer corruption is totally eliminated. The CTS (Common Type System) does not allow any form of pointers, it is simply not possible to create a generalised pointer to a memory allocation for any CTS object.

In the previous chapter we looked at the concept of stack/ heap interaction when considering object instances of CTS reference types, in CTS terms these are not generalised pointers and it is not possible to allocate heap specific usage programmatically. With this removal from the CLR of programmatic heap manipulation and the automation of the identification of discarded objects this means that applications executing in the CLR are no longer subject to the difficult to find software bugs associated with memory leaks.

In having automatic garbage collection the development process is far more straightforward with regard to memory management, but unfortunately this improvement has created anomalies.

- Automatic garbage collection is totally asynchronous to the application, i.e. the compacting and clearing of the heap has no relationship in absolute or relative time to when any object actually went out of scope

- In languages such as C++ the destruction and removal of an object was synchronised to the application by the use of an objects destructor method.

A potential problem of synchronisation can therefore be created if the application does not provide adequate safeguards for the interaction of objects as they go out of scope.

In the next section we will look at the basic mechanism of the automatic garbage collection service, specifically to identify when an object is considered as garbage, as well as the strategy that the collection service uses to remove such objects. In understanding these two factors it is possible to ensure that any asynchronous collection problem is avoided.

Automatic garbage collection

At startup of a .NET application the framework allocates two important areas of memory designated as the managed stack and the managed heap. During the lifetime of the application every instance of a reference object (refer to Chapter 2 for the definition of a reference object) is allocated space on the managed heap with a corresponding object entry on the managed stack.

Obviously, as the application runs, the space on the managed heap will slowly be used up. Therefore as any new instances of objects are required before they can be created the free space on the heap must be checked and if necessary heap compaction must take place, this is the service provided by automatic garbage collection in the .NET Framework.

The automatic garbage collection runs as a system-level process in the CLR itself, there is also a mechanism available that allows an application to request garbage collection at any time, such requests are generally only issued by specialist applications that make excessive use of the heap, this feature will not be considered in this discussion.

In order to fully understand how the garbage is collected we must first review the topic of reference variables looked at in the previous chapter.

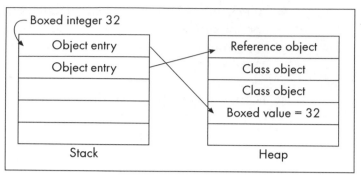

Figure 3.3   *Garbage objects left on the heap*

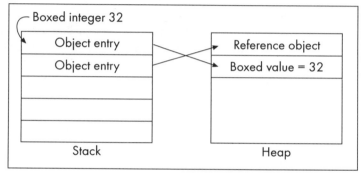

Figure 3.4   *The changes on the heap after the garbage is collected*

In Figure 3.3 we see that for each reference variable allocated on the heap there is a corresponding reference entry on the stack. Figure 3.3 shows that the object variable and the boxed integer have both these entries while the two class instances on the heap appear to be orphans. The question of how these two items got orphaned on the heap is unimportant, but probably they were created and used in a method that has been called and terminated. These two class objects are garbage and need removal.

The automatic collection will identify these extra objects on the heap, it will remove the allocation and at the same time compact the heap space, moving the correctly referenced items to the bottom end. Once this action has been successfully completed the heap will look like Figure 3.4.

This example identifies that long-lived instances of objects on the heap will slowly migrate towards one end. Such a consequence of heap compaction should not be a problem; in fact it should improve the heap-scanning algorithm used by the automatic garbage collector. If short-lived objects (those recently created) always reside above the long-lived objects on the heap then these short-lived objects which will go out of scope first are always found and dealt with quickly by the garbage collector service.

The full garbage collection algorithm Microsoft describe for heap management in the .NET Framework tries to free up enough space for the new object being created, by only looking at the short-lived objects end of the heap. The garbage collector algorithms will only proceed to the long-lived objects end of the heap when such compacting of short-lived item space cannot create enough free space.

This quick overview takes a very complicated task and makes it sound easy. This book is not trying to design an automatic garbage collection system, the purpose of reviewing it in this chapter is to identify the availability of the service and its possible impact on an application development.

A strategy to avoid any asynchronous object destruction problems

In the traditional memory management model it was the application's responsibility to dispose of dynamically created objects on the heap. The destruction of an object was a programmatic action and any final algorithmic tidyup and possible storage of object data were synchronised to the release of the heap space.

Comparing this traditional approach to the .NET Framework's automatic garbage collection service, the .NET asynchronous approach provides no timing relationship between the object going out of scope and its eventual destruction.

In order to eliminate any possible problems such an asynchronous destruction could create, it is important that applications ensure that data within an object is correctly handled (stored elsewhere if necessary) before that object goes out of scope. There is a default standard method available to all objects, the finalizer(..), which is called as the garbage collector removes the allocation from the heap.

A possible solution would be to override this generic .NET method and provide specific cleanup code for each object. However, due to the asynchronous nature of garbage collection and the identified collection algorithm, the fact is long-lived items awaiting destruction may remain on the heap longer than short-lived items, this could make it difficult to generalise the design of these override methods. A more realistic solution is to write a pseudo destructor method for all objects and ensure this is called programmatically prior to the object going out of scope.

.NET process management

When an application is executing in the .NET Framework the process management of that application can no longer be viewed as simply another process in the operating system environment. Investigation of the full technical specification of the CLR indicates that it is built from Windows DLLs. In a Windows environment a DLL is not an executable piece of code in its own right (Tanenbaun, A., *Modern Operating Systems*, 2001, Wiley, London) we must therefore assume that the CLR is supported by some form of host executable environment.

In the .NET architecture terms this host executable is called the run-time host. These run-time hosts load and initialise the CLR and subsequently transfers control to the managed code environment itself. This is a very similar scenario to the way Windows 95 used a form of DOS to get the overall Windows package loaded and executing. There are currently three .NET run-time hosts:

■ Internet Explorer for web-based forms etc.

■ ASP.NET, which is driven by the relevant web server

■ The actual Windows GUI shell process.

These run-time hosts create regions called .NET domains or .NET application domains directly within the hosts' native operating system process. Once these domains are created assemblies can be loaded, this can be viewed as the equivalent of loading a process in a traditional operating system. Figure 3.5 shows a typical .NET process.

The application domain within the run-time host isolates one .NET application from any other. Within any run-time host (a single process on the operating system) there can be multiple application domains and each of these will contain a .NET executable. This arrangement enables .NET processes to communicate with each other with far less difficulty than two native operating system processes.

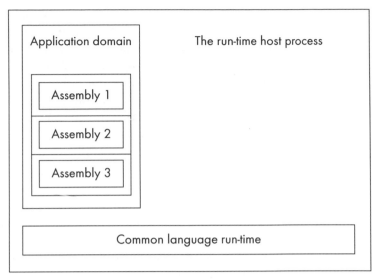

Figure 3.5   *A run time host with an assembly loaded*

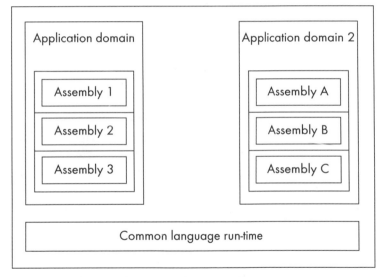

Figure 3.6   *A run-time host with two applications domains*

A major concern in this host domain model as shown in Figure 3.6 is that two .NET applications are executing in a single operating system process leading to the question: how is the isolation of both code and data between the two .NET executables maintained? The inbuilt operating system process isolation model is being bypassed, these two .NET executables are in a single operating system process.

The answer to the question lies in the managed code concept of the .NET Framework itself. All code is subject to verification during loading; in the chapter dealing with the overall structure of a .NET application, we identified that the executable code includes metadata describing not only the CTS objects etc., but also the attributes of methods and actions on the objects. The CLR loader can verify this metadata, in doing such verification the loader makes it impossible for any application to directly access anything beyond its assembly manifest boundary.

The final issue to consider on process management in the .NET Framework relates to part of the original specification of the virtual machine. It was identified in a previous chapter that the .NET Framework environment must be based on:

providing an unambiguous general purpose, language and operating platform independent virtual machine design.

The process management concept of .NET application domains running inside a run-time host removes any dependence on a particular operating system definition of a process. These application domains are totally encapsulated, such domains control .NET process management and it is only the run-time host that directly interfaces with the native operating system. This .NET domain-based execution model is quite bulky when compared to any conventional process execution model. However, in taking this approach the final element in the required virtual machine design is complete and the implemented .NET Framework has no major design compromises.

File IO services

As with all software development there will come a point where data will need to be stored locally onto secondary storage (local disks). In our discussion of the framework class library there is a namespace called System.IO which provides the necessary functionality. It could be argued that this topic should be dealt with in the discussion on supported languages in the next chapter; however, file IO functionality is required across all languages.

In this section we will briefly look at the techniques that the .NET Framework uses to access file systems. Although we have yet to look at the syntax of the compliant languages it is obvious that such languages will have suitable syntax to manipulate system level objects.

The fundamental CTS derived type available for file access within the .NET Framework is a stream, where a stream is actually defined as a series of bytes. The stream will have associated methods to read and write these bytes to/from the file system. As an added facility the namespace System.IO also contains a CTS derived type file, which allows the creation, deletion etc., of files within the operating system file management service. Since streams only work effectively with binary data (a series of bytes), further types are available such as FileInfo, allowing alternative streams to be created, for instance a StreamReader for plain text files. Using such techniques many other types of files can be accessed and applications can derive a new class, based on such standard classes to create streams for any file format that may be required.

To handle the higher functions of the file system the namespace System.IO contains type definitions at directory level, allowing creation, deletion etc. of file directories. Any directory is also considered as a collection of files. This definition allows developers to make full use of the functionality found in the namespace System.Collection.

In the previous section where two applications are executing within a single run-time host we have already seen that since they may be in a single domain they can communicate effectively. If we broaden this to consider two applications in separate domains there is still a requirement for effective communication. If you are familiar with the Windows native memory mapped file techniques used for interprocess communications in conventional Windows applications, it will come as no surprise that a similar technology is available for interdomain communications within the .NET Framework. If you are not familiar with this concept it is the creation of a memory region which to each process appears as a file stream, the processes can then read and write to this common region thereby exchanging information. For more detail on memory mapped file techniques, see B. E. Rector and J. M. Newcomer, *Win32 System Programming*, Addison-Wesley.

Summary

This chapter has identified the second key element in the .NET Framework continuing with the CLR structure derived in Chapter 2 and these .NET class libraries we now have sufficient knowledge to utilise the execution environment within the .NET architecture.

This review of the class library has only just touched upon the overall functionality available; the emphasis here has been to identify the requirements of the examples in the subsequent chapters.

This level of detail should be sufficient to stimulate your interest and encourage you to search for other class definitions that you may wish to use in your investigation of the .NET class library.

In the chapter we have also looked at three very important .NET Framework support functions that are quite often overlooked in books dealing with a programming topic only:

■ Automatic garbage collection – The whole subject of automatic garbage collection could have possibly been ignored. Automatic garbage collection is intrinsic to the .NET architecture. However, without at least some overview of its operation, the limitations it can impose, and possible side effects, a lot of hours can be wasted on difficult to find software problems associated with object destruction

■ Process management – The topic of .NET process management has little to do with using the .NET environment. However, it is important to identify how a run-time host controls specific application domains. In the future you may wish to look at improvement, for instance on web server performance, and this will include the mechanisms used by the Microsoft web server (IIS), which is the run-time host for web services handles:

■ File I/O – Finally the brief review of the interface between the operating systems, inbuilt file management service and the .NET Framework. This clearly identifies that no longer are we looking at file names and content in a strictly linear manner, such functionality is now handled by objects, these objects offer far morc flexibility to the developer when local file storage is required.

Review Questions

1   Investigate the hierarchical structure of the namespaces and draw a diagram of those referenced in this chapter.

2 What are the benefits to a developer of having namespaces?

3 Design a hierarchical structure for your own namespace, the functionality within the namespace should be based on a card game; dealing, shuffling, displaying and rules.

4 Investigate in more detail the Sytem.Security namespace and draw a hierarchical diagram of the functionality available.

5 Outline how you would schedule automatic garbage collection, as a starting point consider that the process is given a fixed memory allocation of say 4 Kbytes of heap space. At what level of space left would you trigger garbage collection?

6 If you are not familiar with conventional process management on an operating system investigate how this is generally arranged. Now compare this model with the .NET model and identify how the concepts of context switching must be modified in this new model.

7 A memory mapped file technique is just one of the options for interprocess communications on a conventional process model, what are the others? How do you think .NET handles these alternatives?

Supported programming languages

Objective

Given that in the last three chapters we have identified how the virtual machine is designed and supported within the .NET Framework, in this chapter, the objective is to:

■ Consider the impact on programming languages of the need to conform to the Common Language Runtime (CLR) specification

■ Identify how the Common Type System (CTS) forms the basis of the derivation of any CLR compliant language.

We have already seen that to design programming languages, which satisfy the prescriptive set of rules laid down for the virtual machine within the .NET Framework, requires that these languages be designed, not in the traditional approach of defining syntax and semantics rules that allow programming statements to manipulate data, but that they must be designed using the perspective that they can only manipulate CTS data types, have inbuilt syntax for these data types and are able to derive algorithmic solutions to solve real world problems.

In order to become proficient in developing solutions within the .NET Framework, the relationship between the supported programming language structure and the underlying .NET Framework needs to be fully understood. The CTS defines a large core of the semantic needs of any programming language, this leads to the conclusion that a great deal of commonality will exist between all of the CLR compliant languages.

It is with this in mind that this chapter provides an overview of two common CLR compliant languages, C# and VB.NET. It must be emphasised that this is only an overview, if you have previously studied any 'OO' methodology or programming practice most of this chapter will be familiar to you.

If you are not familiar with 'OO' programming techniques then I suggest that before you look at the detail in this chapter you utilise the notes I have prepared on basic 'OO' design and programming on the support website for the book.

The syntax of these two languages differs, C# has its roots firmly within the C/C++ family, while VB.NET has evolved from the need to provide a programming environment that is fairly friendly.

Introduction

Within this chapter the descriptions of C# and VB.NET will not be exhaustive, the goal is to give an appreciation of the look and feel of programming using the core functionality provided by the .NET Framework.

The omission of J# from this chapter is intentional, Visual Studio .Net 2003 includes J#.NET (J#.NET can also be downloaded from Microsoft and integrated into Visual Studio 2002 professional).

J# has been introduced as a CLR compliant implementation of the Java programming language; however, student books on Java programming tend to introduce the Java class libraries, with associated interfaces such as Swing and JavaBeans etc. These specialist technologies are unlikely ever to be supported in the CLR since the .NET Framework implicitly has its own similar inbuilt functionality. I therefore felt that J# need not be considered in a book that is dealing with the .NET architecture. If you extend your study to encompass J# you will find that its derivation is very similar to that of C#.

Although it may have been more logical to look at C# and VB.NET on a point-by-point basis, I felt this would have probably become quite confusing to the reader. Instead I have looked at the two languages separately; this approach unfortunately does lead to some duplication of information in this chapter. However, it offers the reader the opportunity to concentrate on one or the other language, so if you are only interested in one of the languages then I would suggest you concentrate your study on that particular section. If you prefer the approach of comparing the two languages then you may wish to study both sections even with the duplication of information. A direct comparison approach will in fact greatly assist in your understanding of the overall .NET architecture.

The C# language

As its name suggests C# firmly has its ancestry within the C/C++ family of programming languages. The C# language was designed explicitly to conform to the requirements of the CLR and CTS requirements. It should be noted that C# has been dramatically simplified when compared to C++.

The flexibility of C and its extension to C++ offers experienced programmers a degree of programming freedom unrivalled by any other modern programming language. This flexibility came with a very high price, a very unfriendly set of syntax and semantics and a steep learning curve for inexperienced programmers.

The designers of C#, because it was to be a CLR compliant language, took the approach adopted previously by the developers of languages such as Java. Although the syntax is similar to C/C++, the CTS semantic rules define how data can be manipulated, this fact alone results in a flexible language structure, which has similarities to most previous object-oriented languages, but a vastly reduced set of syntax rules.

In an attempt to get standardisation, the definition of C# and a subset of the CLR called the CLI (Common Language Interface) have been submitted to ECMA in conjunction with the CTS definitions and form the ECMA – 355 specification.

This standard covers not only the syntax but also the semantics and the metadata, used to describe the variables and the actions that the code will perform on those variables. We will continue to expand on the role of metadata within the .NET Framework in other chapters.

There are two basic roots for the development of a C# application that can execute in the .NET Framework, the first is Visual Studio.NET, this is a complete integrated development environment (IDE), and should be the most popular route for students. The alternative is a set of command line tools, the SDK (Software Development Kit), which includes a compiler called 'csc.exe' designed to be used as a stand-alone application in a Windows environment.

The open source world has also embraced C# and under the GNU licence agreement, a suite of compilers and tools are being developed, along with the .NET Framework for other operating systems in the project codenamed **Mono**.

We have already identified that any programming languages must contain a set of keywords, which when combined correctly allow a real world problem to be defined as a set of algorithmic program steps that manipulate data.

C# has such a set of keywords but unlike older languages all manipulation of actual data is accomplished by building onto the CTS definitions for the data type, rather than being specifically constrained by the keyword definitions.

In the previous chapters I have highlighted that an understanding of the CLR provides a solid foundation for proficient C# programming. The examples in this chapter demonstrate some basic C# coding within a console application. The focus is to provide solutions that demonstrate use of the language to solve basic games requirements. Nothing very complex, the examples are intended to demonstrate the use of the language and the CLR:

```
// Example 1 C#
// CopyRight Tony Grimer Essential .Net for Students
// August 2003
    interface Number
    {
        int GetRandom(int MinValue,int MaxValue);
    }
    class ComputeRandom  : Number
    {
        public int GetRandom(int MinValue,int MaxValue)
        {
            int temp;
            System.Random randomNumber= new System.Random ();
            temp = randomNumber.Next(MinValue,MaxValue);
            return (temp);
        }
    }
    class DisplayValue
    {
        static void Main()
        {
            ComputeRandom cr = new ComputeRandom();
            int v;
            v = cr.GetRandom(1,52);
            System.Console.WriteLine ("Random Value {0}",v);
            System.Console.ReadLine();
        }
    }
```

The program begins with some comments, indicated by the two slashes (the standard C++ inline comment syntax), these give a brief description of the purpose. The body of the program consists of three types: an interface named Number and the two classes ComputeRandom and DisplayValue.

All C# programs consist of a number of types, the outermost of which must be classes, interfaces, structures, enumerators, or delegates. A namespace has also been declared, we have already seen the concept of namespaces when we looked at the .NET class library structure. (You can review any definitions of these 'OO' concepts on the support website).

The first important difference between C and C# is that C# does not permit any global variables or methods, this is obvious as we are dealing with an 'OO' methodology which by its nature has no concept of globals. All instances of variables and methods to manipulate the variable must be contained within a class or similar object and in the case of .NET this must be derived from one of the CTS data types.

The Number interface is the C# incarnation of the CTS definition of an interface type and in this case defines a single method GetRandom(..). This method takes two parameters and returns an integer. The parameters are passed by value, this is the default in C#; passing by value means that any changes made to the parameters in the method won't be seen by the calling method. We will return to this topic in various examples throughout the book.

If you want a parameter to be passed by reference, an option that allows any changes made by the called method to the parameter values to be seen by the calling method itself, then the **ref** keyword must be placed before the parameter, the syntax change to the method if we needed reference passing would be:

```
int GetRandom(ref int MinValue,ref int MaxValue);
```

At this point, if you are unsure of the difference between value and reference, you should review the discussion in Chapter 2 regarding value and reference data types and the subject of boxing and the possible impact on the performance of the final system.

Each class definition in the first example demonstrates the syntax used by C# to declare the CTS class type. Within C#, classes can implement one or more interfaces, they can inherit from at most one other class and have available all the other attributes associated with the CTS core class type. The first class in the example implements the Number interface, as indicated by the syntax of a colon between the class name and the interface.

```
class ComputeRandom : Number
```

In C# this syntax implies that the full implementation of the Number interface and its associated methods must be present within the class ComputeRandom.

The method GetRandom(..) declares a local instance of an integer type that we will call temp, this variable is used to store the result of a method. The second declaration uses a .NET Framework class library to create an instance of an object from the system namespace Random. Once this object is created it uses a method from within system.random to create a new random number and store the result into temp.

The class DisplayValue contains one single method named Main(..). In a similar manner to C and C++, a C# program execution always starts from a fixed point and in C# this is the method Main(..). Although not shown in this example but highlighting the C/C++ ancestry of C#, the Main(..) can have command line arguments, these will need to be interrogated as execution starts. In this example Main(..) returns a value called void, this is a C# keyword which when used in this context indicates that no value is going to be returned. The purpose of a return value for Main(..) is that once again like C/C++ when the application terminates, it could be useful to inform the host operating system that it was successful or it failed etc.

The use of keyword **void** in the example denotes that no value is going to be considered when the application terminates. It must be noted that unlike C/C++ the keyword **void** cannot be used to identify an empty parameter list, it only has one purpose to indicate a method returns no value. In C# the declaration of a void return and an empty parameter list is:

■ void Main();

In C/C++ the corresponding declaration would have been:

■ void main(void);

The use of a capital 'M' in C# is simply a change to the keyword definition and has no relevance to the keyword **void**.

In the example, Main(..) creates an instance of the ComputRandom class using C# syntax, as a point of information the cr = new ComputeRandom(); will be translated to the MSIL newobj described in Chapter 2.

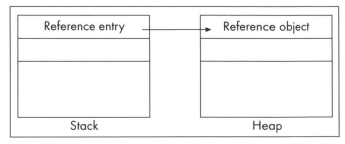

Figure 4.1   *The managed stack and heap relationship*

To create an instance means that we will have an object reference on the local managed stack and the object itself will have storage on the managed heap, as shown in Figure 4.1.

The variable v declared as an integer is assigned the value returned by the method GetRandom(..), in this case the parameter values used in GetRandom(..) have been set to 1 and 52, so the number will be in the correct range for a playing card.

The result is written using the WriteLine(..) method from the .NET Framework console class, an extremely useful subordinate namespace to System, as discussed in the previous chapter. This method has two parameters, the first is a string format identifier, with curly brackets to specify the position of variables, the second a value parameter to display. A typical output from this example would be:

```
Random Value 12
```

The last statement in Main(..) is simply a mechanism to ensure that the console window remains open, without this the Main(..) would terminate and we would not be able to see the value written as the application terminates. To stop this happening the call to the console ReadLine(..) method will wait for any type of keyboard input.

The goal of this simple example is to give you a feel for the general structure and style of C#. There is much more to the language and the CLR environment than such a simple example could possibly indicate, but it is your first real .NET application.

The C# data types

As discussed in the second chapter all supported languages must map their data types to the CTS type system to gain access to the

CLR and the .NET class library support. All of the core data value types are defined in the System namespace, the C# equivalents used in the examples are in fact shorthand synonyms for the complete definitions:

```
int I;          // shorthand form declaration for a 32 bit integer
```

This could have been fully defined as:

```
System.Int32 I ;
```

An important factor for any students who have not worked with a case sensitive syntax before, a declaration of **Int** is not the same as **int**.

Classes

C# classes use a C/C++ derived syntax to expose the functionality etc. of the CTS core class type. For example, the CTS specification defines that a class can implement one or more interfaces, but only inherit from one other class.

So a class DealCards that implements Shuffle and Count and inherits from class ComputeRandom would be declared as:

```
Class Dealcards : ComputeRandom, IShuffle, ICount {…}
```

In the above syntax, the class comes first; any class may be labelled as sealed or abstract, and can also be assigned attributes such as public or only internally visible. These class attributes map to the basic CTS definitions, this attribute information is stored in the metadata for the class and is held in the assembly manifest. Although our simple example contained only a method, C# classes can contain fields methods and properties, once again mapping to the relevant CTS specification.

In following this CTS mapping, accessibility is controlled by the relevant access modifier, for instance private and public. Any C# class can contain one or more constructors, the constructor will be used during the creation of an instance of the class, the correct constructor being called, based on parameter lists. The class will also contain a destructor; however, in the CLR terminology this is a finalize(..) method and because of the automatic garbage collection a finalize(..) is not the same as a destructor. The possible problems associated with the automatic garbage collection available within the .NET Framework were discussed in the previous chapter. If a class inherits from another, the new class can potentially override one or more type members in its parent, the only syntax requirement is that the method in the parent is declared to be virtual. Any virtual methods that are overridden will take preference over the base class method. In C# the base class method can be called by using the **base** keyword to qualify the method call.

Interfaces

The first example showed the use of interfaces; in basic C# syntax interface declaration is quite straightforward. Within the CTS, multiple interface inheritance is possible, the syntax for this being:

```
Interface Card : Shuffle, Count {...}
```

In such a case the interface called Card will contain all the methods, properties and any other type members declared within the two parent interfaces plus anything defined within the implementation of Card itself.

Structures

Since the CTS defines a basic value data type for a structure, any structure is very similar to a class, so as you would expect C# reflects this commonality. A structure can contain methods, fields and properties and it can implement interfaces. Structures are value types rather than reference types, the importance of this distinction is fully discussed in Chapter 2. As previously reviewed, value types in the CTS cannot participate in inheritance, meaning that unlike a class, a structure cannot inherit from another type. It is also not possible to define a type that inherits from a structure. In C# a structure has the form:

```
struct CardType
{
    string suit;
    int facevalue;
}
```

In the example we only have values within the structure, this resembles traditional C/C++ structures, in fact a structure can be far more complex. If we go back to our first example, simply changing the keyword class to struct would change the class ComputeRandom to a structure and the program would function in exactly the same way.

Delegates

Passing a reference to a method in the Windows environment is a major requirement. For example, to identify which method we wish to execute when for instance a button event occurs requires some form of reference pointer to that method.

In C/C++ this was a basic operation, the syntax of C/C++ allowed the passing of an address of the method via a general pointer type. The concept of a pointer type is simply not an alternative in the CTS, a pointer by its very definition can contain a raw memory address, and in the type safe world (review the metadata manifest of an assembly if you are unsure of why it is type safe) of the CLR any form of pointer data type would defeat the whole concept.

However, the CTS does define a reference data type called a delegate. The delegate type is mapped into the C# language to satisfy this pointer to a method concept. A delegate is defined in the CTS specification as a reference object; the data it can contain may be a reference to a method with a specific signature. It is the concept of the specific signature that differentiates a CTS delegate type from a generic pointer type.

Once a delegate is created and initialised, it can be passed as a parameter into another method and used to invoke the method reference in the delegate signature. An example of the use of a delegate in C# would take the form:

```
/// Example 1a C#
// CopyRight Tony Grimer Essential .Net for Students
// August 2003

delegate void MyDel(string s);
class DemoDelegate
{
    static void Main()
    {
        MyDel Del1 = new MyDel (WriteString);
        TestDelegate(Del1);
        System.Console.ReadLine ();
    }
    static void TestDelegate(MyDel WriteTest)
    {
        System.Console.WriteLine("In the call to TestDelegate");
```

```
            WriteTest("Written by the delegated call");
    }
    static void WriteString(string s)
    {
    System.Console.WriteLine
                    ("Delegated method Parameter passed in :- {0}",s);
    }
}
```

In this example the first definition is the template (specific signature) for the delegate, in this case the method referenced by the delegate is defined to have a single string parameter. Within the Main(..) an instance of this delegate is created, this delegate instance is then assigned to the method WriteString(..) which conforms to the specific delegate signature. In the method TestDelegate(..) we use a reference to this delegate, it is passed into the method as the parameter WriteTest. The result of such syntax is that the statement WriteTest(....); is equivalent to WriteString (....);.

Obviously delegates can get far more complex than this, one of the most interesting aspects of delegate use is the ability for a single delegate to be assigned to multiple methods allowing a single delegate call to activate these methods in a particular order.

Such flexibility is exploited when we consider event handling in a GUI environment. If specific event handling is required in any application, the new method will conform to the event handling delegate's signature and the new handler will be attached to the system delegate event handler.

In taking this approach our new handler will be called as part of the delegate chain for that event:

```
// Example 1b C#
// CopyRight Tony Grimer Essential .Net for Students
// August 2003
// multiple delegates
delegate void MyDel(string s);
class DemoDelegate
{
    static void Main()
    {
        MyDel Del1 = new MyDel (WriteString);
        Del1+= new MyDel (WriteStringExt);
        TestDelegate(Del1);
        System.Console.ReadLine ();
    }
    static void TestDelegate(MyDel WriteTest)
    {
```

```
        System.Console.WriteLine("In the call to TestDelegate");
        WriteTest("Written by the delegated call");
    }
    static void WriteString(string s)
    {
    System.Console.WriteLine("1 st method Parameter passed in {0}",s);
    }
    static void WriteStringExt(string s)
    {
    System.Console.WriteLine("2nd method string length is {0}",s.Length);
    }
}
```

This is exactly the same as the previous example but in this case the delegate WriteTest has been assigned not simply to WriteString(..) but also to WriteStringExt(..); when the delegate is called both methods are activated. The order of activation is determined by the order of the two assignments:

```
MyDel Del1 = new MyDel (WriteString);
Del1+= new MyDel (WriteStringExt);
```

The above order produces the output 1st method followed by 2nd. If we reverse this chaining order to:

```
MyDel Del1 = new MyDel (WriteStringExt);
Del1+= new MyDel (WriteString);
```

Then the output is changed to 2nd method followed by 1st.

Arrays

As with other programming languages, C# arrays are considered as ordered groups of elements of the same type.

However, since in the CTS an array is defined as a reference data type, then an array in C# is a single object, rather than the more conventional definition of a collection of value instances of a variable. We can view an array in memory as shown in Figure 4.2. The syntax declaration of arrays is straightforward, but you must remember that as the array is an object it will not exist until an instance of the type is created.

```
int [] values;         // this does not create or give a size
                             to this integer array
values = new int [20];  // now an instance is created
                           with 20 elements
```

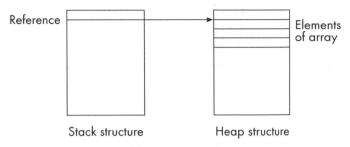

Figure 4.2   *Value type array structure in C#*

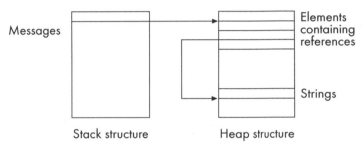

Figure 4.3   *Reference type array structure in C#*

Obviously arrays of value types are simple. In Figure 4.2 the heap allocation would contain the values of the integer in each element. Arrays of reference types are more complex:

```
string [] messages;        // defines an array of strings
messages = new string[20]  // create an instance
                              with 20 elements
```

The allocation on the heap in this case is for 20 references to the strings that in turn will also be stored on the heap, as shown in Figure 4.3.

Multiple dimension arrays are available, the syntax for the declaration is:

```
int [,] positions;         // this does not create or give a
                              size to this integer array
positions = new int[10,20]  // this creates the instance and size
```

The arrays in C# are built from the core type in the CTS, so all arrays in C# inherit from the Sytem.Array namespace. The base type provides various useful methods and properties that can be accessed from any instance of an array.

- **GetLength**(..) method determines the number of elements in a particular dimension of an array

- **CopyTo**(..) method allows a one-dimensional array to be copied to another.

The C# language control structures

I have included a very simple overview here of the C# language control structures, obviously if you are familiar with C/C++ control structures then you can skip over this section.

Conditional execution

```
if ( condition )
    {......}
else
    {......}
```

Note that the condition must evaluate to a value of type Boolean (true or false), the implied then clause is executed for a true and the else clause for a false. If we extend this to the standard multiple condition control.

The switch structure

```
switch (TestValue)
{
case testvalue1: {......} break;
case testvalue2: {......} break;
case testvalue3: {......} break;
default : {......}
}
```

Dependant on the actual numeric value in TestValue, will dictate which of the case options is activated. The break after each case ensures that after execution of the case, control is passed to the next statement following the switch.

Note: Unlike C/C++ the break in C# is mandatory, you cannot allow particular values to run into the next case statements.

Iteration mechanisms

```
while (condition)
{......}
```

While and Do

The condition of the while statement must evaluate to a value of type Boolean (true or false), the loop will continue if it evaluates to true and will exit to the statement after the while when it evaluates to false:

```
do
 {......}
while (condition);
```

The condition of the while statement must evaluate to a value of type Boolean (true or false), the loop will continue if it evaluates to true and will exit to the statement after the while when it evaluates to false.

For loop

There are in fact two versions of the for loop. The first is the standard C/C++ format.

```
for (StartCondition; EndCondition; Increment)
{......}
```

As with C/C++ the control variable used to control the loop must be declared before it is used. The StartCondition defines the first value to use for the control variable, the EndCondition defines the test that will be carried out to terminate the loop, this EndCondition must evaluate to a value of type Boolean (true or false), the loop will continue while it is true and will exit to the next statement below the for loop when it becomes false. The Increment is required to determine how the control variable will be changed at each iteration of the loop. For example:

```
for ( i = 0; i <=10 ; i++)
{......}
```

This will set up a loop which will run for values from i = 0 to i = 10, on each loop the value on i will be incremented by one each time, the loop will exit when i is incremented to 11.

The second version of the for loop is the foreach structure, this is a variation of the basic for loop designed to allow iteration through a collection. The use of this structure is best explained by looking at a simple example:

```
// Example 1c C#
// CopyRight Tony Grimer Essential .Net for Students
// August 2003
// for each

    class ForEach
    {
        static void Main(string[] args)
        {
```

```
int [] Temperature = {20,50,30,10,75,45,66};
int lowTemp = 100;
foreach (int Temp in Temperature)
{
    if (Temp< lowTemp)
        lowTemp = Temp;
}
System.Console.WriteLine ("Lowest temperature was {0}",
                                lowTemp);
System.Console.ReadLine();
}
}
```

In this simple example we have declared a single dimension array Temperature; it is possible using the foreach structure to step through the array values and extract the lowest in this case. Notice the syntax of the foreach, it is important that the type of the value being considered is declared within the statement itself, otherwise you will get a syntax error.

Obviously this simple example could have been written using a traditional structure in the form:

```
for (int Temp= 0 ; Temp <= 6 ; Temp++)
{
    if (Temperature[Temp]< lowTemp)
        lowTemp = Temperature[Temp];
}
```

However, using this standard for-loop structure requires that we access the array elements themselves and that the size of the array is known or can be calculated prior to starting the loop.

Having got this far with the basic structure of C# and since it is not the purpose of this book to teach you how to program in C#, it is left to the student to attempt the review questions and the suggested examples to familiarise themselves more fully with the C# language.

TheVB.NET language

As its name suggests VB.NET has its ancestry firmly within Visual Basic. Visual Basic was originally conceived as a simpler programming environment for Windows applications, offering the non-specialist programmer the ability to develop fairly sophisticated Windows programs without needing to fully understand the Windows architecture. VB.NET has been redesigned to conform to the requirements of the .NET Framework model.

It could be argued that in having to meet the .NET Framework requirement the migration from VB6, the last incarnation of Visual Basic, has actually made VB.NET more complex than its predecessors. VB.NET is now a fully object-oriented language rather than its event driven procedural predecessors, the designers of VB.NET were not able to take the same approach used by C#. They have had to be consistent with the requirements of the CTS structure while trying to maintain the keywords and feel of previous versions of Visual Basic. The result of this design creates a fairly flexible language structure, with much of the syntax of the earlier versions of Visual Basic but which now has similarities to other object-oriented languages.

The syntax should be fairly understandable to anyone with a Visual Basic background, but of course the fact it is now constrained to the CTS structure and must therefore conform to 'OO' design methodology, there is a fairly steep learning curve to migrate from Visual Basic 6 to VB.NET. I have provided an overview of 'OO' programming techniques etc. on the support website for this book.

There are two basic roots for the development of VB.NET application: the first is Visual Studio.NET, this is defined as a complete integrated development environment (IDE), and should be the most popular route for students. It includes all the tools needed to produce solutions in VB.NET. The alternative is a set of command line tools, the SDK (Software Development Kit), which includes a compiler called 'vbc.exe' designed to be used within the Windows environment.

We have already defined that any programming languages must contain a set of keywords, defined by specific syntax rules, that when combined correctly will allow a real world problem to be defined as a set of algorithmic program steps that manipulate data.

VB.NET has such a set of keywords but unlike its predecessors in the VB family manipulation of actual data is accomplished by building onto the CTS definitions for the data type:

```
Module Module1
    '' Example 1 VB.NET
    '' CopyRight Tony Grimer Essential .Net for Students
    '' August 2003
    Interface Number
    Function GetRandom(ByVal MinValue As Integer, _
                    ByVal MaxValue As Integer) As Integer
    End Interface
```

```
      Class ComputeRandom
          Implements Number
   Function GetRandom(ByVal MinValue As Integer, ByVal MaxValue _
          As Integer) As Integer Implements Number.GetRandom
              Dim temp As Integer
              Dim RandomNumber As System.Random
              RandomNumber = New System.Random()
              temp = RandomNumber.Next(MinValue, MaxValue)
              Return temp
          End Function
      End Class
      Sub Main()
          Dim cr As New ComputeRandom()
          Dim v As Integer
          v = cr.GetRandom(1, 52)
          System.Console.WriteLine("Random Value {0}", v)
          System.Console.ReadLine()
      End Sub
   End Module
```

The programme begins with a Module definition common to most VB.NET simple applications, then comments indicated by the single quote, these give a brief description of the purpose.

The body of the program consists of two types: an interface named Number and a class called ComputeRandom and Sub Main(). All VB.NET programs consist of a number of types, the outermost of which must be classes, interfaces, structures, enumerators, or delegates. A namespace can also be declared; we have already seen the concept of namespaces when we looked at the .NET class library structure.

The first important difference to older VB code is that VB.NET does not permit any global variables or methods, this is obvious as we are now dealing with an 'OO' methodology which has no concept of globals. All instances of variables and methods to manipulate such instances must be contained within a class or similar object derived from one of the CTS data types.

The Number interface is the VB.NET incarnation of the CTS definition of an interface type and defines a single method GetRandom(..), this method takes two parameters and returns a numeric value, in this case an integer. These parameters are passed by value, within VB.NET the keyword **ByVal** is used to denote passing by value. Passing by value means that any changes made to the parameters in the method won't be seen by the calling method, we will return to this topic in various examples throughout the book.

At this point for the VB6 programmers it should be noted that VB6 always passed parameters by reference, unless you specified otherwise. If you want the parameter passed by reference, i.e. allowing any changes made by the called method to the parameter values to be seen by the calling method, then the **ByRef** keyword must be placed before the parameter, the syntax change to this method to use reference parameters would be:

```
Function GetRandom(ByRef MinValue As Integer,
                   ByRef MaxValue As Integer) As Integer
```

While on the subject of reference parameter passing, you should review the discussion in the previous chapter regarding the difference between value and reference types and the subject of boxing and the possible impact on the performance of the final system.

The class definition in this example demonstrates the syntax used by VB.NET to declare the CTS class type. Within VB.NET classes can implement one or more interfaces, they can inherit from at most one other class and have available all the other attributes associated with the CTS core class type. The class in the example implements the Number interface, as indicated by the syntax:

```
Class ComputeRandom Implements Number
```

In VB.NET this syntax implies that the full implementation of the Number interface methods must be present within the class ComputeRandom.

Before we leave the syntax issues of an interface within a class, the syntax for this in VB.NET is slightly clumsy requiring that within the class the method is declared as:

```
Function GetRandom(ByVal MinValue As Integer, ByVal MaxValue _
                   As Integer) As Integer Implements Number.GetRandom
```

Notice that the interface name and the method name must be explicitly defined on the end of the method declaration before the implementation, failure to do this produces a very obscure error message. The method GetRandom(..) declares a local instance of an integer type that we will call temp, this variable is used to store the result of a method. The second declaration within the class is using the .NET Framework class library to create an instance of the object from the system namespace random. Once this object is created the class then uses a method from within the system.random object to create a new random number and store the result into temp.

The Sub Main() contains some simple statements. Much like C/C++, and C# programs there must be a start point for an application, in the case of this console VB.NET application this is always the Sub Main(..).

Within the example, Sub Main() creates an instance of the ComputRandom class using VB.NET syntax, as a point of information the cr = new ComputeRandom(); will be translated to the MSIL newobj described in a previous chapter. The variable v declared as an integer is assigned the value returned by the method GetRandom(..), in this case the parameter values used in GetRandom(..) have been set to 1 and 52, so the number will be in the correct range for a playing card.

The result is written using the WriteLine(..) method from the .NET Framework console class, one of the .NET class library subordinate namespaces to System discussed in the previous chapter. This method has two parameters, the first is a string format identifier, with curly brackets to specify the position of variables, the second is a value parameter to display. A typical output from this example would be:

```
Random Value 32
```

The last statement in this method is simply a mechanism to ensure that the console window remains open, without this the Sub Main() would terminate and we would not be able to see the value written as the application would terminate. To stop this happening the call to the console ReadLine(..) method will wait for any type of keyboard input. The goal of this simple example is to give you a feel for the general structure and style of VB.NET. There is much more to the language and the CLR than such a simple example could possibly indicate, but it is your first real VB.NET application.

The VB.NET data types

As identified in the second chapter all supported languages must map to the CTS type definitions to gain access to the CLR and the .NET class library support. All of the main value data types are defined in the System namespace, the VB.NET equivalents used in the examples are in fact shorthand synonyms for the complete definitions.

One interesting consequence of its Visual Basic ancestry is that VB.NET omits a definition of unsigned types. This is because historically Basic as a programming language has never had the concept of unsigned variables. The omission from VB.NET of these data types does not preclude the usage of the available CTS versions, they can be accessed by simply declaring them as:

```
Dim I as System.UInt32;  '' use the fully qualified CTS definition
```

As would be expected in any version of basic, VB.NET is not case sensitive, a hangover from previous original design definition of basic itself. However, this case insensitivity does cause a problem for students when swapping between compliant languages, remember C# is case sensitive whereas VB.NET is not.

Classes in VB.NET

VB.NET has had to derive an entirely new syntax for the declaration of classes that conform to the CTS data type definitions. Although previous versions of Visual Basic have had a class data type, these were very much Visual Basic specific and the syntax has had to be revised to conform to the requirements of using the CTS definitions and be fully compatible with the CLR. Therefore a class DealCards that implements Shuffle and Count and inherits from class ComputeRandom would be declared as:

```
Class DealCards
     Inherits ComputeRandom
     Implements Shuffle
     Implements Count
......
End Class
```

In the above syntax, the class comes first with any base class that is inherited, followed by any interface that is implemented within the class. Obviously as with any CLR supported language any of these definitions can have attributes defining, for instance, visibility in terms of public or private. These class attributes map to the basic CTS definitions and this information is stored in the metadata for the class within the assembly manifest discussed in the previous chapter.

In following this CTS mapping, accessibility is controlled by the relevant access modifier, for instance private and public. Any VB.NET class can contain one or more constructors, the constructor will be used during the creation of an instance of the class, the correct constructor being called, based on parameter lists. The class will also contain a destructor, however in the CLR terminology this is a finalize(..) method and because of the automatic garbage collection a finalize(..) is not the same as a destructor. The possible problems associated with the automatic garbage collection available within the .NET Framework were discussed in the previous chapter. If a class inherits from another, the new class can potentially override one or more type members in its parent, the only syntax requirement is that the method in the parent is declared to be virtual. Any virtual methods that are overridden will take preference over the base class method, in VB.NET the base class method can be called by using the **MyBase** keyword to qualify the method call.

Interfaces in VB.NET

The first example showed the use of interfaces. In VB.NET, syntax interface declaration is quite straightforward. Within the CTS, multiple interface inheritance is possible, the syntax for this being:

```
Interface Card
Inherits Shuffle
Inherits Count
......
End Interface
```

In such a case the interface called Card will contain all the methods, properties and any other type members declared within the two parent interfaces, plus anything defined within the implementation of Card itself.

Structures in VB.NET

Since the CTS defines a basic value data type for a structure, this definition is very similar to a class, so as you would expect VB.NET reflects this commonality. A structure can contain methods, fields and properties and it can implement interfaces. Structures are value types rather than reference types, the importance of this distinction was fully discussed in Chapter 2 when we looked at the CTS in detail. As previously reviewed value types in the CTS cannot participate in inheritance, meaning that unlike a class, a structure cannot inherit from another type. It is also not possible to define a type that inherits from a structure. In VB.NET a structure has the form

```
Structure CardType
    Public suit As String
    Public facevalue As Integer
End Structure
```

In the example we only have values within the structure, this resembles traditional legacy Visual Basic user defined types, in fact a structure can be far more complex. If we go back to our first example simply changing the keyword would change the class ComputeRandom to a structure and the program functions in exactly the same way.

Delegates

Passing a reference to a method in the Windows environment is a major requirement, for example to identify which method to run when a button event occurs. In traditional Visual Basic this was not a feature very often used although VB6 has got the **'addressof'** operator.

The CTS defines a reference type called a delegate and this can be mapped into VB.NET to augment the full visibility to the developer of a mechanism of mapping event code-oriented callback functions etc., in a conventional GUI interface environment. In the previous versions of Visual Basic, although event-oriented coding was supported, the basic mechanism was hidden within the platform specific run-time library. An example of the use of a delegate in VB.NET:

```
'' Example 1a VB.NET
'' CopyRight Tony Grimer Essential .Net for Students
'' August 2003
Imports System.Console
Module Module1
    Delegate Sub MyVBDel(ByVal s As String)
    Sub TestDelegate(ByVal WriteTest As MyVBDel)
        WriteLine("In the call to TestDelegate")
        WriteTest("Written by the delegated call")
    End Sub
    Sub WriteString(ByVal s As String)
        WriteLine("Delegated method Parameter passed in :- {0}", s)
    End Sub
    Sub Main()
        Dim ThisDel As New MyVBDel(AddressOf WriteString)
        TestDelegate(ThisDel)
        System.Console.ReadLine()
    End Sub

End Module
```

In this example the first definition is the template for the delegate, the delegate definition refers to the fact that the method referenced by the delegate must have a single string parameter, using this template the delegate has been uniquely defined.

Within the Sub Main() an instance of this delegate is created and this instance is then assigned to the method WriteString(..). This method WriteString(..) is defined within the same module. In the method TestDelegate(..) we have a reference to this delegate passed, it is passed into the method as the parameter WriteTest.

The result of such syntax is that the statement WriteTest(..); is equivalent to WriteString.

In VB.NET there is no mechanism for the multiple delegate handling found in C# as described in the previous section, there are techniques for multiple invocation lists when an event occurs but we will be looking at the event driven programming paradigm in the chapter dealing with Windows Forms, so for now we have to say that the flexibility of pure delegate handling in VB.NET is significantly reduced when compared to the C# language.

Arrays

As with other programming languages, VB.NET arrays are considered as ordered groups of elements of the same type. However, since the CTS defines an array as a reference data type, then any array in VB.NET must be considered as an object, rather than a collection of value instances of a variable. So we can view an array in memory as shown in Figure 4.4.

The syntax declaration of arrays is quite different in VB.NET to the mechanisms used in C# discussed in the last section and bears a far closer resemblance to the more traditional Visual Basic syntax:

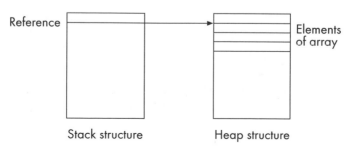

Figure 4.4   *Value type array structure in VB.NET*

```
Dim values(20) As Integer '' this both instances and creates the actual array
```

Comparing this to C# we can see that within VB.NET we can use syntax far more familiar to a Visual Basic programmer. One further difference is that in VB.NET redimensioning an array is totally acceptable.

```
Dim values() As Integer ''an empty array size
ReDim values(10)  '' redefine the array dynamically.
```

The syntax for a multidimensional array is simply:

```
Dim ThesePlots(120,20) As Integers
```

Once again this will create an instance of the array, unlike the C# syntax where we would need to explicitly create a new instance from a base declaration.

Obviously arrays of value types are relatively simple, in the above the heap allocation would contain the values of the integer in each element. However, arrays of reference types are more complex. In Figure 4.5 the allocation on the heap is for 20 references to the strings that in turn are also stored on the heap.

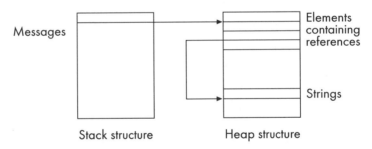

Figure 4.5   *Reference type array structure in VB.NET*

The VB.NET language control structures

I have included a very simple overview here of the VB.NET language control structures, obviously if you are familiar with VB control structures then you can skip over this section.

Conditional
execution

```
If condition Then
    ......
Else
    ......
End If
```

Note that the condition must evaluate to a value of type Boolean (true or false), the then clause is executed for a true, and the else clause for a false.

Select Case

```
Select Case TestValue
Case testvalue1 ......
Case testvalue2 ......
Case testvalue3 ......
Case Else ......

End Select
```

Dependent on the actual numeric value in TestValue, the variable will dictate which case of the select is activated. The natural end of a selection is when the next Case is defined.

Iteration mechanisms

```
While condition
......
End While
```

The condition of the While statement must evaluate to a value of type boolean , (true or false), the loop will continue if it evaluates to true and will exit to the statement after the While when it evaluates to false.

Do…While

As in previous versions of VB there are four variants:

Option 1.
```
Do While condition
......
Loop
```

Option 2.
```
Do Until condition
......
Loop
```

Do…Loop

Option 3.
```
Do
......
Loop While condition
```

Option 4.
```
Do
......
Loop Until condition
```

The condition control of all these 'do loop' structures must evaluate to a value of type Boolean (true or false). It is beyond this simple description of the VB.NET language to spend any more time investigating the algorithmic nature of each of the four options, it is left to the student to test and understand the fundamental difference between testing a loop on entry or exit.

For...Loop

```
For counter = start To end [ Step step ]
......
Next counter
```

The start defines the first value to use for the control variable, the end defines the test that will be carried out to terminate the loop, optional defines how the control variable is handled, the loop itself is terminated by the Next keyword.

The second version of the for loop is the foreach structure, this is a variation of the basic for loop designed to allow iteration through a collection. The use of this structure is best explained by looking at a simple example:

```
'' Example 1c VB.NET
'' CopyRight Tony Grimer Essential .Net for Students
'' August 2003
'' For each
Module Module1
    Sub Main()
        Dim temperature() As Integer = {20, 50, 30, 10, 75, 45, 66}
        Dim lowtemp As Integer = 100
        Dim Temp As Integer
        For Each Temp In temperature
            If Temp < lowtemp Then
                lowtemp = Temp
            End If
        Next Temp
        System.Console.WriteLine("Lowest temperature was {0}", lowtemp)
        System.Console.ReadLine()
    End Sub
End Module
```

In this simple example we have declared a single dimension array Temperature, it is then possible using the For Each structure to step through the array values and extract the lowest in this case. Notice the syntax of the For Each, it is important that the type of the value being considered is declared, otherwise you will get a syntax error.

Obviously this simple example could have been written using a traditional structure in the form:

```
For Temp = 0 to 6
  If Temperature(Temp) < lowTemp
    lowTemp = Temperature(Temp)
  End If
Next Temp
```

However, using the standard for-loop structure requires that we access the array elements themselves and that the size of the array is known or can be calculated prior to starting the loop.

Once again here we could spend a great deal longer discussing the programming concepts in VB.NET but, as with the previous section looking at the C# language, that is not the purpose of this book. So it is left to the students to attempt the review questions and the suggested examples to familiarise themselves more fully with VB.NET.

Other features common to both the C# language and VB.NET

The two previous sections have dealt with the basic data types and control structures that are key to all programming languages. The data types reviewed have been derived from the core definitions within the CTS, so we have now identified in this brief overview of both C# and VB.NET that there is a great deal of commonality between these two compliant languages. Any student with a background in 'OO' programming should have the key skills to undertake simple VB.NET or C# programming tasks. For completeness the following topics identify other aspects of the commonality of the compliant languages.

Namespaces

The underlying .NET class libraries within the CLR are fundamental to any development in either VB.NET or C#. In the examples so far the syntax used has defined the totally qualified name of the form.

```
System.Console.WriteLine (......);
```

Although this is the most basic syntax solution it does have a number of drawbacks; first, it is a large typing overhead and second, it is prone to errors within the syntax. To assist a new keyword has been adopted. In C# it is 'using', by applying this keyword we can refine the above as:

```
using System;
Console.WriteLine(......);
```

Or to more fully qualify the reference we could in fact use the syntax:

```
using System.Console;
WriteLine (......);
```

C# code can contain multiple **using** statements, allowing many aspects of the .NET class library to be referenced using this short form notation. In VB.NET the keyword is **'imports'** which has the same effect allowing the previous code to be changed to:

```
Imports System
Console.WriteLine(......)
```

Or to more fully qualify the reference we could in fact use the syntax:

```
Imports System.Console
WriteLine (....)
```

Multiple **'imports'** statements can be used to access more than one .NET class library from within the overall hierarchy.

Structured exception handling

Structured exception handling is not unique to the .NET Framework, a number of high-level programming languages have had structured exception handling as part of their functionality for a number of years. These implementations relied on using platform specific run-time libraries to provide this feature. The .NET Framework structured exception handling is integrated into the CLR, it is vital therefore that the .NET compliant languages have a consistent exception handling syntax.

Software development always incurs the possibility of leaving run-time errors within the final implementation; run-time errors being defined as logical errors within the algorithmic flow of the solution that cannot be identified by syntax or semantics. Such errors may be due to poor design/implementation or more realistically poor initial problem analysis. The syntax presented here relates to both C# and VB.NET, the underlying consistent approach is built into the CLR itself. Structured error handling is fully defined within CTS specification with suitable reference data types allocated. The CTS defines structured exception handling as:

**some unusual event during the execution of a
piece of code.**

The CLR itself defines a large set of possible exception conditions, but since any CTS type always has the ability to be inherited, it is possible for any application to create custom exception types specifically designed for a particular implementation. The syntax for trapping an exception is quite straightforward. In C# form:

try…catch

```
try
{......}            // some code which could cause an error
catch
{......}            // code that will be executed when the
exception occurs
```

In VB.NET we would use:

```
Try
......               ' some code which could cause an error
Catch
......               ' code that will be executed when the
                     ' exception occurs
End Try
```

If no exception occurs then the catch clause is simply not executed. As a simple example consider the following. In C# we would have:

```
try
{value = number/divisor;}
catch
{System.Console.WriteLine(" Divide by zero attempted);}
```

While in VB.NET it would be:

```
Try
value = number/divisor
Catch
System.Console.WriteLine(" Divide by zero attempted)
End Try
```

In this case, if the value of the variable divisor becomes zero, rather than the application terminating with a system error of divide by zero, the catch block would execute, inform the user of the problem, and the execution of the code will continue at the next statement after the end of the catch block. The question such an approach raises is what happens if the error is not a divide by zero?

Using the code above it would not be possible to identify that a different error had occurred. To overcome such a restriction any try block can have a number of specific catch blocks associated with it, each of these catch blocks has to identify which exception it is intended to process. So, for example, we could extend the above example to the following. In C# the coding would be:

```
try
{ value = number/divisor;}
catch (System.DivideByZeroException)
{System.Console.WriteLine(" Divide by zero attempted");}
catch (System.Exception e)
{System.Console.WriteLine(" Error occurred : {0}", e.Message);}
```

While in VB.NET it would be:

```
Try
value = number/divisor
Catch ex DivideByZeroException
System.Console.WriteLine(" Divide by zero attempted")
Catch ex
System.Console.WriteLine(" Error occurred : {0}", e.Message)
End Try
```

In this case the first block will identify the divide by zero condition, while the second catch will trap any other error and report it. Application execution will continue in either case following the last catch block after the try. As exceptions are defined by CTS data type any exception condition can be inherited from the basic CTS object and as such has access to inbuilt methods and properties. To complete our discussion on structured exception handling in both VB.NET and C# two further keywords need consideration, **throw** and **finally**.

Any application may wish to pass specific exceptions back through the inherent calling hierarchy of the methods. This is accomplished by using a throw statement either to pass back the caught system exception to the next level up the calling hierarchy, or if needed to pass back a user defined exception derived from the base object in the CTS. The whole topic of user defined exception derivation and its use in large system design is a little beyond the scope of this book, the reader is directed to the references on C# programming details. The optional finally keyword and the associated code block in the try / catch structure is used to create code which will be executed irrespective of the result of the try clause. In C# the structure is:

try...catch...
finally

```
try
{......}                    // some code which could cause an error
catch
{......}    // code that will be executed when the exception
//         occurs
finally
{......}                    // code will be executed here even if no exception
                           // occurred
```

In VB.NET the structure is:

```
Try
......                  ' some code which could cause an error
Catch
......    ' code that will be executed when the exception
         ' occurs
Finally
......          ' code will be executed here even if no exception
               ' occurred
End Try
```

So far we have been looking at VB.NET and C# code that will execute totally within the CLR and its managed code environment. This means that, as we saw in the previous chapter, the automatic garbage collection will always be taking place and application defined pointers cannot be used.

Some die hard C/C++ programmers will want to use pointers. Since a pointer holds a reference to user memory, if garbage collection occurred and the heap was rearranged it is quite possible that the pointer would no longer be holding a valid address. So blindly mixing managed code in the CLR with pointers is a terrible option. However, there may be situations where pre-CLR code is used simply because it is not economically viable to rewrite it totally in managed form. Another scenario often quoted for not using managed code with its inherent automatic garbage collection is for solutions in which some critical timing and performance characteristics are required. This situation will never occur with legacy Visual Basic since there was never the true concept of a pointer in Visual Basic, so this additional feature only relates to the C# language.

To enable such code this legacy arrangement of allowing pointers in managed code, a C# keyword of **unsafe** is available, when a C# class is defined as unsafe the methods etc. can use pointers and pointer arithmetic. To further ensure that heap data is not compacted, variables in unsafe code can be marked as **fixed** ensuring that garbage compaction will not move the physical memory address of this variable. Once again I have included a reference to this only for completeness, it is a very advanced topic and should only be investigated if you are looking to utilise code that would fall into one of the above categories.

Summary

C# is an attractive option for a modern high-level language in the managed code environment of the CLR. With its ancestry firmly in the C/C++ family it offers a great deal of flexibility to the developer.

The fact that VB.NET is totally proprietary to Microsoft means that C# offers the best options for future open source implementations of free compilers and future developments of the .NET Framework running on other operating system platforms.

However, the contrary argument can also be put forward for VB.NET; Visual Basic has made a place in history for itself, it is relatively easy to learn the basic structure and although in the CLR framework it has become fully object oriented it is still probably less of a steep learning curve for a legacy Visual Basic programmer than to convert to C#.

Obviously the open source world is not going to provide much support for VB.NET, but the proliferation of freeware and shareware ActiveX controls for Visual Basic highlights how much serious development in this proprietary language has taken place. We will in a later chapter look at .NET component design, this is the .NET Framework equivalent of ActiveX and without a doubt many of the .NET components developed in the future will use VB.NET as the route.

The situation this time is far clearer, development of components or for that matter any other shared implementations in VB.NET will offer 100% compatibility with the .NET Framework and hence with C#.

The great divide previously seen by C/C++ component design and Visual Basic component design will be removed once and for all, the .NET Framework makes it possible to utilise the best tools for the job.

Review questions

There are hundreds if not thousands of examples that you could take from both C/C++ and VB6 books and translate into C# or

VB.NET. Up to this point in the book we have only looked at console-based application, in the next chapter we will be extending this into Windows Forms.

1   For the review topics I suggest you write a couple of console applications only:

   (a) A simple program that throws a dice, or multiple dice and displays the result; try to write it in both C# and VB.NET irrespective of your programming background.

   (b) A program that tries to help you win the lottery, generate six random numbers between 1 and 49, use structured exception handling maybe on validity of number checking; see how easy it is to write a try catch block. Try to implement this in both VB.NET and C# to get a feel for the commonality of the languages. The amount of extra syntax you will have to learn is quite small.

   If you wish to experiment further then try to translate an application that you have written before in either VB or C/ C++.

2   Answer the following questions about the process:

   (a) If you started with an 'OO' solution did it map across to the .NET Framework easily?

   (b) If it was a C program did you manage to create a reasonable C# clone of the application?

   (c) If you started with a VB6 program was it easy to convert to 'OO' and code as VB.NET?

5 Windows Forms

Objective

Up to this point we have not attempted to develop a traditional GUI-based application.

The windows form namespace in the .NET class library can be considered as equivalent to the visual forms programming model used by previous versions of Visual Basic.

The major improvement of the .NET Windows Forms class model over the original Visual Basic model is its ability to support any CLR compliant language. This means that the .NET Windows forms class model, rather than just supporting VB.NET, now fully supports C# and for that matter any future developed CLR compliant language.

The use of visual programming is probably the most common mechanism for the design of any Graphical User Interface (GUI)-based modern application. Much of the popularity of Visual Basic can been attributed to its inherent visual programming technology, using a visual programming model allows non-specialist programmers the ability to quickly produce acceptable solutions to non-trivial real world problems.

The only viable alternative to the use of visual programming techniques requires the use of resource editors, which describe visual components using a pseudo language. The disadvantage of the resource technique is that the relationship between the resources and any related event programming code must be maintained by the developer, while if a visual programming technique is used this relationship is generally maintained from within the development environment itself.

In this chapter we will start to investigate how to use the visual programming model available within the .NET class library. The .NET Windows forms class maintains the outward appearance and basic functionality of the original visual programming environment found within Visual Basic, it is important to remember that the .NET Windows forms class is constrained to execute within a managed code area, i.e. the CLR and the inherent CTS definitions. The combination of these two features:

■ functionality inherited from the visual programming environment of VB

■ constraints imposed by CLR

creates a need that the new .NET Windows forms class has to be fully object oriented in structure while offering the visual flexibility. These two key elements lead to a definition for the .NET Windows form class.

It can be considered as a blend of two inherently different design philosophies.

The remainder of this chapter will investigate how such a blending has been accomplished and identify that the .NET Windows forms class offers developers working in any CLR compliant language a visual programming environment that is fully structured.

Introduction

Any windows form usually contains controls to obtain input from and display output to the user. The CLR Windows forms class contains a comprehensive set of such controls. To effectively use the controls on an applications form requires an environment such as Visual Studio .NET that allows the control to be dragged from a toolbar onto the form. The control once placed onto the form can then be programmatically positioned, interrogated and manipulated to suit the need of the application.

Comparing the above description with the original Visual Basic model, nothing has outwardly changed. In both cases an automatically generated code behind file is created when the user places a control onto a form. In the original Visual Basic model

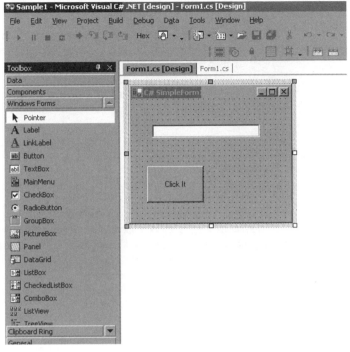

Figure 5.1   *Typical toolbar in Windows Form design view available in VS.NET*

much of the automatically generated code was hidden making it impossible for a developer to modify or track the layout programmatically.

Comparing this to the .NET visual model we find that in the .NET model the automatically generated code is fully exposed and commented. This fully commented source code is generated in the appropriate compliant language based on the original selection by the developer and offers far more flexibility than in the original Visual Basic technique.

Investigation of the generated code behind file for a form with controls shows that all the controls on a particular form are handled as a collection.

Extract from a simple VB.NET form with a button and textbox

```
#Region " Windows Form Designer generated code "
    Public Sub New()
        MyBase.New()
        'This call is required by the Windows Form Designer.
        InitializeComponent()
```

```
                    'Add any initialization after the InitializeComponent() call
            End Sub
        'Form overrides dispose to clean up the component list.
    Protected Overloads Overrides Sub Dispose(ByVal disposing As Boolean)
            If disposing Then
                If Not (components Is Nothing) Then
                    components.Dispose()
                End If
            End If
            MyBase.Dispose(disposing)
    End Sub
        'Required by the Windows Form Designer
        Private components As System.ComponentModel.IContainer
        'It can be modified using the Windows Form Designer.
        'Do not modify it using the code editor.
        Friend WithEvents ClickIt As System.Windows.Forms.Button
        Friend WithEvents Text1 As System.Windows.Forms.TextBox _
        <System.Diagnostics.DebuggerStepThrough()> _
            Private Sub InitializeComponent()
            Me.ClickIt = New System.Windows.Forms.Button()
            Me.Text1 = New System.Windows.Forms.TextBox()
            Me.SuspendLayout()
            '
            'ClickIt
            '
            Me.ClickIt.Location = New System.Drawing.Point(24, 104)
            Me.ClickIt.Name = "ClickIt"
            Me.ClickIt.Size = New System.Drawing.Size(88, 56)
            Me.ClickIt.TabIndex = 0
            Me.ClickIt.Text = "Click It"
            '
            'Text1
            '
            Me.Text1.Location = New System.Drawing.Point(32, 40)
            Me.Text1.Name = "Text1"
            Me.Text1.Size = New System.Drawing.Size(168, 20)
            Me.Text1.TabIndex = 1
            Me.Text1.Text = ""
            '
            'Form1
            '
            Me.AutoScaleBaseSize = New System.Drawing.Size(5, 13)
            Me.ClientSize = New System.Drawing.Size(248, 189)
            Me.Controls.AddRange(New System.Windows.Forms.Control() _
                            {Me.Text1, Me.ClickIt})
            Me.Name = "Form1"
            Me.Text = "VB SimpleForm1"
            Me.ResumeLayout(False)

        End Sub


    #End Region
```

In order to show the commonality in the automatic generation code behind file the following extract looks at the same form and controls in C#.

```
#region Windows Form Designer generated code
    /// <summary>
    /// Required method for Designer support - do not modify
    /// the contents of this method with the code editor.
    /// </summary>
    private void InitializeComponent()
    {
        this.ClickIt = new System.Windows.Forms.Button();
        this.Text1 = new System.Windows.Forms.TextBox();
        this.SuspendLayout();
        //
        // ClickIt
        //
        this.ClickIt.Location = new System.Drawing.Point(24, 104);
        this.ClickIt.Name = "ClickIt";
        this.ClickIt.Size = new System.Drawing.Size(88, 56);
        this.ClickIt.TabIndex = 1;
        this.ClickIt.Text = "Click It";
        //
        // Text1
        //
        this.Text1.Location = new System.Drawing.Point(32, 40);
        this.Text1.Name = "Text1";
        this.Text1.Size = new System.Drawing.Size(168, 20);
        this.Text1.TabIndex = 2;
        this.Text1.Text = "";
        //
        // Form1
        //
        this.AutoScaleBaseSize = new System.Drawing.Size(5, 13);
        this.ClientSize = new System.Drawing.Size(248, 189);
        this.Controls.AddRange(new System.Windows.Forms.Control[] {
        this.Text1,this.ClickIt});
        this.Name = "Form1";
        this.Text = "C# SimpleForm1";
        this.ResumeLayout(false);

    }
    #endregion
```

These two extracts clearly identify the flexibility of the .NET Windows forms class, both listings implement the same functionality and the similarity between the two, other than basic syntax changes, is very obvious. These listings are only an extract from the source files, both show how to position etc. a button called ClickIt and an edit control called Text1. As an example of the similarity we can consider the declaration for the button control in each language is:

C# declaration

```
this.ClickIt = new System.Windows.Forms.Button();
```

VB.NET declaration

```
Friend WithEvents ClickIt As System.Windows.Forms.Button
```

There are only minor differences in the above, we discussed in a previous chapter that basing the CLR on the CTS means that the semantics of any object derived from a base type would be common and programming languages only require specific syntax to support the objects semantics.

This button control requires that the application can detect standard events associated with user actions on that button, for instance clicking the button with the mouse. As noted previously visual programming environments handle the relationship between the control and specific events by creating event handler methods. An event handler for a button click in VB.NET:

```
Private Sub ClickIt_Click(ByVal sender As System.Object, ByVal e As _
System.EventArgs)Handles ClickIt.Click

End Sub
```

In C#, before the event handler can be created a new delegate entry must be formed; refer to the previous chapter for the definition of a delegate:

```
this.ClickIt.Click += new System.EventHandler(this.ClickIt_Click);
```

Once the delegate is attached to the handler, in C# the button click event handler will have the form:

```
private void ClickIt_Click(object sender, System.EventArgs e)
```

This event mechanism is handled within the .NET Framework itself, the actual detail of how the mechanism is implemented is beyond an introductory text such as this and the reader can refer to the message handling architecture within Windows itself (Petzold, C., *Programming Windows*, Fifth Edition, 2000, Microsoft Press), to gain a fuller understanding of the event driven nature of the Windows environment.

The actual handling of routing of an event to the correct handler is carried out within the CLR. If no user defined event handler has been created in an application (this is commonly because the application only requires a default action to occur), there are default event handlers in the CLR.

The ability to chain delegates and hence event calling was discussed in the previous chapter when we looked at the delegate data type. Generally event handler written specifically in an application will be attached to an event handler chain, the final method on the chain will be the .NET default handler.

There are far too many user controls available in the Windows forms class to look at each individually. The most common controls will be investigated when we discuss the implementation of the examples in the following sections.

Before looking at any more detail on user controls, two further aspects of the Windows form class need consideration.

■ The parent–child architecture

■ Modal and non-modal display of a window.

Parent–child architecture

Generally a Windows application contains a parent window that is sometimes called the main window. When an application starts it displays its main window, then during the execution of the application further child windows are displayed normally within the confines of this parent window. These child windows are normally used to display information specific to some aspect of the application. Child windows can be constructed and defined as either a standard window or in some cases a dialogue box. A dialogue box uses a special system management layer within Windows called the Dialogue Manager that organises the use and placement of controls within any form identified to be a dialogue box. It is this Dialogue Management that requires the concept of modal display.

Modal/non-modal

Typically we can define

■ Always modal – special dialogue boxes/message boxes

■ always non-modal parent windows.

Any windows form specified to be opened as modal is displayed in a special manner, when a form is modal it must be closed before the user has the ability to access any other window on function on the desktop. Another way of looking at this is that the focus of the user input is locked onto a modal window form until that form is closed. In the non-modal display of a windows form the focus of user input can be moved away from the currently active window to any other window or function on the desktop.

SDI/MDI applications

An application can be defined as being Single Document Interfaced (SDI), or Multiple Document Interfaced (MDI).

This relates to the manner in which the parent–child architecture is implemented. In a SDI application there will normally be only one active child window per parent at any one time. In an MDI application multiple child windows can be active within a parent, a typical MDI application is a word processor where multiple documents can be open in the application at the same time and the user has the ability to simply switch between them with no regard for closing or saving information.

The .NET Windows forms class as you would expect supports all of these features; the inclusion of multiple controls within any form, opening a form as modal or non-modal, specifying that a form should act as a dialogue and defining the architecture of an application as either SDI and MDI.

Window form controls

There are a great number of standard Windows forms controls, these have been developed from the so-called standard Windows classes originally conceived for the C/C++ programming model that uses application programming interface (API) (Petzold, C., *Programming Windows*, Fifth Edition 2000).

Windows form controls can be divided into basic categories; action controls such as a button, tabbed forms etc., user input controls which include text boxes, combo boxes and list boxes, user display controls that include simple labels as well as more complex graphical capability and finally specialist controls among which we could include database grids etc.

It would be quite simple at this point in the discussion to take the approach of exploring some of the controls from each category. Such an approach allows the investigation of programmatic property changing and the concept of specific event handling. This would have led to some probably trivial examples of specific controls used in tediously boring application examples. However, the overall goal of this book as outlined in Chapter 1 is to show how the .NET architecture can be used to generate suitable solutions for real world problems; this approach in my view stimulates a much more rewarding learning experience.

In order to take this approach and to demonstrate the .NET Windows forms and controls, the examples in this chapter and to some extent the extensions in subsequent chapters lead towards the overall objective of this book, that by the last chapter you will be able to follow and understand the development of a simple multi-tier solution of a web-based service that provides the basic functionality of the card game '**Pontoon**'.

In the previous chapter on compliant programming languages we started along this path. The console application used to look at the compliant programming languages generated a deck of cards, it had methods to shuffle the deck and deal a hand of cards to a player. This console application can now be extended using Windows forms to add a Graphical User Interface (GUI) which has action buttons and a simple text output to display the hand being dealt. In a later chapter on the design of .NET components we will further extend this application to include graphical representation of the playing card.

This first simple example will look at the basic design of a .NET Windows forms base solution. In addition to the basic GUI components mentioned other options such as a menu will be added allowing you to investigate how the .NET Windows forms class offers not only the simple GUI components but also contributes to the solutions architecture. The subsequent examples in this chapter will look at other common problems in simple games programming, the generation of a playing surface (a simple 8 × 8 games board), a very simple animation based on a shoot the aliens game and a sliding block puzzle which includes the ability to save and restore a game's status. Aspects common to many Windows forms applications will be used in all of the examples including menu bars, and common dialogues such as file control and colour selection. In subsequent chapters further refinements to these examples will be made again within the .NET Windows forms class allowing, for instance, user definitions for painting (the clever way of saying drawing) on the form as well as the use of other controls.

The examples

The format of the description of the examples is common throughout the book. The description will first define a simple set of design requirements, followed by the implementation details in terms of class definitions and extracts of relevant source code with suitable descriptions. I have not listed the source code fully since much of this is common to all of the examples and in my view you will learn far more by loading the source down from the support site and trying it out yourself.

Example 1

Objective

To demonstrate a basic Windows GUI application

Specification

A simple graphical user interface extension to dealing a hand of cards. The specification for the GUI can be summarised as:

- A menu bar to select actions

- A button to request a shuffle

- A button to request a deal

- A display panel to identify the hand dealt

The actual playing card deck class will use the implementation from the previous console example and will not be reconsidered here.

This following discussion on the implementation of this example is based on the C# solution, the VB.NET solution is identical other than in the language specific syntax.

Implementing
basic menus

The menu system on the example has been kept to a minimum, there are only four menu entries and only two of these have any event handlers associated with them.

```
public class MainForm : System.Windows.Forms.Form
{
private System.Windows.Forms.MainMenu CSMenu1;
private System.Windows.Forms.MenuItem FileAction;
private System.Windows.Forms.MenuItem FileExit;
private System.Windows.Forms.MenuItem HelpAction;
private System.Windows.Forms.MenuItem HelpAbout;
....
}
```

These data declarations identify the variable names for the actual menu bar and the components associated with the menu bar. I have derived the variable names from within the visual programming environment, the default names are 'MenuItemN' where 'N' is simply an incremented numeric value. Using such default names provides you with very little help when you are trying to find errors in your code. I have derived useful names based on adding the word **Action** to the File entry so that the menu item 'File' is associated with the variable 'FileAction'.

Once declared as variables the automatic code generates actual instances, this simple menu and its associated menu items.

```
this.CSMenu1 = new System.Windows.Forms.MainMenu();
this.FileAction = new System.Windows.Forms.MenuItem();
this.FileExit = new System.Windows.Forms.MenuItem();
this.HelpAction = new System.Windows.Forms.MenuItem();
this.HelpAbout = new System.Windows.Forms.MenuItem();
```

The following code extract from the automatically generated file shows how the menu items are placed onto the menu bar itself:

```
this.CSMenu1.MenuItems.AddRange(new System.Windows.Forms.MenuItem[]
                                {this.FileAction, this.HelpAction});
```

The automatically generated file then details the entries for each of the menu items

```
// FileAction
//
this.FileAction.Index = 0;
this.FileAction.MenuItems.AddRange(new System.Windows.Forms.MenuItem[]
                                   {this.FileExit});
this.FileAction.Text = "File";
//
// FileExit
```

```
//
this.FileExit.Index = 0;
this.FileExit.Text = "Exit";
this.FileExit.Click += new System.EventHandler(this.FileExit_Click);
//
```

This structure is repeated for each of the items on the main menu bar itself.

Although this may look complicated it is quite straight-forward, as previously identified all controls are held in a collection so we find that menu items themselves are added to the collection by the AddRange() Method. Then the applications event handler for the click event on a menu item is added to the delegate list for the standard control event.

The remainder of the automatically generated code for this example identifies the naming, positioning and event handler for the two buttons and a simple text box. This is very similar to our very first basic Windows forms example, where we looked at the commonality between a form definition in either of the compliant languages. I will therefore ignore this code and leave it to you to investigate it in more detail.

The other important area to consider within this example is how to use the previously created class for the actual deck of cards, the original solution used a console output routine meaning that the whole application including the IO was contained within a single class structure. As noted previously in a .NET Windows forms application we are going to have a parent form and hence a parent class:

```
public class MainForm : System.Windows.Forms.Form
```

We need to declare variables within this parent form to interact with the original DeckofCards class as well as some other variables to maintain control of the number of cards dealt for each hand:

```
private DeckOfCards ThisDeck;   // an instance of the card deck
private int PHandSize;          // local size of the deck
```

The first of these declarations is quite straightforward, the second identifies a private integer that we will expand to become a public property of the class. In order to become a property we need to define a property get and set method of the form:

```
public int HandSize
{
    get {return PHandSize;}
    set {PHandSize = value;}
}
```

Using this property approach it is possible for an external class to access the private data within this forms class, the only other alternative would have been to make the variable PHandSize public within the forms class; this later technique of course is not good 'OO' design practice (allowing direct public access to variables within a class).

The use of the MessageBox() object is a very convenient mechanism for displaying user information such as the Help About.

```
private void HelpAbout_Click(object sender, System.EventArgs e)
{
    MessageBox.Show(" CopyRight Tony Grimer \n Date November 2003 \n Simple
    Example 1 of a Deck of Cards \n For Chapter 5 Students Essential Guide to
    .NET \n Version 1.0.0","C# Examples About");
}
```

It must be noted in the previous code extract that the string constants have been split for printing convenience and that C# does not support the syntax of string constant splitting. The version of a message box used is only one of the options available, in this option all that is specified is the message itself and the message box title, missing parameters that can be specified in the alternative versions are defaulted and in this case the user simply has an OK button.

We have previously defined the term modal dialogue, the following code extract from the example shows how such a modal dialogue is used. This extract is from the event handler for the 'Deal' button on the main form.

```
Form NCardDialog;    // declare a variable for the dialog box itself.
DialogResult result; // declare a variable to capture any dialogue
                     // result if needed.
NCardDialog = new NumberOfcardsDialog (this); // instance the dialogue form
result = NCardDialog.ShowDialog(); // request a modal show of the dialogue.
```

Figure 5.2   A modal dialogue

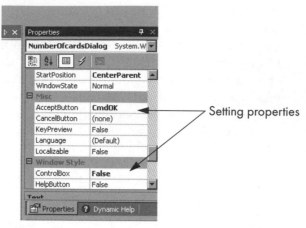

Figure 5.3   *Design view showing Property setting*

In order to act as a modal dialogue the form design for NumberOfcardsDialog requires that some of the basic properties of the form itself are modified:

■ The ControlBox property is set to false

■ The BorderSize property is set to FixedDialogue

■ The AcceptDialogue property is set to the name of the OK button on the form

■ The OK button on the dialogue form has its DialogueResult property set to OK.

Once these properties have been altered, the Dialogue Manager will control the action of this modal form. When the user clicks on the OK button on the form the Dialogue Manager will allow the OK button event handler to run as normal; however, once this handler is completed the form will be automatically terminated. If this form had not been set to execute as a dialogue box then the termination of the form etc. has to be carried out programmatically from within the application. In the code extract, the line:

```
NCardDialog = new NumberOfcardsDialog (this); // instance the dialogue form
```

shows that the default constructor for the form has been overridden, the automatically generated code derived when the form is being visually designed always has a constructor that takes no parameters. The constructor in this case is taking a single parameter allowing the form to have access to its parent's instance. The **this** pointer was discussed when we looked at the C# language, it contains the instance of the currently active object. In this case the active object is the main form so we are passing to the child from the instance pointer of its parent. The code of the revised constructor for the dialogue form being:

```
public NumberOfcardsDialog(MainForm parent)
{
//
// Required for Windows Form Designer support
//
InitializeComponent();
MyParent = parent; // reference to the object that called me
//
}
```

The availability of the MyParent variable within the dialogue form allows the following code to be implemented in OK button event handler for the dialogue form that directly updates the property value in its parent form:

```
private void CmdOK_Click(object sender, System.EventArgs e)
{
    MyParent.HandSize = Cards.SelectedIndex + 5;
}
```

Using a combo box to allow the user to select between various options is quite normal, the standard mechanism for determining which value has been selected from the combo box is to use the combo box list index property. The first item in the combo box list has an index offset of zero (0), and in this case relates to a request to deal a five (5) card hand, the other items on the combo box list increments the size of the card hand by one each time and the index offset on the list increments by one. Using the technique of adding the constant 5 to the index we will get an integer value for the number of cards to deal and this is then stored back, using the property methods, into the variable stored in the main form class.

Figure 5.4   *Combo box*

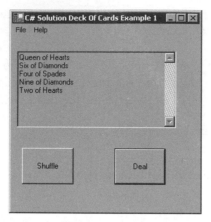

Figure 5.5   *The final application*

The remaining code within the example simply checks that there are enough cards left in the pack to satisfy the size of a deal. It then loops and requests from the DeckOfCards class the next card from the pack and displays the result into the text box. In this example we have investigated a fairly simple GUI application, the key features identified being:

- To create a simple form

- To add a simple menu structure

- To implement a modal dialogue

- To add the previous defined class dealing with a pack of cards and derive some algorithmic code to create and deal a hand of cards.

You should try to modify this example to:

1 Change the basic form design by experimenting with form properties such as colour, size or border style

2 Add additional items to the combo box

Example 2

Objective   To investigate the derivation of a user Class inherited from a User Control, this includes:

- To implement specific event handlers for both Size and Paint events

■ To investigate event handling for mouse clicks and how specific event handlers can be written

■ To integrate into the application Common Dialogue Boxes.

Specification

To look at a possible solution to the problem of drawing a simple 8 × 8 games board and identifying where on the board a user is requesting an action to take place. The basic specification in this case being:

■ A simple menu bar

■ The ability to draw an 8 × 8 games board

■ The ability to change the colour of the squares on the board

■ Identification of the row and column on which a user requests an action to take place based on a mouse click.

The following discussion on the implementation of this example is based on the VB.NET solution, the C# solution is identical other than in the language specific syntax.

As menu creation was discussed in the previous example we will not look at the construction of the menu here, we will start by looking at the dynamic creation of the squares that make up the board. In order to create the squares a .NET control class was created called Square1:

```
Public Class Square1 Inherits System.Windows.Forms.UserControl
```

Note: This class inherits from a UserControl template and not a forms template, the reason for this is that each instance of this class will need to be placed on the MainForm as a control and it must also be added to the control collection for the MainForm. If the Square1 class has been derived from a form type this would not be possible; all new forms derived from System.Windows.Forms are defined as a parent type and these cannot be added to the collection of another parent form.

Within MainForm a variable declaration of an array of squares is made:

```
Dim PSqr(64) As Square1 '' the actual squares
```

Within the MainForm constructor this PSqr array is instanced and given some initial properties:

```
Public Sub New()
      MyBase.New()
      Dim i As Integer
      'This call is required by the Windows Form Designer.
      InitializeComponent()
      'Add any initialization after the InitializeComponent() call
      For i = 0 To 63
          PSqr(i) = New Square1(Me)
          Me.Controls.AddRange(New System.Windows.Forms.Control() _
                                  {Me.PSqr(i)})
          PSqr(i).Size = New System.Drawing.Size(10, 10)
          PSqr(i).Location = New System.Drawing.Point(10, 10)
      Next
```

The reason for a parameter being passed to the constructor of the square object will become clearer when we discuss the identification of mouse clicks on the squares later. The **Me** keyword used as the parameter in this case was briefly discussed in the chapter dealing with compliant languages and is the VB.NET equivalent to the C# **this** keyword.

The most import code in the above constructor is the call to the AddRange(..) method, this method will identify that these new instances of the user control will be made part of the overall forms control collection. If you fail to identify this, although the new instances will be created, they are not included as part of the main form and will not be displayed on the main form. The final two lines in the constructor are not strictly required, their purpose was to give the controls an initial size and position. They were used during development to prove that the controls were being instanced. During the constructor of the main form the actual size of the client area of the main form is unknown, leading to the conclusion that we cannot position and size the grid squares.

A key topic to investigate within this example is how can we find out the size of the client area and subsequently draw the squares to form the grid. In order to look at the code required to perform this functionality we need to realise that CLR standard event handlers can be overridden, allowing the standard functionality they supply to be enhanced to provide application specific requirements.

OnSize(..) and OnPaint(..)

When our main form is created or the user changes its size, specific calculations related to the size and location of the game board squares need to be carried out to ensure the game board size is consistent with the size of the client area of the main form.

The OnSize(..) event handler for the main form is called by the .NET Framework following the initial construction of the instance and whenever the user changes the size of a form. In order to provide in our application this consistency of size calculation the OnSize(..) event handler for the main form will require an override. The override event handler used is shown in the code extract below:

```
Protected Overrides Sub OnResize(ByVal e As System.EventArgs)
    MyBase.OnResize(e) '' allways call the basre event first
    Dim Rect As Size
    Rect = Me.ClientSize
    Border = Rect.Width / 100 ' just a simple boarder calculator
    If Rect.Width - (Border * 2) > Rect.Height - (Border * 2) Then
                                                    'Make a square
        SSize = Rect.Height - (Border * 2)
    Else
        SSize = Rect.Width - (Border * 2)
    End If
    '' SSize is the final size of the Grid.
    Invalidate() '' force a repaint event.
End Sub
```

The first important point is that if an application overrides a CLR form event handler the first executable line of code in the new handler should call the inherited base form event handler. In VB.NET this is identified by the **MyBase** keyword, so in this case we call the MyBase.OnResize(..) passing to it the parameters passed into the overridden event handler.

Some experiments have been carried out without this inherited base call and many times there appeared to be no problems and the application ran normally. Microsoft do, however, recommend this call should always be made. They indicate in various knowledge base articles that it avoids possible contention with the default delegate chain assigned within the CLR and that applications that do not make such a call may be prone to 'hard to find' bugs.

The remainder of the code calculates the client size of the main form and stores into two private class variables, a calculated value for a border gap around the playing grid and the calculated size of each square in the playing grid. The final call in the override method is to the Invalidate(..) method. This Invalidate(..) call ensures that any controls belonging to this window will be repainted. Students tend to wonder why they cannot directly call the OnPaint(..) event for the form. It is not possible to directly call the event handler in the Windows event driven environment, for details of the consequence of direct calling of event handlers you will need to further investigate the windows message handling architecture (Petzold, C., *Programming Windows*, Fifth Edition, 2000, Microsoft Press). The action of calling the Invalidate(..) method is to create a queued request for the whole of the client area of the form to be refreshed.

My reason for using this technique rather than any other to get the controls redrawn stems from long experience of application development in C/C++ in the Windows environment and the firm belief that all drawing functionality requested programmatically should take place within the OnPaint(..) event handler.

Since we have requested an OnPaint(..) event the OnPaint(..) event handler must also be overridden. The override event handler used is shown in the code extract below:

```
Protected Overrides Sub OnPaint(ByVal e As
System.Windows.Forms.PaintEventArgs)
        MyBase.OnPaint(e)
        ' always call the base event to complete delegate chain
        '' this is how to ensure qet the controls on the forms surface
        Dim i As Integer
        Dim Row As Integer
        Dim Col As Integer
        Dim Background As Boolean
        Dim SQSize As Integer
        Background = False
        SQSize = SSize / 8
        '' this is needed only once and avoid rounding errors
        ' Position the squares
        For i = 0 To 63
            PSqr(i).Size = New System.Drawing.Size(SQSize, SQSize)
            Row = Border + (i Mod 8) * SQSize
            Col = Border + (i \ 8) * SQSize
            PSqr(i).Location = New System.Drawing.Point(Row, Col)
            PSqr(i).Show()
            If (i Mod 8) = 0 Then   ' swap the colours as each row alternates
                Background = Not Background
            End If
            If Background = True Then ' Select the background colour.
                PSqr(i).BackColor = DarkColour
            Else
                PSqr(i).BackColor = LightColour
            End If
            Background = Not Background
        Next
    End Sub
```

In fact we do no drawing or painting in this event handler, the only items on the forms surface are the Square1 class objects.

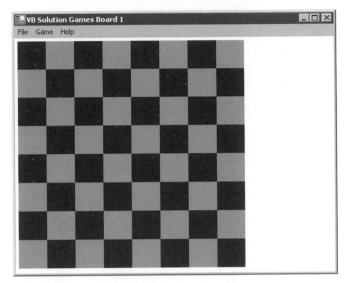

Figure 5.6   *The grid on a typical form*

However, the repositioning of these objects within this OnPaint(..) event will stimulate OnPaint(..) events within all the child controls in the forms control collection and the whole client area of the form will be refreshed. The algorithmic flow of the calculations is very straightforward, the only item that non-Visual Basic programmers may find strange is the calculation (i\8) this syntax ensures we get integer division rather than conversion to a floating or a decimal result. Rounding errors can also occur causing some quite strange effects on the display of the grid if all the calculations are performed dynamically. The solution is to pre-calculate the variable SQSize, and use this value in all the subsequent calculations.

You may wish to experiment with code such as:

```
New System.Drawing.Point(Row, Col)
```

to identify how the object **Point** is derived in the CTS and how this data type can be used to position controls within the client area of a form.

These two overridden event handlers form the basis of this application. The remaining discussion related to this example will first examine how user interaction with the grid was detected and then how you utilise the Windows Common Dialogues in a particular application.

The solution to this problem is extremely straightforward. The derived user control class Square1 was inherited from a .NET class template and as such has standard CLR event handlers. So we can once again override the specific handler that detects a mouse click event in the control:

```
Protected Overrides Sub OnMouseDown(ByVal e As _
                                    System.Windows.Forms.MouseEventArgs)
        '' here we determine they have clicked on a square
        MyBase.OnMouseDown(e)
        MyParent.FindChild(Me)
    End Sub
```

It is the design of this overridden event handler that required the constructor method of the Square1 objects to have a parameter. The parameter you will recall was the instance identifier for the main form. We saw that that this constructor parameter was stored in the private MyParent variable of the Square1 class. With this value we can construct code allowing the instance of a Square1 object to call a method in the main form class:

```
        MyParent.FindChild(Me)
```

This actual calculation of which control in the grid had been clicked could have been placed with the class Square1. Such a design would have required further parameter passing during construction and again local variables in the control class. The technique used here from experience seems to be simpler. The function referenced on the main form is:

```
Public Sub FindChild(ByVal Number As Square1)
        '' here we will search the array and find the squares position
        Dim i As Integer
        Dim Row As Integer
        Dim Column As Integer
        For i = 0 To 63
            If PSqr(i) Is Number Then
                Row = (i \ 8) + 1
                Column = (i Mod 8) + 1
MessageBox.Show(" Row = " + Row.ToString + " Column = " + _
                Column.ToString, "Position Clicked on Board")
            End If
        Next
    End Sub
```

The functionality of this piece of code is quite self-evident, the parameter passed in as Number is the object identifier sent by the MouseDown event in the control. The code then loops and compares this identifier with the array of identifiers created when the 64 square objects were initially constructed, it should be noted that if the condition to compare for equality were expressed using the syntax:

```
If PSqr(i) = Number Then
```

this would have been an error since there is no equality operator available in VB.NET syntax between objects in the .NET Framework. The specific syntax for VB.NET to check two object values for equality is the keyword **Is**, leading to the statement being expressed as:

```
If PSqr(i) Is Number Then
```

Once a match has been found a message box is used to display the row and column information. The final methods within this example use a Windows Common Dialogue to select user Colours.

Common Dialogues

The Windows Common Dialogues available for use by any application are listed in Table 5.1. Each of these common dialogue objects has unique properties but the basic usage is similar for all; key properties for the dialogue box are first set and then the specific dialogue box is instanced. In this example the colour dialogue is required by two of the menu item's event handlers, the first is to set the colour of the light square, the second the colour of the dark square in the game grid.

Rather than duplicating the code a general common dialogue method was written. In order to allow this common method to alter instance variables the parameters were passed to the method ByRef. In using the ByRef technique we allow this method to

Table 5.1

Windows Common Dialogues available for use by any application

Function	Name of Object
Colour Selection	ColorDialog
Font selection	FontDialog
Set Up of a Page	PageSetUpDialog
Set Up a Print	PrintDialog
Open or save a File	FileDilog

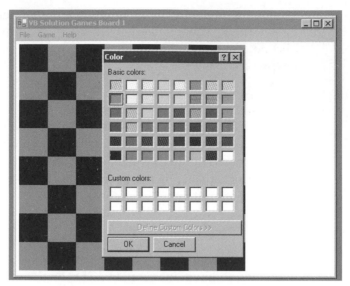

Figure 5.7   *Using the Colour Common Dialogue in the application*

modify the actual value of the calling parameter rather than only seeing a copy of the value. This method is called from either of our two menu event handlers with a ByRef parameter of the appropriate colour. Using this technique when the method terminates the actual value of the colour within the instance variable will have been changed. An example of the calling event handlers passing the class variable DarkColour is:

```
Private Sub GameDarksquare_Click(ByVal sender As System.Object, ByVal e As _
System.EventArgs) Handles GameDarksquare.Click
        ChangeSquareColours(DarkColour)
End Sub
```

The actual method ChangeSquareColours(..) is:

```
Private Sub ChangeSquareColours(ByRef OldColour As Color)
Dim MyDialog As New ColorDialog()
' Keeps the user from selecting a custom color.
MyDialog.AllowFullOpen = False
MyDialog.Color = OldColour
' Sets the initial color select to the current text color,
' so that if the user cancels out, the original color is restored.
MyDialog.ShowDialog()
OldColour = MyDialog.Color
Invalidate()
End Sub
```

The important line of code here is where the calling parameter is assigned the new value as the dialogue closes, OldColour = MyDialog.Color, this updates the ByRef parameter to the returned value from the dialogue box and in doing so updates the class variable which in this case is DarkColour.

In this example we have investigated a slightly more complex GUI application, the key features identified being:

- To create a simple form with a menu structure

- To create a UserControl class and from this create an 8 × 8 grid on the form

- To implement a modal Common Dialogue allowing the user to pick the colour of the squares

- To add a quite simple square detection algorithm, so that when the user clicks on any one square a message box appears that identifies its row and column.

You should try to modify this example to:

1 Change the basic form design

2 Experiment with various UserControl properties, e.g. border style

3 Add menu items to allow other Common Dialogues to be displayed in the application even if you do not actually use the result.

Example 3

Objective

To investigate a solution which has a number of classes and requires us:

- To implement specific event handlers

- To look at the subject of control focus

- To look at the timer control

- To start to gain an understanding of properties and how to expose the properties of one class to another.

Specification   To look at a simple animation of objects in a fixed pattern within the client area, possible usage being to develop a version of the retro video game 'Space Invaders'. The basic specification being:

■ A simple menu bar

■ The ability to draw a group of objects and make them move on the screen

■ To use keyboard actions to move another object at the base of the client area in a constrained fashion

■ To detect collisions between any two or more objects on the screen.

The following discussion on the implementation of this example is based on the VB.NET solution, the C# solution is identical other than in the language specific syntax. This skeleton solution of the game of Space Invaders is the largest example yet of a .NET Windows Forms-based application. It also highlights some common pitfalls when using a class library technique. The implementation is in four classes:

■ The MainForm that controls the application

■ The Alien class that implements the methods associated with displaying and moving, in this case a simple rectangle representing the alien on the screen

■ The Gun class that deals with the movement of an object at the bottom of the screen

■ The Missile class that deals with both the static part that is connected to the gun and the moving part that tracks up the screen to kill the aliens.

The following description deals with each class in turn, because of the size of the application these descriptions deal with specific aspects only, rather than explaining the code on a line-by-line basis.

The MainForm   The creation of the menu is the same as in previous examples and
class   therefore will be ignored, unlike the other examples in this class the approach taken for standard event overrides has been to

The examples

specify a unique new handler for both Resize(..) and KeyDown(..), the latter being the keyboard handling event used to actually control the gun that moves from left to right at the bottom of the screen.

The Resize(..) event handler is very much the same as in the last example; however, in this case it is a unique event handler for this application rather than an override handler as in the last example. If you write a unique handler rather than an override the syntax is slightly different:

on resize(..)

```
Private Sub MainForm_Resize(ByVal sender As Object, ByVal e As _
System.EventArgs) Handles MyBase.Resize
' Calculate the Client size of the Screen and then the size of the Alien Blobs
'                                                 the size of a Gun
'                                                 the size of a Missle
' these are very rough calculations
Dim Rect As Size
Rect = Me.ClientSize
Dim i As Integer
Alien.Width = Rect.Width / 10
Alien.Height = Rect.Height / 11
Gun.Width = (Alien.Width * 3) / 4
Gun.Height = (Alien.Height * 1) / 8
Missile.Width = Gun.Width / 4
Missile.Height = Gun.Height * 3
If GameStarted = False Then
      GunLocation.X = Alien.Width / 2
    MissileLocation.X = GunLocation.X + Gun.Width / 2 - Missile.Width / 2
Else
   '' can't change the X position thats controlled by the keyboard
      GunLocation.X = TheGun.CurrentPosition.X
      MissileLocation.X = TheMissile.CurrentPosition.X
End If
GunLocation.Y = Alien.Height / 2 + ((Alien.Height * 7) / 8 + _
              (Alien.Height)) * 5
MissileLocation.Y = GunLocation.Y - Missile.Width
'' set up the default alien location
Try
   TheMissile.CurrentPosition = MissileLocation
   TheGun.CurrentPosition = GunLocation
   If GameStarted = False Then
   '' Need to ensure Missiles etc. are at the default location
   For i = 0 To 17
     AlienLocation.X = Alien.Width / 2 + _
                     (Alien.Width + Alien.Width / 2) * (i Mod 6)
     AlienLocation.Y = Alien.Height / 2 + Alien.Height / 2 + _
                     (Alien.Height + Alien.Height / 2) * (i \ 6)
     TheAliens(i).InitialPosition = AlienLocation
     TheAliens(i).CurrentPosition = TheAliens(i).InitialPosition
   Next
```

```
    End If
'' always update object size
TheMissile.CurrentSize = Missile
TheGun.CurrentSize = Gun
For i = 0 To 17
    TheAliens(i).CurrentSize = Alien
Next
Catch
  '' empty catch block just in case the objects have not yet been initialised.
  '' We don't want a system error to be generated
End Try
End Sub
```

The calculations are based on the size of the client area of the form, this ensures that as the user resizes the form, all the objects on the form resize dynamically to the new client area. One problem with writing a handler for Resize(..) is that a resize event is created during the form's basic initialisation. However, at initialisation any objects being dynamically created onto the form may not yet be instanced. Any attempt to change properties on a dynamic object that is not yet instanced will result in a run-time error. The solution to this dilemma is to use structured error handling to **Try** the changes and **Catch** any run-time error. In the above code I have simply created an empty catch block since the Resize(..) handler is called again as the form is shown onto the desktop, and by this time the objects on the form are instanced and they will have the properties correctly set.

Experience based on teaching event driven programming leads me to the conclusion that this run-time error is created simply because the student is not familiar with the event driven paradigms.

The event driven paradigm topic related to the actual order of events in for instance Windows architecture is quite difficult to grasp the first time you encounter a problem. Prior to the inclusion of structured error handling in programming languages it was extremely difficult to demonstrate that such problems can exist. It was even more of a problem explaining why they happen. On many occasions such errors in previous development environments, particularly C/C++, are caused by simply not checking that a particular action was successful in the old API programming methodology looking at the API return value.

The new .NET structured error handling environment has greatly improved the ability to describe and demonstrate the problem especially to VB programmers who could not in the past look at returned values.

Table 5.2   *Sequence of event calls during any forms or control construction and activation*

While in method	Events that can occur
Public Sub New()	Load – Load of the form
MyBase.New()	Resize & Paint – Initial creation
InitializeComponent()	1 Activation or Show – After creation as becomes visible 2 Resize & Paint
During your initialisation code	Resize – Based on the properties used during form layout

The sequence of event calls during any forms or control construction and activation can be viewed in Table 5.2.

This is by no means a definitive list since events such as ColorChange and LocationChange also occur as the form is being instanced.

The table highlights that many events occur multiple times, and that the state of a particular object or form cannot be assumed during initialisation.

Remember this is an event driven environment, the events are asynchronous to each other (if you are really interested in the design of such event driven systems then Norton, S., *ThreadTime*, 1998, Wiley, London, looks at the nature of such systems in both a real time and an operating system context).

Keyboard handling

Before looking in detail at the implementation used in this example we can investigate the events generated when a user presses a key on the keyboard. These events are listed in Table 5.3.

Table 5.3   *Event generated when a user presses a key*

Users Action	Event Created
User depresses a key	KeyPress Event KeyDown Event
User releases the key	KeyUp Event

This definition implies any application should look for and handle three events for each keystroke. In this particular example only the KeyDown(..) event is being handled.

This is because the KeyDown(..) event actually contains the key code (an indication of which key was last depressed). The other two events contain important information regarding key modifiers such as the shift key and if a key is being held down for a repeat function. The KeyDown(..) event handler is:

```
Private Sub MainForm_KeyDown(ByVal sender As Object, ByVal e As _
                   System.Windows.Forms.KeyEventArgs) Handles MyBase.KeyDown
If GameStarted = True Then
     If e.KeyCode = Keys.Left Then
          TheGun.MoveGun(True)
          TheMissile.MoveMissile(TheGun.CurrentPosition.X, _
                                        TheGun.CurrentSize.Width)
          If InFlightMissile.Visible = False Then
               InFlightMissile.MoveMissile(TheGun.CurrentPosition.X, _
                                        TheGun.CurrentSize.Width)
          End If
     End If
     If e.KeyCode = Keys.Right Then
          TheGun.MoveGun(False)
          TheMissile.MoveMissile(TheGun.CurrentPosition.X, _
                                        TheGun.CurrentSize.Width)
          If InFlightMissile.Visible = False Then
               InFlightMissile.MoveMissile(TheGun.CurrentPosition.X, _
                                        TheGun.CurrentSize.Width)
          End If
     End If
     If e.KeyCode = Keys.Up Then
          If InFlightMissile.Visible = False Then
               InFlightMissile.Visible = True
               MissileTimer.Enabled = True '' start the missile.
          End If
     End If
End If
End Sub
```

You can see that only three specific key codes are tested and the appropriate action taken. Before moving on to any other aspects of the code in the class MainForm there is one point that requires some further investigation. This topic is not unique to the .NET architecture, problems occur in all Windows environments, it is generally identified as the focus dilemma.

Focus

In-focus is a term attributed by any Windows environment to the control or form that is currently active and to which all user events, both mouse and keyboard derived, are sent. In most cases

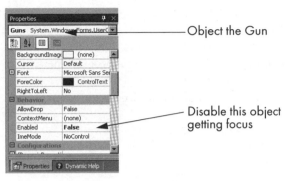

Figure 5.8   *Disabling this object getting focus*

it poses no real problem to an application since, if we are dealing with static situations, the user can see the result of input for instance to a text box immediately. However, in an example such as this some of the controls on the form have been animated, the little alien boxes move across the screen and the missiles run up the screen when fired so a static focus solutions will not work.

All Windows environments shift the focus when an object is changed, so in this case the focus is constantly on the move, but our keyboard KeyDown(..) is implemented in the MainForm class and so we need to ensure all keyboard events are routed to that class. In other Windows development environments (typically C/C++), use has been made of the low-level focus change messages (Petzold, C., *Programming Windows*, Fifth Edition, 2000, Microsoft Press), to determine the focus situation and to keep the focus in the correct place. Within .NET these are not directly available, you can, as we will see in a later chapter, interface to the actual Windows API itself, but such complication would detract from the whole concept of the CLR.

In order to ensure that the MainForm retains input focus all that is necessary is to block focus shift to any of the controls on the form. This can be simply implemented by disabling all controls on a form. There is a distinct difference between disabling and making a control invisible, a disabled control still resides on the form and can be seen by the user, disabling removes the control's ability to interact with the user, so for instance you cannot detect a mouse click over that control. When you make a control invisible on the other hand, the user cannot see it, but if it is enabled it will still generate for instance a MouseOver event when the mouse pointer passes across it.

In this example all controls placed on the MainForm are visible but disabled.

Timer()

The only other controls used on MainForm and not yet discussed are Timers. Two are used, one controlling the alien movement and the other controlling the missile flight. Timers will be familiar to all Visual Basic programmers, they simply create a Timer(..) event when an elapsed time expires, these events will continue to occur while the Timer is enabled:

```
Private Sub Alientimer_Tick(ByVal sender As System.Object, ByVal e As _
System.EventArgs) Handles Alientimer.Tick
'' get here when the alien timer is running.
'' all we do is move the set the aliens on the move.
Dim i As Integer
For i = 0 To 17
        TheAliens(i).MoveAlien()
Next
    '' Need to check here if any of the aliens have got as low as the top of
the gun
    '' Check in the static missiles pass to it the aliens
If TheMissile.AliensOnTop(TheAliens) Then
    MissileTimer.Enabled = False
    Alientimer.Enabled = False
    MessageBox.Show(" You lost please try again!", "Game Over")
    GamseStop.Enabled = False
    GameStart.Enabled = True
    GameReset.Enabled = True
    GameStarted = Not GameStarted
End If
End Sub
```

In the example the Timer(..) event handler calls the AlienMove() method to move objects and then check for collision (missile hits aliens), or other boundary conditions that signify the game is over.

Other classes

The three other classes are basically very similar, each controls a particular object that is used on the MainForm aliens, gun and missiles. These have all been created from .NET Window.Forms.Controls and the important aspect is that once again they have properties exposed. These properties give other classes the ability to modify private data within these controls in a structured manner.

The following extract from one of the classes' shows how to declare private data and then control access via properties:

```
Private mCurrentPosition As Point
Private mCurrentSize As Size

Public Property CurrentPosition() As Point
    Get
        Return mCurrentPosition
```

```
        End Get
        Set(ByVal Value As Point)
            mCurrentPosition = Value
            Me.Left = Value.X
            Me.Top = Value.Y
        End Set
    End Property
    Public Property CurrentSize() As Size
        Get
            Return mCurrentSize
        End Get
        Set(ByVal Value As Size)
            mCurrentSize = Value
            Me.Width = Value.Width
            Me.Height = Value.Height
        End Set
    End Property
```

The syntax for a property's set and get here is quite different to that of C# seen in the previous example. However, the functionality is identical, properties appear as data items when an external class attempts to access or change them. In VB.NET syntax they are handled as method calls, and it is possible to do additional manipulation or set up additional private data modification that is invisible to the calling code. If an instance of another class was, for example, to execute:

```
TheGun.CurrentSize = GunSize
```

what actually occurs in the property set method is that not only is the local variable updated but also the visual properties of the object itself are modified, something that the calling class has no knowledge is happening and could not directly accomplish.

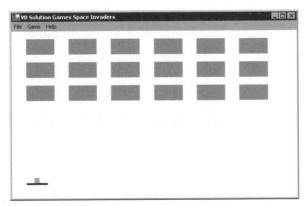

Figure 5.9   *The application running*

In this example we have once again increased the complexity of the application, the key features being:

■ How to write base class event handlers

■ How to overcome event synchronisation problems

■ What to do with input focus in a non-static environment

■ How in VB.NET to expose the properties of one class for use by another

■ How to use the Timer control.

You should try and modify this example to:

1   Investigate how to put an image into the alien control.

Example 4

Objective   The final example introduces two new topics: drawing on the surface of a control object and serialisation the ability to save and restore the status of an object or application. Both of these topics will introduce further aspects of both the .NET + Windows Forms class and the overall .NET architecture. Once again this will only be a skeleton solution, the problem being addressed is the sliding block puzzle. I am sure you have tried one of these. You have a 4 × 4 grid with 15 tiles, i.e. there is one space in the grid. The tiles are numbered 1 to 15 and are in a random order, you have to slide the tiles through the empty space and get them into order.

Specification   Producing a simple sliding block puzzle game. The basic specification being:

■ A simple menu bar

■ The ability to draw on the objects grouped within the main form

■ Use of mouse events to select which block to move

■ The serialisation of a game part way through and the saving and reloading of the data.

This following discussion on the implementation of this example is based on the C# solution, the VB.NET solution is identical other than in the language specific syntax. The implementation is in three classes:

■ The MainForm that controls the application

■ The Tile Class that deals with the characteristics of each numbered tile in the grid

■ The SaveTile Class, this had to be created to allow the actual game data to be serialised. A more detailed discussion on the need to create a specific class for this functionality is given below.

The following description deals with each class in turn, because of the size of the application these descriptions deal with specific aspects only, rather than explaining the code on a line-by-line basis.

The MainForm class

The class is quite simple, the functionality of this game is not complex and the menu options have been limited.

The Resize(..) and Paint(..) handlers have been implemented using the technique of a unique event handler for this class rather than the generic override form. Writing a unique handler here offered the opportunity to ensure that only the application specific functionality was implemented.

MoveBlock()

The only other major method within this class is MoveBlock(..) which is used by the mouse event handler, to calculate, if a block is capable of moving on the grid, moving the block and updating the variables that indicates the empty block position.

You will undoubtedly notice from the listing below that in fact the blocks never move. The technique used is to hide the block at the empty position and simply change the text displayed on the blocks as they apparently move from one position to another:

```
public void MoveBlock(int BlockNumber)
{
// to make this simple when we look at the grid we can check the positions
// +/- 4 from current and check for a match irrespective of the tile clicked
// then we have to look at the columns and if its the first not check -1
// if its the last not check +1
int column ;
next = -1;
column = (BlockNumber-1)%4; // take one off to get back to 0-15
if ((BlockNumber+4) == empty)
```

```
              next = BlockNumber+4;
        else
            if ((BlockNumber -4) == empty)
                next = BlockNumber-4;
            else
            {
                switch(column)
                {
                case 0:if ((BlockNumber+1) == empty)
                        next = BlockNumber+1;break;
                case 3:if ((BlockNumber-1) == empty)
                            next = BlockNumber-1;break;
                default :
                    if ((BlockNumber+1) == empty)
                            next = BlockNumber+1;
                    else
                        if ((BlockNumber-1) == empty)
                            next = BlockNumber-1;
                    break;
            }
        }
    if (next != -1)
        {
        // we have one to sort..
        TheTiles[empty].DNumber = TheTiles[BlockNumber].DNumber;
        TheTiles[empty].TVisible = true;
        TheTiles[empty].TEnable = true;
        empty = BlockNumber;
        TheTiles[BlockNumber].TVisible = false;
        TheTiles[BlockNumber].TEnable = false;
        TheTiles[BlockNumber].Invalidate ();
        TheTiles[empty].Invalidate ();
        }
}
```

You will also notice in the above code that rather than use the direct properties references of a control such as 'visible', the references are to user defined properties, the reason for this will become more obvious when we look at the serialisation of the game data.

The Tile class   The tile class is probably the most interesting part of this implementation, the class has been inherited directly from the standard .NET class System.Windows.Form.label:

```
public class Tile : System.Windows.Forms.Label
```

The reason for this is to use the functionality of a very simple control (labels are probably the simplest forms control available), as the only requirements for this Tile class are:

■ To be able to display a block in the grid

■ To have the ability to detect a mouse event on the block.

We could have used a .NET form here but again we are looking at a design that uses a parent–child architecture; if the Tile class had been inherited from a form then the Tile class would be a parent and as such could not be added to the control collection of the MainForm class. In order to simplify the serialisation issue (the ability to save and restore an object), which we will look at in the next section, this class has a number of properties declared. The C# syntax for this being:

```
private Size mCurrentSize = new Size();    //Current size
private Point mCurrentPosition = new Point(); //Current position in grid
private int mDNumber;          // Displayed number
private int mTNumber;       // Tile number in grid
private bool mTVisible;  // Visibility indicator
private bool mTEnable; // Eanabled indicator
private int mEmpty;  // Number of the empty tile space
public int Empty
{ get {return mEmpty;}
 set {mEmpty = value;}}
public bool TVisible
{ get {return mTVisible;}
  set {    mTVisible = value;
    this.Visible = value;}}
public bool TEnable
{ get {return mTEnable;}
  set {    mTEnable = value;
    this.Enabled = value;}}
public int TNumber
{ get {return mTNumber;}
  set {mTNumber = value;}}
public int DNumber
{ get {return mDNumber;}
  set {mDNumber = value;
     this.Text = mDNumber.ToString();}}
public Size CurrentSize
{ get {return mCurrentSize;}
  set {    mCurrentSize = value;
    this.Width = mCurrentSize.Width;
    this.Height = mCurrentSize.Height; }}
public Point CurrentPosition
{ get{return mCurrentPosition;}
  set{mCurrentPosition = value;
       this.Left = mCurrentPosition.X;
    this.Top = mCurrentPosition.Y;}}
```

The syntax for these properties should be familiar; we had properties in the last example. The difference is the specific syntax for the C# language, which in my opinion is far more logical.

Constructor()

```
public Tile(MainForm Parent, int Number,int Legend, Size CSize, Point  CPos,
bool Vis)
{
    MyParent = Parent;  // parent object used to send Mouse messages back
    InitializeComponent();
    CurrentSize = CSize;
    CurrentPosition = CPos; // set up first
      if (!Vis)
         this.TVisible = false;
    else
    this.TVisible=true;
    this.TEnable = true;
    this.DNumber = Legend;
    this.TNumber = Number;
}
```

The only other methods in this class are:

- Two unique event handlers for the Tile_Size () and Tile_Paint events

- An overridden event method to handle OnClick() event.

Tile Paint()

```
private void Tile_Paint(object sender,
                             System.Windows.Forms.PaintEventArgs e)
{
//Draws a simple Blue Rectangle around the edge of the control
 Graphics Draw;
 Pen Cpen = new Pen(Color.Blue ,3); // Blue pen 3 pixels thick
 Draw = e.Graphics ;          // get the device context.
 Draw.DrawRectangle (Cpen,0,0,this.Width-3,this.Height-3);
}
```

Tile Resize()

```
private void Tile_Resize(object sender, System.EventArgs e)
{
// Ensure a Paint event is called if we get a tile resize
  Invalidate();
}
```

OnClick()

```
protected override void OnClick(System.EventArgs e)
{
 base.OnClick (e); // call the standard label onclick
 MyParent.MoveBlock (TNumber); // link back to the mainForm method.
}
```

The TileSave class The final class TileSave is only required because the specification stated that we needed to load and save the current status of a game at any time. In the past when dealing with a load and save of an application status, the developer would normally have derived some data structure unique to the application and then implemented a file load and save option to deal with such a structure.

Within 'OO' programming design the concept of streaming the properties of objects (serialisation) to and from a file structure is a key requirement. However, in 'OO' languages such as C++ a very detailed understanding of the concepts of serialisation and streaming was required to implement the feature effectively.

Within the .NET architecture the whole problem has been simplified, the .NET class library offers two serialisation techniques, binary and XML (Extended Markup Language). In this example we will only be considering a binary stream serialisation of the data; in a later chapter dedicated to XML we will investigate the XML stream serialisation in detail and revisit this example to look at the implication of XML streaming.

Binary serialisation Binary serialisation is defined as being the ability to take the public and private data of an object and store the result in a suitable file format. It is then possible to use a deserialisation technique to take that data and to rebuild the original object.

Our first objective in this example is to identify the object to serialise, the obvious choice is the TheTiles array. The .NET Framework will allow us to serialise an array because an array is a basic data type of the CTS, the fact that this is an array of instances to a class has no relevance.

However, if you try to serialise an object that references a visual component, as is the case this time since the class was created by inheritance from the standard label class, you will find that these visual components are marked internally as not suitable for serialisation and you get a serialisation run-time error.

The reason for this restriction seems to be that visual components within the .NET class library are placeholders for any application data and do not constitute the application data itself, they are also vast classes inheriting one from another until we arrive at a basic object, the amount of data in the serialisation of such a class would be enormous.

The solution to this problem in the example was to create another class that only contains game data references. This class will then serialise and can be marked with the serialisation attribute.

```
[Serializable]
public class SaveTile
{
private int mTNumber;
private Size mCurrentSize = new Size();
private Point mCurrentPosition = new Point();
private int mDNumber;
private bool mTVisible;
private bool mTEnable;
private int mEmpty;
public int Empty
{get {return mEmpty;}
set {mEmpty = value;}}
public bool TVisible
{get {return mTVisible;}
set {mTVisible = value;}}
public bool TEnable
{get {return mTEnable;}
set {mTEnable = value;}}
public int TNumber
{get {return mTNumber;}
set {mTNumber = value;}}
public int DNumber
{get {return mDNumber;}
set {mDNumber = value;}}
Public Size CurrentSize
{get {return mCurrentSize;}
 set {mCurrentSize = value;}}
public Point CurrentPosition
{get{return mCurrentPosition;}
 set {mCurrentPosition = value;}}
public SaveTile()
{
// Empty constructor
}
}
```

The class contains the private data and properties of the actual tile array discussed above in the Tile class. Obviously this duplication is not strictly necessary, the two classes could have been designed to share this data in other manners (by inheriting from another class or using another simple class to define this data). However, to demonstrate serialisation this technique offered a simple explanation. Having both the SaveTile class and the actual Tile class allows the application to track the data in two separate arrays, the first TheTile[] based on the Tile class holds the references to the objects currently in use in the game, the second STile[] based on the SaveTile class is used to store or retrieve only the information that is going to be serialised.

Figure 5.10 The serialisation Save As Dialogue

Now all we need to look at is the implementation of the load and save event handlers:

```
private void FileSave_Click(object sender, System.EventArgs e)
{
 int i;
 IFormatter formatter = new BinaryFormatter();
  for (i =1;i<17;i++)
    {
    STile[i].CurrentPosition = TheTiles[i].CurrentPosition ;
    STile[i].CurrentSize = TheTiles[i].CurrentSize ;
    STile[i].DNumber = TheTiles[i].DNumber ;
    STile[i].TNumber = TheTiles[i].TNumber ;
    STile[i].TVisible = TheTiles[i].TVisible  ;
    STile[i].TEnable = TheTiles[i].TEnable ;
    STile[i].Empty = empty;
    }
if (saveFileDialog.ShowDialog ()==DialogResult.OK)
    {
    Stream stream = new FileStream(saveFileDialog.FileName, FileMode.Create,
    FileAccess.Write, FileShare.None);
    formatter.Serialize(stream, STile);
    stream.Close();
    }
}
```

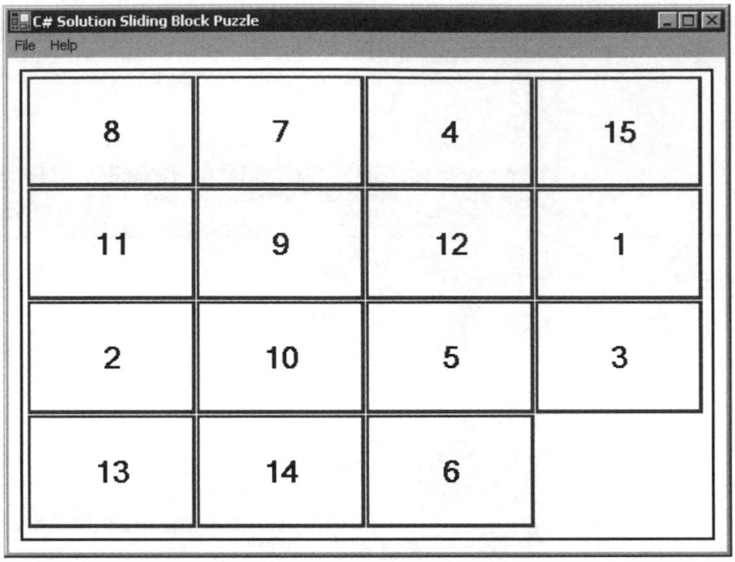

Figure 5.11   *The application running*

The functionality of the above code can be split into two parts, the first is to ensure that the STile[] is up to date with the status of the game itself. In the second part a Save Common Dialogue is used to get a file name and using the binary formatter the data is serialised from the STile[] into the file specified.

To read back a saved file the serialisation code structure is reversed, first an Open Common Dialogue is used to request the file name, the data is deserialised into the STile[] object and then the game object TheTile[] is updated from STile[]:

```
private void FileLoad_Click(object sender, System.EventArgs e)
{
 int i;
 IFormatter formatter = new BinaryFormatter();
 if(openFileDialog.ShowDialog () == DialogResult.OK )
    {
    Stream stream = new FileStream(openFileDialog.FileName, FileMode.Open,
FileAccess.Read, FileShare.Read);
STile = (SaveTile[]) formatter.Deserialize(stream);
    stream.Close();
    }
for (i =1;i<17;i++)
    {
        TheTiles[i].CurrentPosition = STile[i].CurrentPosition ;
        TheTiles[i].CurrentSize = STile[i].CurrentSize ;
        TheTiles[i].DNumber = STile[i].DNumber ;
        TheTiles[i].TNumber = STile[i].TNumber ;
        TheTiles[i].TVisible = STile[i].TVisible ;
```

```
        TheTiles[i].TEnable = STile[i].TEnable ;
        empty = STile[i].Empty ;
    }
    Invalidate(); // force a repaint
}
```

Summary

The whole topic of the .NET class library for the namespace Windows.Forms is enormous, this brief introduction should have shown you how stand-alone Windows applications can be built quite simply using the Windows forms concepts. It has also looked at tailoring functionality of both forms and controls to the specific needs of a particular application. The examples given have demonstrated some basic design strategies you can adopt, showing the concepts of:

■ Unique and overridden event handling to provide unique functionality within CLR standard event handlers

■ Common dialogue boxes

■ UserControls

In subsequent chapters other features of the .NET Windows class library will be used to illustrate further aspects of the .NET overall architecture. In this chapter I have endeavoured to cover the basic knowledge you need to understand these other features, at least in principle.

Review questions

After each of the examples there are suggestions for further enhancements or extensions to these basic solutions:

1 Another simple game that lends itself to Windows Forms is Pac Man, try to create a simple example

2 There are numerous simple card games that you could investgate and produce some simple solutions using the card deck class

3 The topic of 2D drawing with the drawing functionality available in the .NET class library offers many options for

simple Windows Forms examples. Try to add graphical objects to the space invaders example

(a) Does this cause a problem to the resize event?

(b) What options are available, to position a fixed-size image, into a window that can be any size?

6 .NET components

Objective

In the previous chapter when we looked at the namespace Windows Forms we have in fact been using .NET components. Rather than calling them components they were referred to as members of the .NET class library (and as controls).

In fact any new Windows forms control derived or inherited from one of the standard controls is in fact a .NET component. A component as was discussed in an earlier chapter offers a developer the ability to use the functionality of the object without being aware of how that functionality was derived.

The reason that the .NET Framework can offer component transparency to a particular application is intrinsically built into the design goal 'of the unambiguous virtual machine design' investigated in the earlier chapters. This .NET Framework virtual machine environment allows all aspects of the .NET executable code to be operating system and hardware platform independent.

By basing the virtual machine design on the CTS definitions, all programming language dependency is eliminated; interoperability between .NET components irrespective of the implementation programming language is therefore guaranteed. The ability to develop in such a generalised environment will undoubtedly lead to a proliferation of additional .NET components from third party suppliers.

Historically once Visual Basic became reliant on the ActiveX control design technology, countless numbers of specialist ActiveX controls started to appear, some very generalised while others were application specific from third party vendors. We will investigate in the next chapter how these controls or components can still interoperate within the .NET architecture.

The problem with the ActiveX technology was that, in general, it required specialist knowledge to develop effective solutions and many controls were designed specifically for the Visual Basic environment. This chapter will show how in the .NET Framework any such constraints are removed, we will also be considering how, if you have previously developed a suitable class, for instance within a .NET stand-alone application, the translation of this class into a more generalised .NET component is quite feasible and does not mean a complete redevelopment.

Once again we must remember that the CLR supports the concept of application development language independence, and by implication therefore componentware developed independence, so any component created is expected to function correctly, in any application developed to run within the .NET Framework.

Introduction

In the previous chapter we defined that a Windows form usually contains controls to obtain input from, and display output to, the user. Within this chapter we are going to extend the definition slightly to encompass the fact that any control (component) used within an application in the .NET Framework could in addition to obtaining input or displaying output perform complex manipulations on the data itself.

The whole philosophy of 'OO' program design is that the objects created would be self-contained and that once such an object was designed it could be reused in many future applications. In a later chapter when we look at other aspects of componentware design and multi-tier solutions, we will investigate why such a design goal tends to fall down in practice. The .NET component model, however, does enable us to build complex algorithmic manipulation into the user-designed component and then reuse the component in other solutions.

For the purpose of these discussions I am going to divide .NET components into two categories, those with a visual interface and those without. The reason for this division is that there are many other aspects of the design that need considering when the component has a visual interface than when it does not.

In order to demonstrate our user-designed components we are going to need to build test applications that will assist in the development and testing of the component itself. In order to demonstrate this effectively the early examples in the chapter will use the same programming language for the component and the test application.

In the later examples the test application will be developed in a different programming language to the component, to demonstrate the language independent nature of the .NET Framework.

Before commencing on our first component design the configuration of the Visual Studio .NET must be reviewed.

In the previous examples we have been developing a single project (an application) within a .NET Framework solution space (namespace). When you start to consider the development of a component and a test application, it is usual to have both projects within a single solution. This idea of multiple projects in a single solution brings with it the topic of project dependency. Our test application is going to be dependent on the component project so we must ensure that any changes made to the component development files are rebuilt to ensure the test application is always using the latest version. Similarly in the Visual Studio .NET solutions set up we must set the test application as the startup project. A .NET component is built as a Dynamic Link Library (DLL) and DLLs cannot be executed directly, they must have an executable host.

Setting up Visual Studio .NET

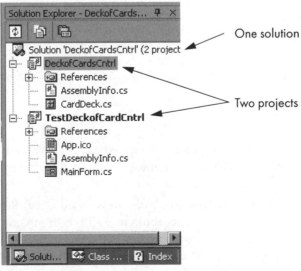

Figure 6.1   *A Multi-project solution*

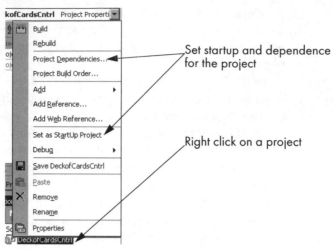

Figure 6.2   *Setting dependencies and start up options*

In the chapter on Windows forms a number of useful pieces of functionality were developed in the examples. These included the handling and dealing from a deck of cards and the generation of a board game surface. This type of functionality is common to many simple games; it would therefore seem appropriate to look at developing some .NET components using such ideas.

The examples

Example 1

Objective   To take a previous designed class and modify it to become a useful .NET component.

Specification   The first component to be developed is a full card game control; however, such a component will require major functionality and to jump straight into the development would make any explanation of the implementation so complex and confusing that it would be nearly impossible to follow. To make the discussion useful the design will be carried out in three stages.

1   The basic deck of playing cards as a component

2   The dealing of a user-defined hand of cards as a component

3   A complete card game component that monitors multiple hands of cards.

In taking this approach the individual aspects of each component design will be reviewed and a simple test application written that will exercise the functionality at each stage.

There are a number of approaches that could be taken to progress from stage to stage but for simplicity the approach taken is to redefine the previous component class solution as a new class totally encapsulated within the next design. This approach is a little clumsy and does obviously have the requirement to cut and paste some of the implementation from one source file to another.

The most obvious technique that could have been used would have been to make use of the previously developed component in the implementation of the next stage. Such a technique would have offered an incremental design approach but, the added complication in the description of the overall solution, ruled it out in this introductory text.

Stage 1

The component can be thought of as requiring the following functionality:

- No visual requirement

- Create and maintain a pack of playing cards

- Ability to shuffle the pack of cards at any time

- Ability to a deal single cards on demand.

There is little change here to the stand-alone Windows application other than the fact there is no visual interface. However, any .NET component must be configurable and indicate, by raising an event, if certain conditions occur. The following properties and events will therefore be needed.

Properties

- The name of the suit for the card

- The name of the face value of the card.

■ No events, although it could be improved by an event when the deck of playing cards is exhausted.

■ Constructor – create pack and populate a playing card pack

■ Shuffle the pack – randomise the order of the cards in the pack

■ Deal a Single Card – return the value as a string that can be displayed.

The overall implementation is based on the original console application and the Windows Forms version from the last chapter. Only some minor changes have been made to the storage of the card values etc. compared to the original stand-alone version. These changes reflect some of the needs of the component design when it is interfaced in a later chapter with its visual counterpart. The component is designed to have two classes, the first is:

```
public class PlayingCards
{
 private string[] faces = { "Ace", "Two", "Three", "Four",
     "Five", "Six", "Seven", "Eight", "Nine", "Ten",
             "Jack", "Queen", "King" }
private string[] suits = { "Clubs","Diamonds","Hearts", "Spades" };
private CardFace face;
private CardSuit suit;
public CardFace Face
{ get {return this.face;}
  set {this.face = value;}}
public CardSuit Suit
{ get {return this.suit;}
  set {this.suit = value;}}
public PlayingCards(CardFace face,CardSuit suit)
    {
      this.face = face ; // just default the card deck here
      this.suit = suit ;
    }
public override string ToString()
    {
    return faces[(int)face] + " of " + suits[(int)suit];
    } // end method ToString
}
```

There is nothing very different about this class, it has some properties, a basic constructor and an override on the fundamental CTS object method ToString(..). Overrides on this method are very common especially in component designs since anything, other than a simple value type, generally requires that the ToString(…) method be implemented to return some meaningful and formatted data. The second class is the actual control itself:

Card Deck class

```
public class CardDeck : System.Windows.Forms.UserControl
```

It inherits from a .NET class of Windows.Form.UserControl, this allows it to have a visual component, if required. If we had inherited say from a visual control then we would have had to override some other standard methods such a Paint(..) as in this design we have specified no visual attributes to this component.

Something that may be new to you is the definition of some enumerating types of the form:

```
public enum CardFace
{// First we need a definition of the 13 cards in a suit.
    One, Two, Three, Four, Five, Six, Seven, Eight, Nine,
    Ten, Jack, Queen, King
}
public enum CardSuit
{// definition of the card suits
    Clubs = 0, Diamonds = 1, Hearts = 2, Spades = 3
}
```

These enumerations allow the component to define names to counted values. In the second case of CardSuit, I have shown what actually happens when you enumerate, the assignments are not required but they should indicate how the C# language deals with an enumerated data type.

The remainder of the class, with some of the extra coding associated with Visual Studio .NET removed for clarity, has the form:

```
private PlayingCards[] cards = new PlayingCards[52];
private int nextcard;
public CardDeck()
{
// order 1,2,3,...(Clubs), 1,2,3,...(Diamonds), 1,2,3,...(Hearts),
// 1,2,3,...(Spades).
Random rand1, rand2;             // a random number generator.
int counter = 0;
int face = 0;
int suit = 0;
int aNumber;
bool[] used = new bool[52];      // an array of flags to tell which card is
used.
```

```
while(counter<52)
{
    rand1 = new Random((int)DateTime.Now.Ticks);
    // initiates a random ganerator
    rand2 = new Random(rand1.Next(int.MaxValue));
    aNumber = rand2.Next(52);     // get a value within the 52 cards.
    if(!used[aNumber])            // if the selected card was not used
      {
        used[aNumber] = true;        // set it assosiated flag to true;
        face = aNumber % 13;
        suit = aNumber / 13;
        cards[counter] = new PlayingCards((CardFace)face, (CardSuit)suit);
        counter ++;
      }
    }
    nextcard = 0;
}
public void Shuffle()
{
Random randomNumber;
PlayingCards temporaryValue;
int i,j;
randomNumber = new Random();
    // swap each card with random card
for ( i = 0; i < cards.Length; i++ )
    {
    j = randomNumber.Next( 52 );
        // swap cards
        temporaryValue = cards[ i ];
        cards[ i ] = cards[ j ];
        cards[ j ] = temporaryValue;
    }
    nextcard = 0;
}
public string DealACard()
{
string Card;
Card = cards[nextcard].ToString() ;
nextcard++;
return Card;
}
```

The constructor uses a random number to create all the values
from o to 51. A second array of Booleans ensures that all cards are
unique, the values are then split and instanced into the playing
card class each being given a face value and a suit. The variable
nextcard is initialised to zero and is used to track the position of
the cards as they are extracted from the pack. It is this portion of
the simple original design that required revision since, if any
application using this component did not track how many cards
are being consumed, the nextcard variable would increment

beyond the maximum of 51 and a run-time exception would result.

The Shuffle(..) method simple reorders the cards in the array, while the DealACard(..) method extracts a single card and using the overridden ToString(..) method in the playingcards class, returns a formatted string representing the card value. This component offers any application that wishes to use it, the ability to create a deck of playing cards and request, via the DealACard(..) method, a string containing a valid description of a random playing card.

Test for Stage 1 component

To test the functionality of this stage 1 component, a small .NET windows form application has been written which exercises the component. Again I have extracted from the source file the parts of the implementation that relate to the control and have removed all aspects associated with the menu, the layout of the form etc:

```
using DeckofCardsCntrl;
public class MainForm : System.Windows.Forms.Form
{
//... code removed
    CardDeck Pack ;    // declare the object
    public MainForm()
    {
    InitializeComponent();
    Pack = new CardDeck(); // create the instance
    }
    private void CDeal_Click(object sender, System.EventArgs e)
    {
    textBox1.Text = Pack.DealACard ();// display the result
    }
//... code removed
}
```

The using directive identifies the control so we can instance it with the simple line. We will see later in the chapter that if the component has a visual interface we must inform Visual Studio of its existence as well as providing some basic property values for the components that are used when it resides on the toolbar:

```
    Pack = new CardDeck(); // create the instance
```

The form itself has only a text box and a button, the click event on the button causes the text box to recover the result, via a request to the control for the next card from the pack of cards. I have not tried here to check if the error condition outlined previously is about to occur, so if you run the test application and

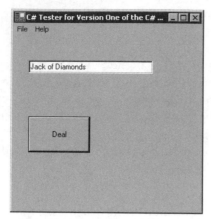

Figure 6.3   *The test application checking Stage 1 component functionality*

click the button more that 52 times, the application fails with a run-time exception of array boundary exceeded.

Stage 2   Enhancement so the control maintains a hand of cards.

Objective   To extend the functionality of the component.

Specification   The component can be thought of as requiring the following functionality:

- All those of Stage 1

- The ability to accept a parameter to set up the size of the card hand

- The ability to deal a hand of cards

- The ability to return details of the hand of cards.

There is no major change to the classes derived in the Stage 1 implementation, the enhancements to Stage 2 adds a new class that encapsulates the functionality from Stage 1, and exposes more complex functionality concerned with a total hand of cards rather than a single card.

Properties
- The Hand size, i.e. how many cards are in a player's hand

- The Player Number as an integer identifier

■ A further property to return the player's hand could have been implemented but instead a Display method was introduced to recover the detail of the hand.

Events

■ Again no events, although once again the component would be improved by an event when the deck of playing cards would be exhausted if another hand were dealt.

Methods

■ Constructor – create the player's hand structure

■ Deal a hand to a player

■ Display the deal hand.

The overall implementation is based initially on the Stage 1 solution, some minor changes were made to the original DeckOfCards class, to allow the component to request that a hand of cards is dealt programmatically, rather than just returning a string variable with a description of the card value:

```
public PlayingCards DealToHand()
{
    PlayingCards HCard = new PlayingCards();
    HCard = cards[nextcard];
    nextcard++;
    return HCard;
}
```

HandOfCards class

The HandOfCards class has the required properties added to it along with a local private variable that is used to hold the card values associated with an instance of the class. The constructor was overloaded for the class to ensure that if an instance were created without the size of hand variable being set, a default hand would be created:

```
public HandOfCards()
{
int i;
Pack = new CardDeck ();  // create a pack
if (HandSize !=- 1)
    for (i=0;i<HandSize;i++)
    mCardHand[i] = new PlayingCards();
}
public HandOfCards(int ThisHandSize)
{
int i;
Pack = new CardDeck ();  // create a pack
HandSize = ThisHandSize;
```

```
mCardHand = new PlayingCards [HandSize];
for (i=0;i<ThisHandSize;i++)
    mCardHand[i] = new PlayingCards();
}
```

This constructor code creates the pack of cards using the CardDeck class and either using defaults or the constructor parameter creates the basic HandofCards instance. Two methods to populate and display the card hands are then available:

```
public void DealAHand()
{
 int i;
 if (HandSize !=-1)
    {
    for (i=0;i<HandSize ;i++)
        mCardHand[i] = Pack.DealToHand();
    }
    else
MessageBox.Show(" You must set a Card Hand Size before Dealing",
"Error on Deal a Card Hand");
}
```

Note a message box has been included here to catch any attempt to deal a hand to an uninitialised version of the HandofCards instance. This is really only for testing purposes but can be left in the final version to avoid any possible run-time errors at this point; it may be an advantage to modify the control to issue an event if this condition occurred. The topic of issuing events has been left to a later section of this discussion:

```
public override string ToString()
{ // must construct a string to handle this..
string SHand= "";
int i;
if (HandSize !=-1)
{
    for (i=0;i<HandSize ;i++)
        SHand = SHand + mCardHand[i].Face + "&" + mCardHand[i].Suit+ " ";
    }
    else
    MessageBox.Show(" You must set a Card Hand Size before Dealing",
"Error on Deal a Card Hand");
return SHand;
}
```

The ToString(..) method for this object has again been overridden to allow formatting of the HandofCards. The string produced uses the '&' to delimit between suit and face value for each card and a 'space' character to delimit between cards. Any application will need to write a piece of parser software to split the string if it needs to identify the individual cards more completely.

Test for Stage 2 To test the functionality of this Stage 2 component, another small .NET Windows Forms application has been written which exercises the component.

Once again I have extracted only the parts of the implementation that relate to the control and have removed all aspects associated with the menu, the layout of the form etc.

```
using HandofCardsCntrl;
public class MainForm : System.Windows.Forms.Form
{
private HandofCardsCntrl.HandOfCards  CardHand;
public MainForm()
{
    InitializeComponent();
    CardHand = new HandOfCards(5);  // set hand size to 5.
}
private void CDeal_Click(object sender, System.EventArgs e)
{
    CardHand.DealAHand ();
    label1.Text = CardHand.ToString ();
    }
}
```

The form itself in this case has a label and a button, the click event on the button causes the label text to recover the result from a request to the control for the card hand details. Once again I have made no attempt here to check if an error occurs with the deal request.

If insufficient cards remain in the pack when the request is made for a new hand, an array out of bounds error will occur.

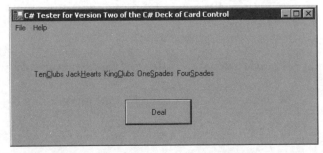

Figure 6.4 *The test application checking Stage 2 Component functionality*

Stage 3	The final Card Game control.
Objective	To finally have the complete component available
Specification	The component can be thought of as requiring the following functionality.

- All those of Stages 1 & 2

- The ability to set up the size of the card hand (range 1–13)

- The ability to set up how many players (range 1–4)

- The ability to maintain the card hand for each player selected

- The ability to deal a hand to each player selected

- The ability to deal single additional cards selectively to each player

- The ability to return detail of each player's hand selectively.

This final control automates the basic card handling process for a card game with up to four players, this selection of four players was purely arbitrary as was the range of size for the actual card hands.

Properties	

- The Hand size, i.e. how many cards are in a player's hand

- The Number of Players.

Events	

- Again no events, although once again the component would be improved by events indicating if any error conditions occur. This would be a very good topic for students to look at for future enhancements.

Methods	

- Constructor – create the basic structure of the game control

- Deal – construct hands for all players

- Deal selectively a single card to a selected player

- Display hand selectively by player

■ NewHand – reinitialise to properties and deal a new hand.

There was no need to make any major changes to the classes defined at Stage 1 and Stage 2, some enhancements were added to allow the HandOfCards default constructor, to create a full thirteen card empty hand structure:

```
public HandOfCards()
{
int i;
mCardHand = new PlayingCards [13];
for (i=0;i<13;i++)   // Define a default for now and set up a hand of 13
    mCardHand[i] = new PlayingCards();
}
```

In doing this any player would always have the maximum hand size available, so in games where players draw, or are dealt additional cards, the only check needed is that the maximum card hand size is not exceeded. The alternative meant creating a new version of the HandOfCards each time an additional card was added to the selected player's hand.

The CardDeck class was altered to allow access to two new properties the SizeofPack and nextcard, the first identifies how many cards are in a pack and the second the number of the next card to deal. With this information the GameOfCards class can check if there are enough cards left for the next game, and can request a shuffle which resets these variables if insufficient cards are left.

Within the DeckOfCards class therefore we now have:

```
private int mSizeOfPack;
private int mnextcard;
public int nextcard
{get {return mnextcard;}
set {mnextcard = value;}}
public int SizeOfPack
{ get {return mSizeOfPack;}
  set {mSizeOfPack = value;}}
```

GameOfCards class

The actual class of GameOfCards performs the majority of the manipulation to ensure the component performs the functionality required.

The private data and properties are handled with the following:

```
public static CardDeck Pack;
private HandOfCards[] CardHands= new HandOfCards [4];
private int mNumberofPlayers;
```

```
private int mSizeofHand;
public int NumberofPlayers
{get {return mNumberofPlayers;}
 set
{ if ((value>1)&& (value<5))
        mNumberofPlayers = value;
  else
            // raise an event error
        mNumberofPlayers = 1;
}
}
public int SizeofHand
{ get {return mSizeofHand;}
  set
   { mSizeofHand = value;
    int i;
    if ((value>1)&& (value<14))
    {
      for (i=0;i<4;i++)
      CardHands[i].HandSize = value;
    }
    else
    // raise an event error
      for (i=0;i<4;i++)
        CardHands[0].HandSize = 1;
    }
}
```

These property access methods now have far more logic than simply getting and setting private variables; they ensure that, should the calling application make a change that is invalid, then a default value is inserted to avoid possible run-time error.

There is only one constructor that takes, as its parameters, both the number of players and the size of the basic hand for each player:

```
public GameOfCards(int NoPlayers, int SizeHand)
{
int i;
InitializeComponent();
Pack = new CardDeck (); // As game initialises need to create a pack of cards
for (i=0;i<4;i++)
    this.CardHands[i] = new HandOfCards ();
this.NumberofPlayers = NoPlayers;
this.SizeofHand =SizeHand;
}
```

The methods available for controlling the component are first, a basic deal of cards to all players:

```
public void Deal()
{
    // deal a hand to each player
  int i;
  for (i=0;i<NumberofPlayers;i++)
    CardHands[i].DealAHand ();  // Thats a deal.
}
```

and second, a method to deal a single card to a specific player:

```
public void DealACard(int Player)
{
// deals an extra card to a given player
    CardHands[Player].HandSize++; // add one to this players hand size
    CardHands[Player].DealACard (); // Add a card.
}
```

Notice that the hand size for that player has been incremented, so an external application can keep track of the hand size for each player by looking at the property value. To recover the details of any player's hand and recover a string variable as we have seen before, we have the following method:

```
public string GetHand(int Player)
{
    return CardHands[Player].ToString ();
}
```

The final new method allows for dealing a new set of hands from the same pack with a check on the numbert of cards etc:

```
public void NewHand()
{
int i;
if ((Pack.SizeOfPack  - Pack.nextcard )< NumberofPlayers * SizeofHand)
    Pack.Shuffle ();
    for (i=0;i<4;i++)
        CardHands[i].HandSize = this.SizeofHand ;
    Deal();
}
```

Test for Stage 3   Once again, the functionality of the final component is tested by a small .NET Windows Form application that exercises the basic functionality.

In this case it was decided that it would be a fixed game format of four players and five cards, with the option that each player could draw an additional single card. The listing of the application has had all the excess code related to Visual Studio .NET graphical component control removed:

```
using GameOfCardsCntrl;
public class MainForm : System.Windows.Forms.Form
{
    private GameOfCards CardGame;
    public MainForm()
    {
        InitializeComponent();
        CardGame = new GameOfCards(4,5);
    }
    private void CDeal_Click(object sender, System.EventArgs e)
    {
        CardGame.NewHand ();
        Player0.Text = CardGame.GetHand (0);
        Player1.Text = CardGame.GetHand (1);
        Player2.Text = CardGame.GetHand (2);
        Player3.Text = CardGame.GetHand(3);
        Add.Enabled = true;
    }
    private void Add_Click(object sender, System.EventArgs e)
    {
        // Add an extra card to each of the hands..
        Add.Enabled = false;
        CardGame.DealACard (0);
        CardGame.DealACard (1);
        CardGame.DealACard (2);
        CardGame.DealACard (3);
        Player0.Text = CardGame.GetHand (0);
        Player1.Text = CardGame.GetHand (1);
        Player2.Text = CardGame.GetHand (2);
        Player3.Text = CardGame.GetHand(3);
    }
}
```

The form has four labels controls named as Playero through to Player3, the text property of these is being used to display the hand of cards for each player.

There are two button controls, one to deal a new hand to each player and the other to add a card to each player's hand. No error checking is being carried out within this application since the GameOfCards component now checks to see if there are enough cards left in the pack for a deal, if not it will shuffle the pack and reset the internal pointers to a full 52 cards remaining.

This has been a fairly complex .NET component development of a fairly extensive user control, considering it has no visual interface. It has been designed to allow it to be extended in future chapters, first to interface it with a further visual component control that will display the playing cards graphically and finally to provide the basis of a web service control for the final case study application.

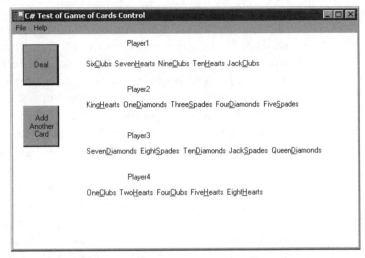

Figure 6.5   *The test application checking Stage 3 Component functionality*

You should try and modify this component example to:

1   Implement the rules of a simple card game into the component itself

2   Have additional functionality, other properties in any one of the designed classes; for instance in which class would you store the player's name

3   Add all the necessary error handling, you could add try .. catch blocks as well as event generation when an error occurred.

Example 2

Objective   To investigate component implementation further and to implement a visual interface on a component

Specification   To investigate how to integrate a user derived visual component in the Visual Studio .NET design environment and to ensure any custom properties are made available within the Visual Studio .NET design environment.

The second component to be developed is a game grid control. It could be used for any standard board game such as chess or draughts. Equally other types of game, for instance battle ships, need a basic grid in which the players both position their craft, as well as planning a strategy for attacking the opponent.

A control design of this type will require both a visual element as well as all the necessary programmatic control associated with user input and output. In this case the visual aspects (i.e. the GUI) have not been analysed fully, the purpose of this example is to illustrate the design and implementation of the .NET component, not how to design visual components. This component will need the ability to use and interact with a typical visual design environment as found in Visual Studio .NET, as well as the ability to be used within the algorithmic solution to the particular problem.

When a component such as this is required to interact with the programming environment and to react correctly when, for instance, it is placed onto a form and sized, there are a number of key issues that need to be considered. The first part of the discussion on the implementation of this example will be based only on these issues.

Once it is possible to place the control on the form then we can look at the programmatic nature of, for instance, the properties of the control being dynamically changed and the raising of suitable events when the end user interacts with the control.

The development of this component is by no means simple; however, it is based on the example from the previous chapter where a stand-alone application was developed which had a simple 8 × 8 grid drawn within the client area. The actual algorithms developed for the sizing and drawing of the squares in that example will be directly transferred to this component design.

When looking to design a component with a visual interface significant time should be spent on the overall architecture, the first area to consider concerns the choice of base control to use for inheritance for the new component. Obviously we could start with a blank sheet and create a unique class, but we are producing a visual component and therefore it will need, as a minimum, colour, position and size information as well as standard events such as Resize(..) and Paint(..). It makes perfect sense therefore to inherit the new component from one of the standard .NET Windows Forms library components.

Once this decision is made we will have the parent class of the control defined but in many cases we will need standard child elements, within this parent, to satisfy the basic functionality. Standard child controls would, if we were not careful, appear to be both amalgamated and part of the new overall control but they could equally appear as new components in their own right.

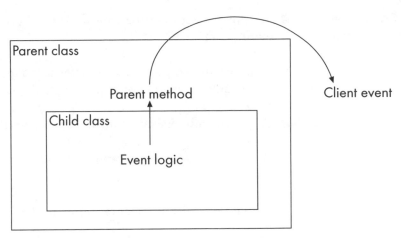

Figure 6.6   *Event handling aggregation*

If the later case were allowed to occur this would cause a great deal of difficulty in a visual programming environment such as Visual Studio .NET.

The overall architecture of this component has been designed to ensure that only the parent class of the component is visible, all other classes are private and do not appear to exist to the visual programming development environment.

Hiding child classes while fully using them in the component is quite an advanced topic. In essence it means all intercommunication related to data items between parent and child must be through a route that involves changes to property values, a major area of misunderstanding in 'OO' design is that internal data in a private class within a parent class is not directly accessible by the parent.

In this example a single child class is defined and this is totally encapsulated by the parent. To limit the degree of interaction the only property changes by the parent on the child are size and position. The event logic for the component is actually implemented in the child class, this is because we are looking for mouse events in the individual squares on the grid.

To ensure that having these events in the child does not expose the child class, all events are passed across a single method interface from child to parent. Such a technique ensures the overall transparency of the child class is maintained and the parent class wholly owns the external event logic that raises an event from the component to the client.

Component functionality

■ To interact with and be controlled by a visual programming environment

■ To have suitable external properties to make it flexible for use in a number of client applications

■ To expose only one component class to the client application

■ To identify user input and provide suitable user output options.

This final control implementation comprises the specification that:

Final specification

■ The board size is defaulted to 8 × 8 squares

■ The colours are defaulted to alternate squares of light and dark (the normal for a chess or draughts board)

■ A Method is available that allows each square to have an individual background colour set

■ A Method is available that allows each square to have unique text

■ It is fully compatible with the pick and place technique found in the Visual Studio .NET Form designer mode

■ A minor irritation is that it does not automatically register itself onto the designer's 'toolbar' but the understanding and programming skills to accomplish this are beyond the scope if this book

■ It has a number of properties that can be set either statically within the form designer, or programmatically by the client application to change its layout and the colour of the squares.

Properties

■ Number of Rows

■ Number of Columns

■ Colour of the Light squares when displaying a chequer board pattern

■ Colour of the Dark squares when displaying a chequer board pattern

■ Standard Board, a Boolean variable to indicate if the board should be standard chequered, or customised with the user being able to select colour and text for each square

■ The inherited properties relating to size and position etc.

Events

1 A single event, that of a mouse click, on any square will return the number of the square in the range 0 to (Row * Columns - 1).

Methods

1 Constructor – create the basic structure of Game Board

2 Get and Set Methods that allow single squares to be set to a unique colour

3 Get and Set Methods that allow single square text to be defined.

The implementation of the control will be discussed below using the VB.NET version, the C# version is very similar except for the specific syntax differences.

The Square1 Class

Each square on the board is constructed as an instance of this class as was discussed in the example in the last chapter. This class is derived from the standard .NET windows.forms.label class allowing it the flexibility of all the properties and methods that the label class offers. It is declared within the body of the main GameGrid class and has the attribute of private, ensuring that when the GamesGrid class is exposed as a .NET component, the Square1 class is not exposed.

Its functionality is quite minimal, it allows a square to be created and has a Paint(..) that draws a bounding rectangle in all cases, and if the overall control is being used in the customised form rather than as a standard board, the Paint(..) will setup the specific background colour and any associated text. It contains one Mouse event handler of MouseDown(..) used to signal back to the main control class that the user has clicked a specific square. This listing has had the Visual Studio specifics removed for clarity:

```vbnet
Private Class Square1  ' the class which deals with each square in turn
    ' this class is hidden from the user of the Control
    Inherits System.Windows.Forms.Label
    Dim MyParent As GamesGrid  ' used to identify who the parent control is
    Dim MyNumber As Integer     ' identifies which tile on the board
    Private mMyColour As Color ' set for the option of indivual colours
    Private mMyString As String ' set for the option of special text disply
    Private mDrawColour As Boolean = False
                                ' used to sort out which type of board is in use
    Public Property DrawColour() As Boolean ' exposed only to the control
        Get
            Return mDrawColour
        End Get
        Set(ByVal Value As Boolean)
            mDrawColour = Value
            Invalidate()
        End Set
    End Property
    Public Property Mycolor() As Color ' exposed only to the control
        Get
            Return mMyColour
        End Get
        Set(ByVal Value As Color)
            mMyColour = Value
            Invalidate()
        End Set
    End Property
    Public Property MyString() As String ' exposed only to the control
        Get
            Return mMyString
        End Get
        Set(ByVal Value As String)
            mMyString = Value
            Invalidate()
        End Set
    End Property
    ' Constructor takes as parameters the parent Control and the Square Number
    Public Sub New(ByVal parent As GamesGrid, ByVal Square As Integer)
        MyBase.New()
        InitializeComponent()
        MyParent = parent
        MyNumber = Square
    End Sub

    Private Sub Square1_Click(ByVal sender As Object, ByVal e As _
                                    System.EventArgs) Handles MyBase.Click
        MyParent.FindChild(Me.MyNumber)
    End Sub
    Private Sub Square1_Paint(ByVal _
                                    sender As Object, ByVal e As _
```

```
                              System.Windows.Forms.PaintEventArgs) _
                              Handles MyBase.Paint
          '' Here we paint a boundary for the squares

      Dim draw As Graphics
      Dim ThePen As New Pen(Color.Black, 1)
      draw = e.Graphics
      draw.DrawRectangle(ThePen, 0, 0, Me.Width, Me.Height)
      If DrawColour = True Then  ' then check if we are going to paint a
              ' Background and set the text.
              Me.BackColor = Me.Mycolor '' draw my own colour
              Me.Text = Me.MyString
      Else
              Me.Text = "" '' make sure string is empty..
      End If
      End Sub
      End Class
```

Having created this quite small class, which totally deals with all aspects of a single square on the final board grid, we can look at the actual GamesGrid class.

This again has been derived from the .NET windows.forms.label root class, once again the functionality of the label class is required within the main class and the only area of concern was the text attribute of a standard label component. The solution to the problem of the label as we will see is to handle the TextChanged(..) event and ensure that the inherited label text is always assigned an empty string.

The first aspect of the implementation to investigate is the local variable declarations for the class.

```
#Region "Some standard values to use for the designer"
    Private Boundary As Integer = 4
    Private NumberofSquares As Integer = 64
    Private Rows As Integer = 8
    Private Columns As Integer = 8
    Private ASize As Integer = (Rows * Columns) - 1
    Private PSqr(1) As Square1   '' the actual squares
    Private BoardWidth As Integer = 0
    Private BoardHeight As Integer = 0
    Private SquareWidth As Integer = 0
    Private SquareHeight As Integer = 0
    Private LightColour As Color = Color.White
    Private DarkColour As Color = Color.Red
    Private ChequerBoard As Boolean = True
#End Region
```

The major difference you will notice about the declaration of variables in this component, when compared to the previous non-visual component, is that all the variables, although they have the private attribute, have been given default values. The reason for this is that we are dealing with a visual component, it can be attached to the toolbar in a visual development environment such as Visual Studio .NET. Once on the toolbar the component can be dragged onto any application form in design mode. When this action occurs the Visual Studio .NET Form designer software will create a new instance of the component and populate the properties window in Visual Studio .NET. The component specific properties will be read from the component itself, as we have seen before the return value from a property read is generally the relevant private variables from the class, and if no initialised value exists for such a property variable, Visual Studio .NET has been known to crash.

I will skip over the properties declaration and code since there is really nothing different in this implementation from properties in other examples. Our first investigation of the GamesGrid class is to consider the constructor:

```
Public Sub New()
    MyBase.New()
    'This call is required by the Windows Form Designer.
    InitializeComponent()
    CreateGrid()      ' actual Build the board
End Sub
```

The actual creation code has been moved out from the constructor to a private CreateGrid(..) method, the reason for this is, if either the row or column property values are changed, once the board has been instanced, we will need to remove and destroy the Square1 objects that constitute the game grid and recreate a new set of Square1 objects based on the new values in row and column. In order to make this a simple exercise two private methods have been implemented, CreateGrid(..) and ClearGrid(..):

```
Private Sub CreateGrid()
  ' Build the grid
  Dim i As Integer
  ReDim PSqr(ASize)
  For i = 0 To (Rows * Columns) - 1
          PSqr(i) = New Square1(Me, i)
          Me.Controls.AddRange(New System.Windows.Forms.Control() _
                                      {Me.PSqr(i)})
          PSqr(i).Size = New System.Drawing.Size(10, 10)
          PSqr(i).Location = New System.Drawing.Point(10, 10 + i * 20)
          PSqr(i).Mycolor = Color.White
          PSqr(i).MyString = ""
      Next
```

```
End Sub

Private Sub ClearGrid()
    ' Delete copmponents on the board when Rows or Columns changed
    Dim i As Integer
    Dim j As Integer
    For i = 0 To (Rows * Columns) - 1
            j = Me.Controls.GetChildIndex(PSqr(i))
            Me.Controls.RemoveAt(j)
            PSqr(i) = Nothing
    Next
    ReDim PSqr(1)
End Sub
```

In both of these methods the ReDim keyword is used in this VB.NET version. Changing the dimension of an array using this type of syntax is unique to Visual Basic; when you look at the C# version you will see we have to completely remove the array and recreate it.

The other important aspect of the .NET Framework in use here is the assigning of an object reference to the keyword **Nothing**. This action is not strictly necessary, since the automatic garbage collection (we looked at this topic in Chapter 4) will identify when an object is no longer in scope; however, if you get into the habit of assigning items to Nothing when they are no longer required, according to the technical specification of the CLR automatic garbage collection algorithm this will improve overall garbage collection performance. When deleting objects from a form you must also remove the object from the forms controls collection, this is a slightly more complex operation than inserting an object with the simple statement:

```
Me.Controls.AddRange(New System.Windows.Forms.Control() {Me.PSqr(i)})
```

To remove an object you have first to find the index in the collection array for the object by:

```
j = Me.Controls.GetChildIndex(PSqr(i))
```

Once this index is located you can remove the object using the recovered index by:

```
Me.Controls.RemoveAt(j)
```

GamesGrid class Since this class has been inherited from the label class we must implement three standard event handlers that perform actions specific to the games board needs.

First the GamesGrid_Paint(..) provides the drawing of our grid:

GamesGrid_Paint(..)

```
Private Sub GamesGrid_Paint(ByVal sender As Object, ByVal e As _
System.Windows.Forms.PaintEventArgs) Handles MyBase.Paint
'' this will deal with the painting of this new control.
Dim draw As Graphics
Dim ThePen As New Pen(Color.Black, Boundary)
Dim Background As Boolean = False
Dim i As Integer
draw = e.Graphics
draw.DrawRectangle(ThePen, Boundary, Boundary, Me.Width - (Boundary * 2),_
  (Me.Height - Boundary * 2))
If ChequerBoard = True Then  '' draw the normal grid
    For i = 0 To (Rows * Columns) - 1
        If (i Mod Columns) = 0 Then  ' swap the colours as each row alternates
                Background = Not Background
        End If
        If Background = True Then ' Select the background colour.
                PSqr(i).BackColor = DarkColour
        Else
                PSqr(i).BackColor = LightColour
        End If
        Background = Not Background
   Next
Else
    '' send an invalidate to the square.
    PSqr(i).Invalidate()         ' square will paint itself
End If
End Sub
```

This paint handling simply draws an external boundary on the board and then, either produces a standard chequer board pattern by changing the background colour of the individual squares or it sends an Invalidate() to specific squares so they will redraw the custom information as required.

Second, the GamesGrid_Resize(..) calculates dimensions etc. for our grid:

GamesGrid_Resize(..)

```
Private Sub GamesGrid_Resize(ByVal sender As Object, ByVal e As
System.EventArgs) _
Handles MyBase.Resize
' calculate the basic sizes.
Dim Rect As Size = New Size(0, 0)
Dim i As Integer
Dim row As Integer
Dim col As Integer
Rect = Me.ClientSize
BoardWidth = Rect.Width - (Boundary * 2)
BoardHeight = Rect.Height - (Boundary * 2)
```

```
SquareWidth = BoardWidth \ Columns
SquareHeight = BoardHeight \ Rows
    For i = 0 To (Rows * Columns) - 1
        PSqr(i).Size = New System.Drawing.Size(SquareWidth, SquareHeight)
        row = Boundary + (i Mod Columns) * SquareWidth
        col = Boundary + (i \ Columns) * SquareHeight
        PSqr(i).Location = New System.Drawing.Point(row, col)
        PSqr(i).Show()
    Next
Invalidate() ' make sure we gat a paint
End Sub
```

As in the stand alone solution of the similar problem it is quite simple integer maths, you will find that certain sizes with strange row and column values can create a rounding error and cause the board to look not quite correct on the screen. I leave it to you to make the necessary correction.

Finally GamesGrid_ TextChanged(..)

The GameGrid class inherited from the basic label class and a label can have text. This text can be set programmatically or alternatively in the Visual Studio .NET designer by changing the text property. The board does not have any overall text requirements, the individual squares when the board is set up for custom colours can have text but we have no need for any board-based text to appear. To ensure that no text can appear within the actual board, the handler GamesGrid_TextChanged(..) is added to ensure any attempt to set text is converted to an empty string:

```
Private Sub GamesGrid_TextChanged(ByVal sender As Object,ByVal e As _
System.EventArgs)_
Handles MyBase.TextChanged
'' make sure user can't set up text as part of the grid properties.
Me.Text = ""
End Sub
```

Event Handling

The requirement specification for this component is to raise an event when a mouse click occurs on any one square. In the description of the Square1 class we have already identified that an event handling for the mouse click event will pass back to the GamesGrid class an indicator of the square. Remember as well this passback will ensure that the click event will only be visible from the GamesGrid class ensuring any client will have no visibility of the child class in the component.

We must now set up the external event within GamesGrid by first declaring the event within this class:

```
Public Event SquareClicked(ByVal SNumber As Integer) ' the only event
```

This is a standard delegate template as was discussed in the chapter on the compliant programming languages in the .NET Framework. This template identifies the event name that will be exposed to client and any parameters that will be passed with the event:

Event Name　　　SquareClicked

Parameter　　　An Integer Value

The GamesGrid method called from the Square1 class can then raise the event:

```
Public Sub FindChild(ByVal Number As Integer)
  '' here we raise an external event to indicate the square clicked
RaiseEvent SquareClicked(Number)
End Sub
```

Any client application using the component GamesGrid must declare an event handler for this event. Typically this will have the form.

```
Private Sub XXXXXX_SquareClicked(ByVal SNumber As Integer) Handles _
                                XXXXXX.SquareClicked
End Sub
```

The XXXXXX_ is the name of the instance of the GameGrid class within the client application. The creation of specific events and their associated handlers is something students find very confusing but with a little careful thought it is quite simple, the key stages are:

■ Define a public delegate template of the event in the class that will raise the event

■ Use the RaiseEvent keyword as required, ensuring the delegate template form of the call is maintained

■ Within the client that is going to consume the event, write a handler for the specified event.

Special Method and Properties

The only other aspects of this visual control that we need be concerned about are the specialist methods that allow the client application access to properties within the Square1 class. It was noted earlier that the Square1 class must not expose properties publicly because to do so would expose this class as another component. If it were to do so developers using the GamesGrid could be tempted to bypass the GamesGrid component interface and try to interface directly with the individual squares; the result of such interaction could be totally indeterminate since Square1 was not designed to have external interaction with a client. It is therefore important that GamesGrid has specific methods that interact with the user that allow the user to effectively interact with the individual squares. These public methods allow specific colour and text attributes to be set on a square-by-square basis:

```
Public Function GetSQColour(ByVal Index As Integer) As Color
    '' Get the special Colour of a Tile or square
    Return PSqr(Index).Mycolor
End Function
Public Sub SetSqColour(ByVal Index As Integer, ByVal C As Color)
    '' Set the special colour
    PSqr(Index).Mycolor = C
End Sub
Public Function GetSQText(ByVal Index As Integer) As String
    '' Get the special Text
    Return PSqr(Index).MyString
End Function
Public Sub SetSqString(ByVal Index As Integer, ByVal C As String)
    '' Sets the special Text
    PSqr(Index).MyString = C
End Sub
```

Once again these methods have no error handling so if the square parameter is out of bounds the control will crash; it is left to the reader to improve on this in their own time.

This GamesGrid component has quite complex functionality but if you review the overall implementation detail there is in fact fewer than 400 lines of VB.NET code.

A question quite often asked by students is 'What about all the other functionality associated with a normal .NET component control?' The simple answer is to look at where the component came from, it was inherited from a standard label component, and therefore anything you can do to a label, you can do to this control, either through the properties window in the design environment or programmatically in the application. It has inherited all the standard events associated with a label, so any client using the control can write an override event handler specific to an application on any of these standard events. In order to demonstrate the control now that it is complete, a simple Windows Forms application has been developed which allows the user to manipulate all of the properties and exposed methods.

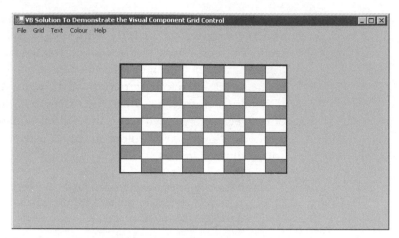

Figure 6.7   *The chequer board grid configuration*

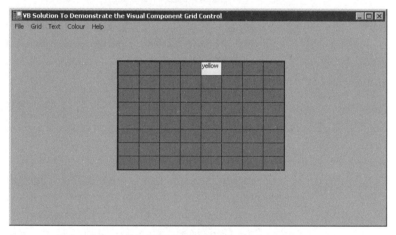

Figure 6.8   *The user defined board grid configuration*

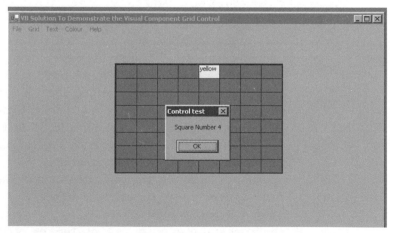

Figure 6.9   *Identifying which grid square was clicked*

The Windows
Form Tester for
the GamesGrid
Control.

First, I would point out this is only a piece of test software so the GUI is purely functional and the dialogue boxes used are quite crude.

The aim of this test application is simple, to offer some menu options that allow the properties and methods exposed by GamesGrid to be set to values and the result seen on the displayed games board. Obviously some of these changes can be seen by using the property window in the form designer window of Visual Studio .NET. If the property window is open, you can simply change the property and view the result.

However, this is not the case for the custom layout option or events generated when a user clicks on a square, to see these working we do require a simple test form running.

Since this is a standard Windows Forms application little explanation of the code is required; I have extracted some snippets of code to demonstrate how, for instance, a single dialogue form can be used to serve more than one purpose.

Rows and
Column Change

From the menu the user can request to change either the number of Rows or the number of Columns on the GamesGrid:

```
Private Sub GridRows_Click(ByVal sender As System.Object, ByVal e As
System.EventArgs)
Handles GridRows.Click
        Dim Dialogue As RowColumSelector
        Dialogue = New RowColumSelector(Me, 0)
        Dialogue.ShowDialog()

End Sub

Private Sub GridColumns_Click(ByVal sender As System.Object,ByVal e As _
System.EventArgs) Handles GridColumns.Click
        Dim Dialogue As RowColumSelector
        Dialogue = New RowColumSelector(Me, 1)
        Dialogue.ShowDialog()
End Sub
```

These two methods are handling the menu selection for both the row size change and the column size change, notice both have identical code except for the creation of the dialogue box itself:

```
Dialogue = New RowColumSelector(Me, 0)
Dialogue = New RowColumSelector(Me, 1)
```

The second parameter in the call to the constructor of the dialogue identifies if we are looking at a change to the row or column property of the component.

This constructor for the RowColumSelector dialogue box can then be implemented:

```
Public Sub New(ByVal Myparent As MainForm, ByVal ind As Integer)
      MyBase.New()
      MParent = Myparent
      'This call is required by the Windows Form Designer.
      InitializeComponent()
      Indicator = ind
      If ind = 0 Then
          '' changing rows
          Me.Text = Me.Text + " Rows"
          Me.Label1.Text = Me.Label1.Text + " Rows"
          Me.InValue.Text = Myparent.GamesGrid1.RowsOnBoard.ToString()
      Else
          Me.Text = Me.Text + " Columns"
          Me.Label1.Text = Me.Label1.Text + " Columns"
          Me.InValue.Text = Myparent.GamesGrid1.ColumsOnBoard.ToString()

      End If
End Sub
```

Using this indicator parameter to customise the text fields, the user is aware of which value is being requested in the dialogue but unaware that the same code is being used for two purposes. When the user closes the dialogue with an OK button click the stored indicator passed into the constructor can be used to update the correct property on the GamesGrid component:

```
Private Sub cmdOK_Click(ByVal sender As System.Object, ByVal e As
System.EventArgs)_
Handles cmdOK.Click
If Me.Indicator = 0 Then
      MParent.GamesGrid1.RowsOnBoard = Integer.Parse(Me.InValue.Text)
Else
      MParent.GamesGrid1.ColumsOnBoard = Integer.Parse(Me.InValue.Text)
End If
End Sub
```

A similar technique was used in the dialogue box for the custom square colour selection and unique text since in both cases the information to gather was similar:

Colour Selection → Which Square → What Colour
Unique text   → Which Square → What text

The remainder of the code for the tester application is left for the reader to investigate more fully if required.

Summary

This chapter has taken the subject of .NET Windows forms into the area of componentware design and implementation. Once again it is only possible to give a brief glimpse at the potential. In the introduction to this chapter it was stated that when the ActiveX control model became accepted for third party vendor supplied specialist controls in Visual Basic, the floodgates opened and perhaps hundreds of thousands of lines of code were written providing specialist controls for anything you can imagine.

The .NET component model has not made these Active X controls obsolete, in fact in the next chapter we will be reviewing interoperability of .NET with other technologies and one area we will be looking at is ActiveX controls. However, any ActiveX control unless it is very crude and simple, constituted a very complex development and demanded a very high competence and understanding of programming languages such as C++.

The aim of this chapter was to show that anything that can be written as a basic .NET application could, with only some very minor changes, be transformed into a .NET component. This was certainly never the case with technologies such as COM, DCOM or ActiveX, such transformations from a stand-alone executable to a componentware version quite often incurred a complete redesign and implementation of the product.

I have deliberately avoided the topic of component deployment and installation of your component on another machine. This is a far more advanced topic than a book at this introductory level should attempt to investigate and I leave you to research into these topics should you wish to do so.

Review questions

1   Investigate how the ActiveX controls were deployed.

2   What issues would you need to address to deploy a .NET component?

3   There are many other components you could design and implement that relate to games; for instance what about a component for:
    a. Randomly selected questions and answers
    b. Throw and maintain the state of a selected number of dice
    c. The game board for a game of back gammon
    d. The game board for a game of solitaire.

7 Interoperability issues

Objective

Up to now we have basically dealt with .NET as a totally new set of technologies both for the development of stand-alone applications and reuseable components. However, previous techniques for Windows stand-alone solutions as well as Windows distributed applications have created a great deal of legacy code.

Within this chapter we will investigate just a portion of the interoperability available within the .NET architecture to give a feel for the amount of additional work the use of legacy code will involve when designing a new system.

There is of course a trade-off, a new .NET system design could start from scratch if no .NET components existed for the functionality required or alternatively older technology components or libraries could be used. The cost/benefits analysis of each option needs careful consideration, we have already discovered that the .NET class library is enormous and that the learning curve for even a fraction of the functionality provided is long.

Introduction

Many applications exist that have been built using the standard Win32 application interface (API) and of course there are in existence hundreds if not thousands of currently active COM/ActiveX components. Such software plays an important role in the running of a modern business so they cannot simply be ignored. No matter how much the .NET Framework may offer to new developments, the previous technologies used to solve the problems will not be obsolete for many years to come.

With such a vast investment in software development the .NET Framework has to provide a mechanism for any new development to utilise aspects of the older technologies. This interoperability task is certainly non-trivial, the overall architecture of the .NET Framework, as investigated in the previous chapters, is forged around the use of the CLR and the inherent managed code philosophy.

Legacy software of course has no such provision for interoperability with the CLR. None of the earlier componentware technologies of COM or DCOM offered any form of managed code environment and as we will see in this chapter interoperability with COM objects requires that the .NET Framework must revert back to registry-based library metadata descriptions of the object, rather than the far simpler assembly manifest descriptions outlined in a previous chapter.

It is not only componentware that needs consideration when dealing with legacy interoperability. Software development traditionally has been based on building libraries of useful functionality, such libraries may have been static or dynamic but they all have one factor in common, they certainly were not designed to run in the CLR environment.

Such is the need to have a consistent approach to the interoperability problems for the .NET class library structure that a complete subordinate namespace has been developed to offer services to the software developer in an attempt to ensure an apparent seamless integration of legacy code into any new .NET Framework solution.

Use of some of the interoperability options is by no means simply a matter of bolting onto the older technology the .NET class library techniques. Marrying together software technologies has always required a great deal of technical expertise on the part of the software developer, coupled with something that is akin to luck, but which more accurately reflects the attribute of developers to see a complete overall solution before they start to actually write code.

Win32 API interoperability

The simplest interoperability issue is the inclusion of Win32 API-based unmanaged code in a .NET Framework application. In the .NET Framework this comes under the generic title of 'Platform Invoke Services'. However, using such an idea will beg the question 'When would I want to do that?'

Obviously it would be a relatively easy task to write a completely new .NET component to offer specific functionality, but this has just one major drawback. Suppose the functionality already exists in a stable form, suppose it includes for instance graphics that would need to be completely redeveloped? Then if there is an effective mechanism to invoke this older technology from within the managed environment it will be far simpler and more cost effective to use it.

Using an existing system DLL

As an example of Platform Invoke Services, and as a simple introduction to the subject, I have taken as an example the use of the standard cards.dll. This standard dynamic link library has been shipped with all versions of the Windows operating system since Windows 3.0. Its function is quite simple, it provides a consistent implementation of the drawing of playing cards for the game of solitaire which we have all come to either love or hate.

The cards.dll provides the necessary graphics in a form the user is familiar with and even though the final result will have any limitations associated with the original cards.dll it should be much better than any attempt at producing new graphics for a totally new .NET component I might consider implementing.

Windows has always offered many extensions using DLLs these can be used within any application. You only have to review the directory System32 under your Windows installation to see just how many DLLs are installed within a standard Windows operating system.

The cards.dll has actually appeared as two versions. The Windows 95 series of operating systems (this includes Windows 98 and Windows ME) uses the original 16-bit version that was shipped with all versions from Windows 3.0. Obviously this version is not usable within the .NET environment since there is no .NET support for older 16-bit environments. The later version is a 32-bit cards.dll and is shipped with the Windows NT series (Windows NT, Windows 2000 etc.). This is the version discussed here.

Exported functions from 'cards.dll'

As you may be unfamiliar with the concept of a dynamical link library exporting functions, the following brief description should help to clarify the technique. Should you wish to look at dynamic link library exporting in more detail, then further reading will be required and can I suggest you look at Petzold, C., *Programming Windows*, Fifth Edition 2000.

Exporting a function in a standard dynamic link library allowed Win32 applications to link to the functionality either statically or dynamically. The implementation of the DLL used a keyword 'exports' on the functions it wished to expose for external use. This keyword enabled either an imports library to be created to which an application could statically link or the application could at run time use the API Loadlibrary(..) and locate the relevant function dynamically and then call that function.

The following C/C++ code gives an example of performing this dynamic binding to a dll:

```
HINSTANCE TheDLL;                // Handle to DLL
LPFNDLLFUNC1 TheFunc1;           // Function pointer
DWORD Param1; // Some parameters
UINT  Param2, ReturnVal;

TheDLL = LoadLibrary("MyDLL.dll");
if (TheDLL != NULL)       // NULL = we did not find the dll
{
    TheFunc1 = (LPFNDLLFUNC1)GetProcAddress(TheDLL,"TheFunctionToCall");
// find the function in the DLL
    if (!TheFunc1)
    { // Could not find the function handle the error
      FreeLibrary(hDLL);
      return SOME_ERROR_CODE;
    }
    else
    {
      // call the function
      ReturnVal = TheFunc1(Param1, Param2);
    }
}
```

It is this type of technique that we need in the CLR but of course we have to ensure that the parameters and the return value etc. are acceptable to the CTS system.

Cards.dll actually exports five functions that we will use in this example code, these five functions will provide any .NET application with the ability to draw playing card images. These five functions are the only interface that cards.dll provides to draw cards. The functions never let you have access to the actual bitmaps used, rather, you supply a suitable device context and the card functions draw the card bitmaps for you.

Here is a basic description of each function, and the C/C++ prototypes.

1 **cdtInit BOOL WINAPI cdtInit (int *width, int *height)**
This function initialises the cards.dll library for your application. The parameters are passed by reference and comprise two integer variables, these are the width and height (in pixels) of a card, the cards.dll will use these to provide local storage for the application of these sizes. We will see later that using a fixed size improves the graphical representation.

2 **cdtDraw BOOL WINAPI cdtDrawExt (HDC hdc, int x, int y, int card, int type, DWORD color)**
This function specifies how and where to draw the playing card. It requires the device context, i.e. the definition of the output device, and the X and Y position within the device. The type parameter controls whether the front, the back, or the inverted (normally used to indicate that a card is selected) front of the card is drawn.

The integer card controls which card face value or back is actually drawn. There is of course a relationship between this value and the previous type parameter. If a card face is to be drawn (type is set to 0 or 2), and the card must be a value from 0 through 51 representing which actual playing card is required. If type specifies that the card back needs to be drawn (type is 1), then the card value has a range of 53 to 68 (inclusive) to represent one of the possible predefined card backs.

Card faces are organised in increasing order. That is, the aces come first, then the twos and so on. In each group, the cards are ordered by suit. The order is 'Clubs, Diamonds, Hearts and Spades'. This pattern is repeated as the card values increase.

You can use Tables 7.1 and 7.2 to define both face values and card backs. Given the need to specify a particular card face, the following simple calculation identifies the card parameter. The definition for face value is 0 to 12, the 0 represents an Ace and 12 is a King.

This allows us to specify the card parameter = (face × 4) + Suit. Table 7.2 contains a list of the 16 possible predefined card backgrounds that can be used.

Table 7.1   *Card face values*

Suit	Value
Clubs	0
Diamonds	1
Hearts	2
Spades	3

Table 7.2   *The 16 possible predefined card backgrounds*

Card Back	Value	Card Back	Value
CROSSHATCH	53	FISH2	61
WEAVE1	54	SHELLS	62
WEAVE2	55	CASTLE	63
ROBOT	56	ISLAND	64
FLOWERS	57	CARDHAND	65
VINE1	58	UNUSED	66
VINE2	59	THE_X	67
FISH1	60	THE_O	68

Lastly, the colour parameter sets the background colour for the CrossHatch card back, which uses a pattern drawn with lines. All the other backs and fronts are bitmaps, so colour has no effect.

3 **cdtDrawExt BOOL WINAPI cdtDrawExt (HDC hdc, int x, int y, int dx, int dy, int card, int suit, DWORD color)**
This procedure is the same as cdtDraw except that you specify the dx and dy parameters to indicate the size of the card. The card bitmaps are stretched or compressed to the specified size. Some experimentation with this proved it is very difficult to get good graphics if you stretch or compress the default size.

4 **CdtAnimate BOOL WINAPI cdtAnimate (HDC hdc, int cardback, int x, int y, int frame)**
This function animates some of the predefined backs of cards by overlaying part of the card back with an alternative bitmap. It creates effects: blinking lights on the robot, the sun donning sunglasses, bats flying across the castle, and a card sliding out of a sleeve. The function only works for cards of normal size drawn with cdtDraw. The function requires that you start with frame set to 0 and then keep drawing, incrementing the value of frame by one until cdtAnimate returns 0.

5 **cdtTerm void WINAPI cdtTerm (void)**
This function cleans up the card resources from your program. It takes no parameters, and returns no values. It is advisable to call this, to close down the instance of cards.dll, just before the application using it exits.

Having identified these five functions are available for application use and are resident in the cards.dll how can we make use of them within the .NET architecture? There are two options:

1 Import the dll into each of the applications

2 Write a simple interface .NET component that will create a wrapper around this non-managed code and provide a reusable interface for any application that needs to gain access to the cards.dll.

The second option is the most general solution and it will allow the discussion in the previous chapter on writing .NET components to be extended to include interfacing to non-managed code within a component design.

Creating the user control

As in the previous chapter we should first identify the requirement for this component. Most importantly it must in this case have a visual interface. Based on the discussion in the last chapter relating to the instancing of such a component in the Visual Studio .NET designer environment, the most obvious class to derive this new component from is again the standard label.

In the actual component design itself we are going to need

access to the functions in cards.dll and we then need to provide a suitable managed code interface to the five basic functions available. It is also important that we use some simple properties so that any .NET application using this new component will not need to be aware of the complexity of interfacing the cards.dll itself.

Properties

- Width of card

- Height of card

- Face value of card

- Suit of card

- Card back to use

- Boolean controlling face or back.

Additional properties related to animation and selections could also be implemented but since this component is being used to illustrate the interoperability of a Win32 dynamic link library within a .NET component, these have been ignored and the reader is left to extend the component to include this functionality at a later date.

Events

Once again because this example is looking at the interoperability issues rather than component design, no events are being implemented in this example; the obvious choice for an event would be the mouse click on the card.

Methods

Only a single constructor method is required for this component, there is no functional requirement to expose further user methods as the component can be controlled by programmatic changes to property values. Of course we will need to ensure that these property changes are fully qualified by writing set property methods.

In fact this is a far simpler component design than those discussed in the previous chapter, the important aspect of the implementation to consider is the interface to the cards.dll itself. Once again the discussion below relates to the C# solution, the VB.NET solution is very similar and the differences relate to the specifics of the language syntax.

The component implementation

```
namespace DisplayPlayCardCntrl
{
    /// <summary>
    /// Summary description for UserControl1.
    /// </summary>
    public class DisplayPlayCard : System.Windows.Forms.Label
    {
        public enum AFace
        { //first we need a definition of the 13 cards in a suit.
            One, Two, Three, Four, Five, Six, Seven, Eight, Nine,
            Ten, Jack, Queen, King
        }

        public enum ABack
        {// Definition of the backs that are available
         ROSSHATCH, WEAVE1, WEAVE2, ROBOT, FLOWERS, VINE1, VINE2, FISH1,
         FISH2, SHELLS, CASTLE, ISLAND, CARDHAND, UNUSED, THE_X, THE_O
        }

        public enum ASuit
        {// definition of the card suits
            Clubs = 0, Diamonds = 1, Hearts = 2, Spades = 3
        }
    }
}
```

If you refer back to the example of the GameofCards Component in Chapter 6 these enumerations for the face value and suit are identical, the reason being that, in the later chapters we will be using both controls together in one solution and having a common description for the playing cards will greatly simplify the interworking of these .NET components.

In common with the discussions on component design in the previous chapter, the actual properties have been given default values, you should recall this ensures that when this component is dragged from the toolbar to a form in the development environment it will automatically be instanced by the visual designer and without default properties this normally crashes the development environment:

```
private int mWidth = 71;
private int mHeight = 95;
private AFace mFace = AFace.One ;
private ASuit mSuit = ASuit.Clubs  ;
private ABack mBack = ABack.ROBOT ;
private bool mShowback = false;
public int MWidth
{ get {return mWidth;}
```

```
          set {mWidth= value;}}
       public int MHeight
       { get {return mHeight;}
          set {mHeight= value;}}
       public AFace Face
       { get {return this.mFace;}
          set {this.mFace = value;this.Invalidate();}}
       public ASuit Suit
       { get    {return this.mSuit;}
          set {this.mSuit = value; this.Invalidate();}}
       public ABack Back
       { get    {return this.mBack;}
          set    {this.mBack = value; this.Invalidate();}}
       public bool Showback
       { get    {return this.mShowback;}
          set    {this.mShowback = value; this.Invalidate();}}
```

In this class, as it inherits from a basic label, the properties Width and Height, already exist so to uniquely identify the cards.dll Width and Height and because of a possible resize(..) problem that is discussed below, the component design uses two further properties MWidth and Mheight to distinguish the cards.dll required values for display size.

The DisplayPlayCard class constructor in this case only sets up a default instance of the component:

```
public DisplayPlayCard()
{
 InitializeComponent();
 int aWidth = MWidth;
 int aHeight = MHeight;
 if(!DisplayPlayCard.cdtInit(ref aWidth ,ref aHeight))
 {
    throw new Exception("cannot initialize dll (\"cards.dll\"");
 }

}
```

There are two important factors to consider regarding the implementation of the constructor.

The first is when we investigated the available functions in cards.dll the initialisation function cdtInit required two parameters both passed by reference, these represented the width and height of the display size for the cards. Since we have already defined these two values as properties, the most obvious solution is to pass these property values, by reference, to the function. The CLR does not support such operations, a property is a mechanism to gain access to a private data member in a class and as such cannot be used for a parameter pass by reference; it can of course be used for a parameter pass by value, since any property has an implied get and set value method.

The second important factor is the ability to pass back to the client application using the component, the fact that the required cards.dll could not be correctly initialised in this case is accomplished by using the throw to generate a new structured exception that the client can catch. Obviously this constructor is making use of some mechanism to reference the functions in the cards.dll and we will investigate this next.

The code for the interoperability in this case is fairly straightforward for each of the functions in the Win32 dynamic link library, we declare:

```
/// Initializes the cards.dll library for drawing
//  Param one =passed by reference "height" - height of cards to be drawn
/// param two =passed by reference"width" width of card to be drawn
/// returns true if successfull
[DllImport("cards.dll")] // identify source
// identify function fully.
public static extern bool cdtInit (ref int width, ref int height);
```

The DllImport attribute is used to specify the specific location of the required dynamic link library that contains the implementation of an 'extern' method. Specifically, the DllImport attribute has the following requirements that must be followed:

■ It can only be placed on method declarations

■ It has a single parameter: the dynamic link library name

■ It can have up to five additional subparameters:
    ❏ A CallingConvention indicates the calling convention for the entry point. If no CallingConvention is specified, a default of WinAPI is used
    ❏ A CharSet parameter indicates the character set used in the entry point. If no CharSet is specified, a default of Auto is used
    ❏ An EntryPoint parameter gives the name of the entry point in the libary. If no EntryPoint is specified, then the method name is used
    ❏ An ExactSpelling parameter indicates whether EntryPoint must exactly match the spelling of the indicated entry point. If no ExactSpelling is specified, a default of false is used
    ❏ A PreserveSig parameter indicates whether the signature of the method should be preserved or transformed. When

a signature is transformed, it is transformed to one having an HRESULT return value and an additional out parameter named retval for the return value. If no PreserveSig value is specified, a default of true is used

❑ The SetLastError parameter indicates whether the method preserves the Win32 'last error'. If no SetLastError is specified, a default of false is used.

In this example all of the entry points in the dynamic link library cards.dll are declared to take the defaults on these optional parameters, this is quite normal for many of the standard Win32 libraries available and the reader should not concern themselves with the detail of these optional parameters until they have studied related techniques on Dllimports.

The final aspect of this component implementation relates back to our discussions in Chapter 6 on the painting and resizing of a .NET component. This is specifically within the visual designer interface; in common with our previous discussions this component must ensure it does not get itself into any strange modes, the most common of which is recursive calling itself when a property is changed.

During experimentation with the cards.dll, it was found that stretching and compressing the size of the image to fit larger or smaller cards than the default size of 71 × 95 pixels produced unacceptable distortion on the images when using the extended cdtdraw(..) function. To avoid such problems the override method for the resize(..) event handler needed to limit the physical size to the default. This proved a unique opportunity to create the recursive 'stack overflow error', simply because if a change is made to either width or height, when dragging such a component in the visual designer this will create resize(..) events and trying to limit the size in the same routine simply creates more resize events. The solution to the problem is shown in the listing below:

OnResize(..)

```
protected override void OnResize(System.EventArgs e)
{
// needed to be a bit careful here otherwise you disappear up you own !!!
// can only set width or height once
// This is mainly when in design mode they just will keep on trying to change
the size
if (this.Width !=this.MWidth )
    this.Width = this.MWidth;
if (this.Height !=this.MHeight )
    this.Height = this.MHeight ;
base.OnResize (e);
}
```

The resize event is protected from recursive calling by checking that the change that created the call was not caused by the previous call itself:

OnPaint(..)

```
protected override void OnPaint(System.Windows.Forms.PaintEventArgs e)
{
    // here we will draw on the surface of the control the card
Rectangle rect = this.ClientRectangle;
Graphics graph = e.Graphics;
IntPtr hdc = graph.GetHdc();  // get the device context
int card;
int type;
long color = Color.Transparent.ToArgb();
if(Showback)
{
   card = ((int)this.Back)+53;  // explicit type overide
      type = 1;
      }
else
    {
      card = ((int)this.Face)*4+((int)this.Suit);
          type = 0;
      }
if(!DisplayPlayCard.cdtDraw(hdc, rect.X, rect.Y, card,type, color))
    {
        graph.ReleaseHdc(hdc);
        throw new Exception("could not draw selected card");
    }
graph.ReleaseHdc(hdc);
base.OnPaint(e);
}
```

The override OnPaint handler makes use of the namespace graphics and extracts from the paint event arguments the device context:

```
IntPtr hdc = graph.GetHdc(); // get the device context
```

It is then simply a matter of calculating either the playing card back value or the face and suit value to select and call with the correct parameters the cards.dll function to draw the card:

OnTextChanged(..)

```
protected override void OnTextChanged(System.EventArgs e)
{
this.Text ="";
// can't have a text label across the face of the playing card...
base.OnTextChanged (e);
}
```

The new control

As was discussed in the games grid example in the last chapter, as this component is derived from a standard label control we need to eliminate all text change events from the inherited label property. This is accomplished by setting the base text to an empty string with an overridden OnTextChanged(..) event handler.

No specific test program was needed or created for the base line functionality testing of this component. It is only necessary to add the component to the toolbar in the visual designer built into Visual Studio .NET.

Then to drag an instance of the component to a default form in a new Windows application project, when the component has been instanced on the form, the properties window for the component can be used to view the effects of the changes to the properties. No further testing is required after this stage, as the component does not have any events or methods defined.

As previously indicated this display control in conjunction with the GameofCards control, developed in Chapter 6, will be used when we look at web forms and services in the last two chapters.

Interoperability with COM objects

It is far beyond the scope of this book to look at the architecture of the COM model itself. Many excellent texts exist explaining the design philosophy and implementation details for building COM

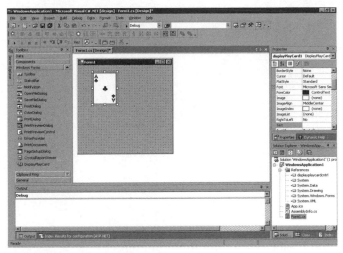

Figure 7.2   *The playing card display control in the graphics design window*

components using both Visual Basic and C++ implementation languages (see Dennings, *ActiveX Controls Inside Out*, 1998, Microsoft Press).

We must remember that the .NET architecture does not mean the end of the COM model, far from it, there are so many third party supplied COM/ActiveX controls available it will be many years before most or all of these are translated into .NET components.

It seems very likely that for quite a number of years development of new solutions within the .NET environment will require access to many of these very specific COM/ActiveX control implementations. Although COM is a proprietary Microsoft standard it is also viewed as a universally accepted mechanism at present, for the generation of componentware products. The specification is frozen, it is very unlikely that any significant changes will ever again be made to the COM/ActiveX architecture, therefore it is possible to define within the .NET Framework an interoperability strategy that is totally acceptable to both old and new developments.

The major problem faced in trying to use COM within the .NET Framework is the age-old problem of type conflicts. The COM model was not defined by the CTS strategy whereas the CLR is totally constrained by the CTS, so mapping the data types is very problematic.

The only viable solution is to use some form of code wrapping technique. Our first example wrapped the Win32 dynamic link library cards.dll using a .NET label class and created a perfectly usable implementation of a .NET component. Componentware

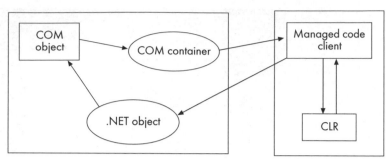

Figure 7.3   *COM to managed code*

written using the COM architecture is far more complex in basic structure than this relatively simple Win32 dynamic link library cards.dll but the same wrapping philosophy can be adopted to allow interoperability.

The fundamental concept involved, in arriving at any interoperability solution, is that each element involved in the merging of technologies sees an interface to the other technology that maps directly to the interface it expects. So when we start to consider the mechanism we must ensure that the COM object sees an emulation of the COM container model it expects, while equally, the .NET client sees an emulation of the .NET component it expects.

In Figure 7.3, the wrapper that needs to be produced must provide two levels of functionality, the first will allow the COM object in use to satisfy its need to see standard COM functionality in terms of source and sink points for its standard COM interfaces such as IUnknown(..). Second, the managed code must see the COM object as a derived .NET component class with its inherent assembly manifest from which this .NET client can derive the available functionality etc.

These two levels of mapping are classified within the .NET Framework by a technique known as the generation of a runtime callable wrapper (RCW) for the COM object. The RCW is a proxy built to expose the relevant COM object. Although the RCW appears to be an ordinary object to .NET clients, its primary function is to marshal calls between a .NET client and a COM object.

The CLR will create exactly one RCW for each COM object, regardless of the number of references that exist on that object. Using metadata derived from the type library belonging to the COM object, the CLR creates both the COM object being called and a wrapper for that object. Each RCW maintains a cache of

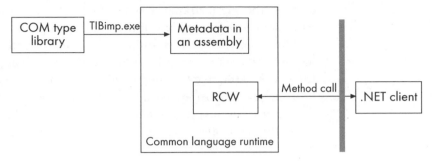

Figure 7.4   *Creating the metadata*

interface pointers on the COM object it wraps, and releases its reference on the COM object when the RCW is no longer needed. The run-time performs garbage collection on the RCW but of course it has no way of collecting garbage from the COM object itself.

Among other activities, the RCW marshals data between managed and unmanaged code, on behalf of the wrapped object. Specifically, the RCW provides marshalling for method arguments and method return values whenever the client and object have different representations of the data passed between them. The standard wrapper enforces built-in marshalling rules.

For example, when a .NET client passes a String type as part of an argument to a managed object, the wrapper converts the String to a BSTR type. Should the COM object return a BSTR to its managed caller, the caller receives a String. Both the client and the COM object send and receive data that is familiar to them. Other types require no conversion. For instance, a standard wrapper will always pass a 4-byte integer between managed and unmanaged code without converting the type.

The utility TIBimp.exe accomplishes the creation of the RCW metadata and the creation of this new assembly manifest. The .NET client can now fully interact with the RCW as if it were a native .NET component rather than a wrapper class for the COM object itself.

Obviously it is very difficult to provide much in the way of an example for this technique. I do not have any simple COM objects and even if I did, proving that the mechanism was working would require a great deal of technical knowledge related to COM and the .NET overall framework structure.

Windows Media Player OCX   However, I have put together a demonstration of using the standard Windows Media Player that is shipped as an ActiveX control, the file msdxn.ocx is the COM Object and is available with most current versions of the Windows operating system.

The example itself is quite trivial but for the technically inquisitive, the following brief look at the RCW manifest derived from the TlBimp.exe, along with the ILDisam.exe output (ILDisam.exe is shipped with the .NET Framework and allows an assembly to be investigated by displaying the MSIL within the assembly) will offer some view of the process. If you are not interested in these technical aspects the next section can be skipped without loss of continuity within the chapter.

The COM example using the Media Player

This is a simple Windows Form application with the ActiveX COM control playing a simple music file.

The first task is to produce the RCW, this can be automatically created within the visual designer of a product such as Visual Studio .NET or alternatively using the TlBimp.exe utility with a command line such as:

TlBimp c:\winnt\system32\media\msdxm.ocx out:c:\xxxxxxx

can create it.

The out option specifies where the files Axinterop.mediaplayer.dll and interop.mediaplayer.dll will be created as the assemblies controlling the RCW for the COM object. Once these are in existence you can then add references to your .NET solution for both and have confidence that you will be able to access the COM object as if it were a .NET component.

If you are interested in the mechanism further then use the ILDisam utility on each of these files in turn. The manifest for the basic interoperability has the form:

```
.assembly extern mscorlib
{
  .publickeytoken = (B7 7A 5C 56 19 34 E0 89 )                    // .z\V.4..
  .ver 1:0:3300:0
}
.assembly extern stdole
{
  .publickeytoken = (B0 3F 5F 7F 11 D5 0A 3A )                    // .?_....:
  .ver 7:0:3300:0
}
.assembly Interop.MediaPlayer
{
```

```
   .custom instance void
[mscorlib]System.Runtime.InteropServices.GuidAttribute::
.ctor(string) = ( 01 00 24 32 32 64 36 66 33 30 34 2D 62 30 66 36
                  2D 31 31 64 30 2D 39 34 61 62 2D 30 30 38 30 63
                  37 34 63 37 65 39 35 00 00 )
   .custom instance void
[mscorlib]System.Runtime.InteropServices.ImportedFromTypeLibAttribute::.ctor
(string) = ( 01 00 0B 4D 65 64 69 61 50 6C 61 79 65 72 00 00 )
   .hash algorithm 0x00008004
   .ver 1:0:0:0
}
.module MediaPlayer.dll
// MVID: {4D30C60B-5F02-4800-ACFC-5C2754183259}
.imagebase 0x00400000
.subsystem 0x00000003
.file alignment 4096
.corflags 0x00000001
// Image base: 0x03260000
```

The manifest for the Axinterop manifest has the form

```
.assembly extern System.Windows.Forms
{
  .publickeytoken = (B7 7A 5C 56 19 34 E0 89 )
  .ver 1:0:3300:0
}
.assembly extern mscorlib
{
  .publickeytoken = (B7 7A 5C 56 19 34 E0 89
  .ver 1:0:3300:0
}
.assembly extern Interop.MediaPlayer
{
  .ver 1:0:0:0
}
.assembly extern System
{
  .publickeytoken = (B7 7A 5C 56 19 34 E0 89 )
  .ver 1:0:3300:0
}
.assembly AxInterop.MediaPlayer
{
  .custom instance void [System.Windows.Forms]System.Windows.Forms.AxHost/
TypeLibraryTimeStampAttribute::.ctor(string) = ( 01 00 13 30 35 2F 30 36 2F
32 30 30 31 20 31 35   // ...05/06/2001 15

3A 32 35 3A 34 38 00 00 )                              // :25:48..
  .hash algorithm 0x00008004
  .ver 1:0:0:0
}
.module AxInterop.MediaPlayer.dll
// MVID: {7ECE2CFA-45B0-491A-9375-CACD58D3B862}
```

Figure 7.5   *The COM component 'Media Player' in a .NET application*

```
.imagebase 0x00400000
.subsystem 0x00000003
.file alignment 4096
.corflags 0x00000001
// Image base: 0x03340000
```

As can be seen on closer examination, it is obvious that these two manifests both relate to the same overall solution; it should also be apparent that some form of translation has taken place between the type library stored in the original ActiveX file and the Axinteroperability manifest. It is quite pointless at this level to try to take this discussion further since you will not have the prerequisite knowledge of the COM architecture to look into the detail of the two assemblies that have been created.

The actual application has a simple File Open Dialog allowing the user to select a suitable media file to play and when the player has the file name, it starts, and reduces itself in size. Notice at the client level the code in C# has no reference to the COM model, it simply treats the component as a standard .NET control:

```
private void FileOpen_Click(object sender, System.EventArgs e)
{
this.openFileDialog1.ShowDialog();
this.axMediaPlayer1.FileName = this.openFileDialog1.FileName;
this.axMediaPlayer1.Size = new Size( this.axMediaPlayer1.ImageSourceWidth,
            this.axMediaPlayer1.ImageSourceHeight );
this.Size = new Size( this.axMediaPlayer1.Size.Width + 20,
            this.axMediaPlayer1.Size.Height + 60 );
}
```

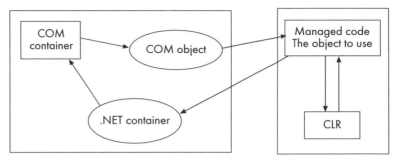

Figure 7.6   *COM using a managed code object*

Other interoperability issues

The only other topic that should be mentioned here is the reverse of the above discussion, the possibility that a COM container is going to be required to use a .NET component. The possibility of this situation seems far more remote than the previous one since it would seem far more logical if you have developed a new .NET component to use it from within a .NET Framework container. However, the situation could occur and once again since the COM architecture is highly unlikely to be altered, a fixed strategy can be adopted to ensure that in a similar manner to using COM within .NET each side will see what it expects rather than trying to fix the data typing on the fly.

In this case the technique is known as a COM Callable Wrapper, the diagram from the last section is still totally valid except we are now looking at the .NET managed code as the componentware and the COM code as the client user.

In this case rather than producing assembly manifests from the type library, the type library information has to be created from the manifest. There is in fact a further complication, the type library information references are held in the registry for the COM object architecture so in creating a type library from a .NET manifest we must then translate, and register the type library details, into the operating system registry.

Once again some basic tools are provided to help the developer to accomplish the tasks, this time, however, the visual programming environment of Visual Studio .NET does not have any automated functionality to assist in the process. The exporting tool to create the type library is called Tlbexp.exe and the Regasm.exe will take this type library information and create the correct registry entries.

It is not possible to investigate the result of a Tlbexp.exe operation since the file created is an extension dll, as would be expected, and although a few tools do exist to explore such files their use is not within the scope of this book.

The final comments on calling code across the boundary between managed and unmanaged code is the expansive nature of the marshalling involved, anything other than very simple data type transfer across the interface between the two types of code is very time consuming. The suggestion given in books specifically written on the interoperability issues is to do as much of the translation on one side or the other and do not allow the automatic marshalling much freedom, in that way you are in control. My suggestion for this book and to students at this level is to avoid like the plague any interoperability requirements unless they are as simple as the first example in this chapter.

Summary

This chapter has taken quite a quick look at a very complex subject. This book is intended as an introductory text and the subject of interoperability is certainly not introductory material. It was important that I gave you an understanding of the issues and the first example is genuinely as simple as it looks. It is once we start to consider interoperating in the COM environment the topic takes on a whole new dimension. My suggestion that you ignore the topic may not be very positive in respect of a learning outcome, but you must feel that you have mastered the basics of the .NET architecture before trying to deal with the intricate subject of marshalling and type mapping, which, although it may sound automated, is never really that simple.

Review questions

1   There are many COM components in the form of ActiveX controls that you can use in the Managed Code environment. Using your imagination, select an ActiveX control and use it in simple applications to evaluate its interoperability. Possible examples:

a. Microsoft Calendar Control – MScal.ocx

b. Microsoft Common Controls – MScomctl.ocx

c. Audio Recorder – Recording.ocx.

Then perform a design requirements analysis to provide the same functionality in a .NET component.

8 The role of XML

Objective

The mark-up language XML can certainly be considered within
the category of important technologies to emerge in the last few
years. The designers of the .NET architecture have recognised
this fact and XML plays a major role within the whole .NET
Framework. XML is used in a variety of manners within any
.NET-based solution and equally XML support is a key aspect of
the .NET class library. In a similar manner to interoperability
there is a whole subordinate namespace, within the class library
structure, dedicated to providing support for XML as a
mechanism for describing information in any application.

   In this chapter we will investigate the key structure of XML,
this will lead into its role within the .NET Framework (covering
the manner in which it is used to describe the solution for an
intelligent development system, such as Visual Studio .NET, to
how a .NET assembly is described and the resultant assembly
manifest description used by the CLR). Finally we will look at
using XML in some typical applications, specifically the subject
of serialisation of an object which we briefly looked at in
Chapter 5, when we used binary serialisation to store a games
status. Serialisation is the ability to extract the key data from a
particular task and stream it to some storage device. The XML
serialisation technique will be compared to the binary option
used previously and we will look at the benefit of XML based on
having human and machine-readable serialised information.

Introduction

The original specification for XML (Extensible Markup Language) was conceived in the mid 1990s. Its goal was to provide a portable and widely supported mechanism that allowed information to be fully described in a uniform manner.

How is this accomplished?

Within an XML structured document the actual data is described using a tagged text based system in a similar manner to that used for a web page. The web page markup language HTML (Hypertext Markup Language) allows the content of a web page to be fully described so that any web browser can reproduce or render the information content on the page, exactly as the author initially intended.

This viewing platform independence has been a key factor in the rapid growth of information retrieval via the World Wide Web (WWW). Just consider for a moment the chaos we would now be facing if HTML were not the standard for web page creation. In order to view specific pages the users would need specific browser software, not a situation anyone could envisage in which WWW growth could have been sustained. One can consider that XML takes the scenario of structure documents a stage further, rather than simply structuring the data for a web page browser. An XML document fully describes the data contained within it, in doing so any user of that document can extract and meaningfully interpret the data without recourse to the originator of the data.

We have already identified, on many occasions, in the earlier chapters of the book, that the .NET architecture was specifically formulated to offer platform and operating system independence to developers. It is not therefore surprising that the .NET Framework utilises XML documents extensively. Within the .NET Framework library a comprehensive set of classes associated with XML are provided allowing developers the opportunity to use XML technology. One of the key benefits such technology offers within application development is the reduced need for either registry or .INI file techniques normally associated with application configurations and data storage needs.

The promoted major advantages of XML are that it is both human and machine-readable. If you have ever tried to find and interpret a specific registry entry for an application, many such entries are obscure in nature and contain binary formatted data so any option that is human readable must be an advantage.

Obviously one alternative to the registry is the '.ini' file technique, it uses plain text formatted, but these '.ini' files are normally sequentially accessed and can only have a rigid data structure, meaning that many common applications simply do not make use of this option.

The techniques available within an XML document map to the .NET architecture when we are looking at its primary focus of distributed applications development. When originally conceived XML was derived as a usable mechanism to support interoperability, it is not therefore a surprise to find a very close integration of XML and the .NET architecture. Within a later chapter we will investigate some of the important aspects of this tight integration when dealing with so-called Multi-Tier distributed applications in terms of XML and the SOAP protocol.

XML documents

This book is not intended to teach you the intricacies of XML and how to use it effectively; the aim is to give you a broad understanding of the technology and its usage. In order to understand how it is used in .NET we must review some basic ideas on the form of a typical XML document structure:

```
<?xml version = "1.0"?>
<!-- A Comment on this Document -->
<gameon>
        <gname>
                First Game
        <date>
                November 2003
        </date>
        </gname>
        <player>
                <nickname>
                        TonytheLecturer
                </nickname>
        </player>
        <stage>
                Stage 1
        </stage>
        <comment>
                Not got far !
        </comment>
</gameon>
```

The above is an example of a simple XML document. It is usual to start the document with an XML declaration, although in fact it is an option. The comment line is also optional but of course comments make the file more readable.

Notice that a comment is always defined as <!-- A Comment on this Document --> The <!-- is the start of the comment and --> ends the comment.

The most important syntax within any XML document is the layout of the tags themselves. The tags are balanced into pairs, so we will always have:

```
<date> November 2003</date>
```

If you have created web pages using HTML the syntax form will be very familiar. The content between the pair of tags is usually called an element, the first simple example shows that the elements can be structured into a hierarchy. The first element (sometimes referred to as the root element) is contained within the first tag and will be either immediately at the start of the document or following the XML declaration.

All other elements will then be contained within the root element and the closing tag of the root element should be the last structure to close in the XML document itself:

```
<root tag start >
        <other elements>
</root tag end>
```

Using a hierarchical structure allows XML documents to contain element groupings. In the example:

```
<gname>
        First Game
<date>
        November 2003
</date>
</gname>
```

the <date> element is fully defined within the <gname> element, meaning that the <gname> element is defined not simply by the text between the tag pairs, but also by the definition of the element within the <date> tag pair.

Figure 8.1 shows that a standard web browser can render the basic structure of an XML document and its data, without any recourse to the meaning of the actual data presented.

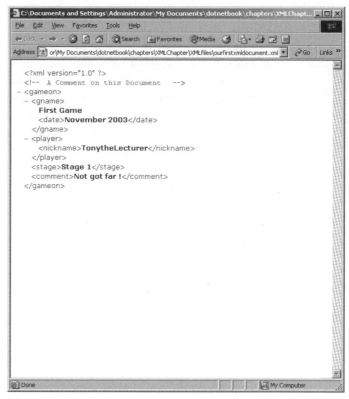

Figure 8.1   *The XML example file rendered in a web browser*

Why is XML so important to us?

The content of our simple example is of course no more than plain text; this already identifies that any XML document is human readable. When this factor is added to the result of displaying the example in a browser window, an XML document can always be defined as both human and machine readable. The software within the browser responsible for the interpretation of the XML is generally called an XML parser. Such parser software is responsible for checking the validity of the XML syntax and then making the data elements available to a specific application. Common standard commercial parsers available include Microsoft's msxml (which is built into Internet Explorer) xerces (the most common parser found in the Apache software foundation products) and xml4J from IBM.

The display of this file within Internet Explorer shows the hierarchical structure we have already identified as common to all XML documents, the – and + symbols identifying where element structures can be expanded or collapsed. You should have identified that in Visual Studio .NET this same − and + hierarchical structure is used within the code editor to define items such as classes, methods etc.

Any XML element can have an attribute assigned; the number of attributes associated with any particular element is the document designer's choice. Attributes allow additional data to be included within a specific element although the relevance of these attributes may not be immediately obvious. In our later discussion we will see that the use of attributes can greatly enhance the machine readable aspects of the XML for specific applications.

However, for now we can look at another simple example to identify how we can improve on our previous XML document with the inclusion of some elements with attributes:

```
<?xml version = "1.0"?>
<gameon>
        <gname>
                First Game
        <date>
                November 2003
        </date>
        </gname>
        <player Number = "1">
                <nickname>
                        TonytheLecturer
                </nickname>
        </player>
        <player  Number = "2">
                <nickname>
                        The Opponent
                </nickname>
        </player>
        <stage>
                Stage 1
        </stage>
        <comment>
                Not got far !
        </comment>
</gameon>
```

The attribute Number added to the element player now identifies for the parser a value that could be interpreted by an application as a unique identifier for each of the player elements. One other important XML feature is the ability to have empty elements. Empty elements have no text between the tag pairs, but can contain attributes. In the next example we have included empty elements:

```
<?xml version = "1.0"?>

<gameon>
        <gname>
                First Game
        <date>
                November 2003
        </date>
        </gname>
        <player Number = "1">
                <nickname>
                        TonytheLecturer
                </nickname>
                <last move= "Right"></last>
        </player>
        <player  Number = "2">
                <nickname>
                        The Opponent
                </nickname>
                <last move= "Up"></last>
        </player>

        <stage>
                Stage 1
        </stage>
        <comment>
                Not got far !
        </comment>
</gameon>
```

We have added an empty element to the element player identifying the direction of the last move:

```
<last move= "Right"></last>
```

Once again the parser will be able to extract this data element and its attribute and an application can then use it as needed. The interpretation of this simple XML document programmatically is probably best demonstrated by a simple Windows form application in VB.NET.

XMLFileDisplay(..) The following extract shows how some of the aspects of the .NET class library are used to parser a typical file and extract the elements and attributes. This extract assumes that the XML file name is in a public variable Filename and then goes on to use the two standard XML objects XmlDocument and XmlNodeReader to extract the elements and attributes and display them in a multi-line text box control:

```vb
Sub Display()
'' Read the file and process the basic element types.
 Dim document As XmlDocument = New XmlDocument()
 Dim i As Integer
 Dim j As Integer
 TextBox.Text = ""  '' clear the previous text box contents
 document.Load(Filename)
 ' create XmlNodeReader for document
 Dim reader As XmlNodeReader = New XmlNodeReader(document)
 ' display each node's content
  While reader.Read
   St1 = ""
   Select Case reader.NodeType
           ' Element?
       Case XmlNodeType.Element
         CurrentTag = "<" + reader.Name + ">"
         St1 = "Element " + CurrentTag + " Start "
         TextBox.Text &= St1 + vbCrLf
         If reader.HasAttributes Then
             i = reader.AttributeCount
             For j = 0 To i - 1
                 reader.MoveToAttribute(j)
                 St2 = reader.Name + " = " + reader.Value _
                 TextBox.Text &= "Element " + CurrentTag + _
                             " Attribute " + St2 +_vbCrLf
             Next
         End If
             ' Comment
       Case XmlNodeType.Comment
          TextBox.Text &= "<!--" & reader.Value & "-->" _
                        & vbCrLf
             ' Text
       Case XmlNodeType.Text
             St1 = "Element " + CurrentTag + " Value = "
             TextBox.Text &= St1 + reader.Value.Trim & vbCrLf
             ' XML declaration
       Case XmlNodeType.XmlDeclaration
             TextBox.Text &= "<?" & reader.Name & " " & _
             reader.Value & "?>" & vbCrLf
             ' EndElement
       Case XmlNodeType.EndElement
             St1 = "Element " + "</" + reader.Name + ">" + " End "
             TextBox.Text &= St1 + vbCrLf
   End Select
  End While
End Sub
```

The result from this example of reading and interpreting the simple XML document is as shown as Figure 8.2.

The above example application is extremely simplified however, it does re-enforce the mechanisms available for identifying and

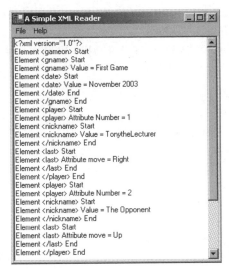

Figure 8.2   *Our simple example XML file interpreted by an XML parser*

extracting elements and attributes. The .NET Framework library class is quite straightforward to use and shows that the available namespace in the .NET class library System.Xml contains objects such as XmlDocument and XmlNodeReader that form the basis for any application XML parser requirement.

Namespaces

Obviously the naming of the elements will be very specific to a particular application and as such the possibility of name duplication is quite high. In common with the .NET class library and other 'OO' languages such as C++ that contain extremely large class libraries grouped together in terms of features and functionality, the use of some form of a namespace technique is advisable to eliminate the possibility of name duplication.

XML has adopted a Namespace technique that ensures that any element has a totally unique identifying tag pair; this is accomplished by attaching a prefix (the namespace) to all element names:

```
<mygame:nickname> Tonythelecturer </mygame:nickname>
```

Here we have qualified the element <nickname> with a prefix <mygame>. In using this syntax we have identified that the element <nickname> belongs to the namespace <mygame>.

Once such a namespace approach is adopted we can have common element names within any XML document, but since each will be identified by a unique namespace, parser software will be able to identify the elements uniquely:

```xml
<?xml version = "1.0"?>

<namesS xmlns ="urn:thisgame:text"
        xmlns:image = "urn:thisgame:images">
<gameon>
      <gname>
              First Game
      <date>
              November 2003
      </date>
      </gname>
      <player Number = "1">
              <nickname>
                      TonytheLecturer
              </nickname>
              <last move= "Right"></last>
              <file filename = "player1.dat"></file>
              <image:file filename = "player2.ico"></image:file>
      </player>
      <player  Number = "2">
              <nickname>
                      The Opponent
              </nickname>
              <last move= "Up"></last>
              <file filename = "player2.dat"></file>
              <image:file filename = "player2.ico"></image:file>
      </player>
      <stage>
              Stage 1
      </stage>
      <comment>
              Not got far !
      </comment>
</gameon>
</namesS>
```

This example, which could be part of some XML description for a multi-user game, uses the element file twice. The file element is first used for a file path to a player's statistics and then again to identify the file path to an icon used to identify this player.

The namespace definitions appear within the XML document as:

```
<namesS xmlns ="urn:thisgame:text"
        xmlns:image = "urn:thisgame:images">
```

The first attribute defines a default namespace for the text, the second attribute defines a second namespace <image: >. This is quite a common technique when only two namespaces are to be defined. If the XML document requires more than two namespaces you would generally find all namespaces fully defined as well as all element tags fully qualified by the appropriate namespace.

A fully defined set of namespaces would have a declaration of the form

```
<text:namesS xmlns:text ="urn:thisgame:text"
        xmlns:image = "urn:thisgame:images">
```

The attribute values in this declaration are assigned to text strings. Such strings in this context are called a URI (Uniform Resource Identifier), and the only requirement for such URI strings are that they are totally unique. A very common practice is to equate these URIs to the more common URLs (Uniform Resource Locators), used on the WWW, i.e. http:// www.wlv.ac.uk. Using such a technique the fully qualified namespace declaration could be replaced with:

```
<text:namesS xmlns:text ="http://www.wlv.ac.uk/~cm1918/text"
        xmlns:image = "http://www.wlv.ac.uk/~cm1918/images">
```

An area that normally confuses students is that when the XML parser sees these URI text strings the only check made is that they are unique within this document, i.e. you must ensure that the URI string is never duplicated in any one document.

It does not matter whether the URL used to represent the URI is correctly formed. The XML parser will not attempt to visit the specified URL. The URL is used simply to represent a series of unique characters to differentiate the namespace. In fact the URL used does not need to represent a valid WWW address and you do not need to correctly format such a URL, i.e. http:fred,work,ac,uk would also be valid, even though the URL has an incorrect form.

It is very important to realise this fact. In the past I have had students worrying about the form of the URI and trying to ensure that a correct URL is formed so that the parser, should it wish to, can visit the relevant address.

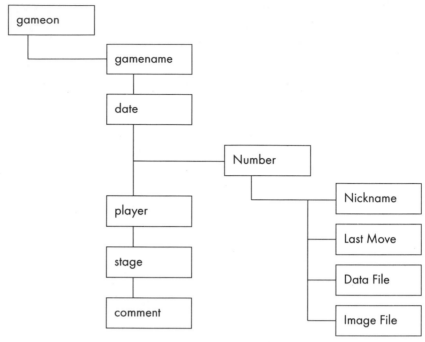

Figure 8.3   *A tree diagram of our example XML*

The DOM

Although any XML document is no more than a formatted plain text file, extracting data programmatically using simple sequential file access techniques would not be a practical solution. We have to consider how we can add and delete information in a dynamic environment. Consider our XML example document, it is a description of the players and state of a computer game, it would be quite useless unless we had dynamic ability to update the status as the player completed sections or levels of the game. A suitable solution is to use the Document Object Model (DOM). The DOM is generally represented as a simple data structure that is loaded with the various element values and attributes, once the XML document has been validated. The application can update such a structure dynamically as required and write back the new element values etc. to the XML document. We can represent such a structure for our simple example file as shown in Figure 8.3.

In Figure 8.3 the player element is duplicated as many times as required. This DOM tree identifies each unique element within the XML as a node. If any node is unique, i.e. no further elements are declared within it, then it is a parent node, if other elements are declared within it then it is a parent node with siblings. If a node is totally contained within another node then that node is a child or sibling of a parent node.

The most important aspect of working with the XML DOM is to have programmatic control of the mechanism used to traverse the hierarchical data structure of the tree. This ability to traverse the DOM tree is available within the .NET class library by using the XPath object and the XPathNavigator.

The XPath functionality is the ability to query a data store for a node or set of nodes within the DOM tree. The XPathNavigator class provides the methods required to implement XPath queries over any data store, and is based on the data model described in the XML Path Language: (XPath) 1.0 Recommendation http:// www.w3.org/TR/xpath.html). A data store is defined as data in a file system, database, or object such as System.Xml.XmlDocument, or System.Data.Dataset; we will in the chapter on ADO.NET look at XML translation from a dataset. The XPathNavigator reads data from any data store using a cursor model that allows forward and backwards movement. It is a read-only cursor, and does not allow editing. If you need editing capabilities then the .NET class library object based on the XML Document Object Model (DOM) should be used. The Document Object Model (DOM) class is an in-memory representation of an XML document. The DOM allows you to programmatically read, manipulate, and modify an XML document.

An XmlNode object is the basic object in the DOM tree. The XmlDocument class, which extends XmlNode, supports methods for performing operations on the document as a whole, for instance loading it into memory or saving the XML to a file. In addition, XmlDocument provides a means to view and manipulate the nodes in the entire XML document. Both XmlNode and XmlDocument have methods and properties to:

■ Access and modify nodes specific to DOM, such as attribute nodes, element nodes, entity reference nodes, and so on

■ Retrieve entire nodes, in addition to the information the node contains, such as the text in an element node.

Node objects also have some basic characteristics:

■ Nodes have a single parent node, a parent node being a node directly above it. The only node that does not have a parent is the Document root, as it is the top-level node and contains the document itself, and document fragments

■ Most nodes can have multiple child nodes, which are nodes directly below it.

As XML is read into memory, nodes are created. However, not all nodes are the same type. An element in XML has different rules and syntax than a processing instruction. So as various data is read, a node type is assigned to each node. This node type determines the characteristics and functionality of the node.

The DOM is most useful for reading XML data into memory to change its structure, to add or remove nodes, or to modify the data held by a node as in the text contained by an element. Using this definition we can see that the root element is the parent of all other elements within the DOM for any XML document, knowing that the .NET Framework library contains a complete set of classes to manipulate any DOM tree. This next example looks at expanding the first simple XML reader example with a graphical output using XPathNavigator to traverse the DOM tree and a 'TreeView' control to allow a visual representation of the DOM for the selected XML file.

TreeView Display(..)

The 'TreeView' control allows a collection of 'TreeNode' objects to be displayed in a hierarchical structure. The example populates the 'TreeView' by navigating the DOM tree using a recursive algorithm, as the 'XpathNavigator' identifies a new item within the DOM a new 'TreeNode' is generated and added at the right level within the 'TreeView'.

```
Private Sub TreeDisplay()
      Dim document As XPathDocument
      Dim xPathM As XPathNavigator
      Dim tree As TreeNode
      document = New XPathDocument(Filename)
      xPathM = document.CreateNavigator
      tree = New TreeNode()
      xPathM.MoveToFirstChild() '' move to first element..
      tree.Text = xPathM.Name
      TreeView.Nodes.Add(tree)
      TreeView.SelectedNode = tree '' set first element
      Populatetree(xPathM, tree)
      TreeView.ExpandAll()
   End Sub
```

This first method creates the 'XpathNavigator' and the root structure of the 'TreeView'. Although the root element could have been called root, in the example the 'MoveToFirstChild(..)' method within the 'XpathNavigator' is used to step to the first actual element in the DOM and the root 'TreeNode' in the 'TreeView' uses the first DOM XML element. To maintain a reference to the current position in the 'TreeView' the SelectedNode is set to this location. The call to Populatetree(..) then uses the recursive method described below and finally the ExpandAll method is used to expand all populated branches in the final 'TreeView'.

Populatetree(..)

```
Private Sub Populatetree(ByVal xpath As XPathNavigator, ByVal pposition As
TreeNode)
Dim CurrentP As TreeNode = New TreeNode()
Dim CurrentT As TreeNode = New TreeNode()
Dim TX As XPathNavigator
If xpath.HasChildren Then
    xpath.MoveToFirstChild()
        Do
        Select Case xpath.NodeType
            Case XPathNodeType.Element
                TreeView.SelectedNode = pposition
        CurrentP.Text = xpath.Name
        TreeView.SelectedNode.Nodes.Add(CurrentP)
                TreeView.SelectedNode = CurrentP ''
                                        set first element
                TX = xpath.Clone
                Populatetree(xpath, CurrentP)
                xpath = TX.Clone
                CurrentP = New TreeNode()
            Case XPathNodeType.Text
                CurrentT.Text = xpath.Value.Trim()
                TreeView.SelectedNode.Nodes.Add(CurrentT)
                CurrentT = New TreeNode()
            End Select
        Loop Until xpath.MoveToNext = False
        TreeView.SelectedNode = pposition '' set first element
End If
End Sub
```

Recursive algorithms are always difficult, when any recursive algorithm fails it normally crashes the system completely with some form of stack overflow failure, the cause of such failures is not always simple to identify.

This recursive algorithm identifies the next node in the DOM tree if the node is an element then, after creating a new node on the 'TreeView', it performs a recursive call. The reason for this is that any element will indicate a new branch in the DOM. However, finding a text node will indicate there is information at this node level and so all that is required is to attach a node at this level. The loop is controlled by the MoveToNext(..) method which, if it returns true, indicates that another sibling (child node) is available at this level down the tree, whereas a return value of false indicates no further children and the loop will exit allowing any recursion to start unnesting. The use of the Clone method just before the recursive call and after the return, i.e. as the recursion unnests, is to ensure that the XPathNavigator is set to the correct parent node position as any unnesting of the recursion takes place..

Figure 8.4   *Looking at the first XML example we get this tree view*

Using this technique on the first simple XML file produces a display as shown in Figure 8.4

In Figure 8.5 we find we have lost the attributes that are in this file. This is because the recursive method requires an additional case to look for element attributes, this modification will give you an ideal opportunity to investigate the recursive algorithm in your own time.

Figure 8.5   *The tree view of the second example XML*

Document Type Definitions

Although in the above discussion we have seen that it is possible to fully define an XML document locally and to read, write and parser the document locally, within a distributed system design this may not be the case. We need to look at the situation where an XML document references optional documents that specify how a particular XML document should be structured.

These optional documents are called Document Type Definitions (DTD) and schemas. When a DTD or schema is provided by an XML document the parser will first need to read the DTD or schema to identify the syntax of the data elements and then parser the actual XML for both basic XML syntax and element structure.

We can therefore define a DTD as a means of type checking an XML document and verifying the validity of the elements (confirming that an element contains the proper attributes, additional elements and sequence). It is well beyond the scope of this book to look in detail at the syntax form of DTD documents. DTDs use EBNF (Extended Backus-Naur Form) grammar to describe the XML document's content.

DTDs arc always optional, but obviously if we are dealing with a distributed system where we are faced with transferring XML documents between various processes then it is important to use DTD techniques to ensure the XML documents are properly formed:

```
<!-- DTD document for the simple XML -->
<!ELEMENT gname ( #PCDATA) >
<!ELEMENT date  ( #PCDATA) >
<!ATTLIST player Number CDATA #IMPLIED>
<!ELEMENT nickname (#PCDATA) >
<!ELEMENT stage ( #PCDATA) >
<!ELEMENT comment ( #PCDATA) >
```

This DTD ensures correctly formed XML in the following file:

```
<?xml version = "1.0"?>
<!DOCTYPE gameon SYSTEM "simple.dtd">
<gameon>
        <gname>
                First Game
        <date>
                November 2003
        </date>
        </gname>
        <player Number = "1">
```

```
                <nickname>
                        TonytheLecturer
                </nickname>
        </player>
        <player  Number = "2">
                <nickname>
                        The Opponent
                </nickname>
        </player>
        <stage>
                Stage 1
        </stage>
        <comment>
                Not got far !
        </comment>
</gameon>
```

The DTD is referenced in the second line and the parameters are
first, the major element names in the XML file, in this case
<gameon>, and secondly the use of SYSTEM to indicate the DTD
is an external file with its qualified path as the optional last string
on the line.

XML schemas

In this section we will look at an alternative to DTD, so-called
document schemas. One major criticism of DTDs is the EBNF
syntax and the inflexibility such syntax implies. EBNF is not
formed using any form of XML so programmatically it cannot be
simply searched, modified or parsered. So schemas were
introduced that again perform the same function as DTDs but
which use XML to describe the element form of a particular
document. Here we will be looking at the Microsoft definition of
such schemas; the reader is directed to the W3C web site if they
wish to look at the more general schema definition.

A schema definition for our simple example would generally
have the form:

```
<?xml version = "1.0"?>
<Schema xmlns = "urn:schemas-microsoft-com:xml-data" >
   <ElementType name = "gname" content = "textOnly"
        model = "closed" />
    <ElementType name = "date" content = "textOnly"
        model = "closed" />
   <ElementType name = "nickname" content = "textOnly"
        model = "closed" />
   <ElementType name = "stage" content = "textOnly"
```

```
            model = "closed" />
  <ElementType name = "comment" content = "textOnly"
            model = "closed" />
</Schema>
```

Notice that the URN for this Microsoft specific schema definition must be: "urn:schemas-microsoft-com:xml-data.

The element-closed attribute is used here since these elements can only exist once. The source file will use the following declaration to indicate that a schema is being used:

```
<?xml version = "1.0"?>
<gameon1 xmlns = "x-schema:simple.xdr">

<gameon>
        <gname>
                First Game
        <date>
                November 2003
        </date>
        </gname>
        <player Number = "1">
                <nickname>
                        TonytheLecturer
                </nickname>
        </player>
        <player  Number = "2">
                <nickname>
                        The Opponent
                </nickname>
        </player>

        <stage>
                Stage 1
        </stage>
        <comment>
                Not got far !
        </comment>
</gameon>
</gameon1>
```

Unlike the DTD declaration for this file, the schema reference has its own tag, it is therefore important that this tag is closed as the last action on the XML document. In a similar manner to the unique definition of the URI in the actual schema definition file, the xmlns = "x-schema:simple.xdr" is also Microsoft specific.

A topic that we could have explored at this point in the discussion is the inbuilt .NET class library dealing with schema checking. This is a very specialist topic and as such probably does not need to be included in this chapter. In the introduction to this chapter the objectives were first to look at a basic overview of XML and the .NET class library support for XML, then to build on this knowledge by looking at two further aspects of XML within the .NET Framework. First, the use of XML in the development environments and assemblies and second, the concept of XML serialisation comparing this technique to the binary serialisation already discussed in Chapter 5. My reason for restating these objectives is simply to ensure you do not proceed to the next sections unless you are quite happy with the overall structure of an XML document. In these next sections there will no overall discussion on the actual XML, the descriptions will purely be concerned with how the XML is being used.

XML in the development world of Visual Studio .NET

So far any look at files used for an application development has been limited to the graphical design resource file created, and the programming language source file.

For the purpose of this investigation I have created two effectively empty applications one in each of the supported languages VB.NET and C#. There is nothing new about the source file content of either of these, they are in the basic form created automatically by Visual Studio .NET when you start a new Windows application.

The reason for the choice of a Windows application is that the XML files created with the basic source files are relatively small and easy to understand; obviously if we were to investigate a .NET component the complexity would increase and jumping ahead to the next couple of chapters where we will be looking at web forms and web services the complexity of the XML increases again.

The first we will look at is Form1.resx. The contents are identical for both VB.NET and C#, the XML defines the basic definition of an empty form. I have had to remove much of the indentation control to allow the contents to fit the page.:

```
<?xml version="1.0" encoding="utf-8" ?>
<root>
xsd:schema id="root" xmlns="" xmlns:xsd="http://www.w3.org/2001/XMLSchema"
xmlns:msdata="urn:schemas-microsoft-com:xml-msdata">
 <xsd:element name="root" msdata:IsDataSet="true">
   <xsd:complexType>
    <xsd:choice maxOccurs="unbounded">
```

```
    <xsd:element name="data">
     <xsd:complexType>
       <xsd:sequence>
    <xsd:element name="value" type="xsd:string" minOccurs="0"
                                    msdata:Ordinal="1" />
    <xsd:element name="comment" type="xsd:string"
                        minOccurs="0" msdata:Ordinal="2" />
       </xsd:sequence>
       <xsd:attribute name="name" type="xsd:string" />
       <xsd:attribute name="type" type="xsd:string" />
       <xsd:attribute name="mimetype" type="xsd:string" />
     </xsd:complexType>
    </xsd:element>
    <xsd:element name="resheader">
     <xsd:complexType>
      <xsd:sequence>
    <xsd:element name="value" type="xsd:string" minOccurs="0"
                                    msdata:Ordinal="1" />
      </xsd:sequence>
       <xsd:attribute name="name" type="xsd:string"
                                    use="required" />
     </xsd:complexType>
    </xsd:element>
   </xsd:choice>
  </xsd:complexType>
 </xsd:element>
</xsd:schema>
<resheader name="ResMimeType">
   <value>text/microsoft-resx</value>
</resheader>
<resheader name="Version">
   <value>1.0.0.0</value>
</resheader>
<resheader name="Reader">
 <value>System.Resources.ResXResourceReader, System.Windows.Forms,
Version=1.0.3300.0,
                       Culture=neutral, PublicKeyToken=b77a5c561934e089
 </value>
</resheader>
<resheader name="Writer">
 <value>System.Resources.ResXResourceWriter, System.Windows.Forms,
Version=1.0.3300.0,
                       Culture=neutral, PublicKeyToken=b77a5c561934e089
 </value>
</resheader>
</resheader>
</root>
```

As you can see, unless you know the meaning of some of the elements we cannot interpret how the data will be used by the Visual Studio .NET form designer but we can very quickly identify the data elements, their individual attributes and in some cases the stream reader and writer that will be used to load and save this file into the form designer. The document has a schema defined and is in the main a well-structured XML document. The fact that it is identical in both the VB.NET and C# indicates that the Visual Studio .NET Form designer is implementation language independent, a fact that was probably obvious from the earlier examples but it is quite helpful to be able to prove it here. The next file is either called SimpleApp.vbproj or SimpleApp.csproj depending on the version being investigated:

```
<VisualStudioProject>
    <VisualBasic
        ProjectType = "Local"
        ProductVersion = "7.0.9466"
        SchemaVersion = "1.0"
        ProjectGuid = "{D42A188F-B9C5-4B8A-8040-1B4A675F796F}" >
        <Build>
            <Settings
                ApplicationIcon = ""
                AssemblyKeyContainerName = ""
                AssemblyName = "SimpleApp"
                AssemblyOriginatorKeyFile = ""
                AssemblyOriginatorKeyMode = "None"
                DefaultClientScript = "JScript"
                DefaultHTMLPageLayout = "Grid"
                DefaultTargetSchema = "IE50"
                DelaySign = "false"
                OutputType = "WinExe"
                OptionCompare = "Binary"
                OptionExplicit = "On"
                OptionStrict = "Off"
                RootNamespace = "SimpleApp"
                StartupObject = "SimpleApp.Form1" >
                <Config
                    Name = "Debug"
                    BaseAddress = "285212672"
                    ConfigurationOverrideFile = ""
                    DefineConstants = ""
                    DefineDebug = "true"
                    DefineTrace = "true"
                    DebugSymbols = "true"
                    IncrementalBuild = "true"
                    Optimize = "false"
                    OutputPath = "bin\"
                    RegisterForComInterop = "false"
                    RemoveIntegerChecks = "false"
                    TreatWarningsAsErrors = "false"
                    WarningLevel = "1" />
                <Config
```

```
                        Name = "Release"
                        BaseAddress = "285212672"
                        ConfigurationOverrideFile = ""
                        DefineConstants = ""
                        DefineDebug = "false"
                        DefineTrace = "true"
                        DebugSymbols = "false"
                        IncrementalBuild = "false"
                        Optimize = "true"
                        OutputPath = "bin\"
                        RegisterForComInterop = "false"
                        RemoveIntegerChecks = "false"
                        TreatWarningsAsErrors = "false"
                        WarningLevel = "1"  />
                </Settings>
                <References>
                    <Reference
                        Name = "System"
                        AssemblyName = "System"  />
                    <Reference
                        Name = "System.Data"
                        AssemblyName = "System.Data" />
                    <Reference
                        Name = "System.Drawing"
                        AssemblyName = "System.Drawing" />
                    <Reference
                        Name = "System.Windows.Forms"
                        AssemblyName = "System.Windows.Forms" />
                    <Reference
                        Name = "System.XML"
                        AssemblyName = "System.Xml"/>
                </References>
                <Imports>
                    <Import Namespace = "Microsoft.VisualBasic" />
                    <Import Namespace = "System" />
                    <Import Namespace = "System.Collections" />
                    <Import Namespace = "System.Data" />
                    <Import Namespace = "System.Drawing" />
                    <Import Namespace = "System.Diagnostics" />
                    <Import Namespace = "System.Windows.Forms" />
                </Imports>
            </Build>
            <Files>
                <Include>
                    <File
                        RelPath = "AssemblyInfo.vb"
                        SubType = "Code"
                        BuildAction = "Compile"/>
                    <File
                        RelPath = "Form1.vb"
                        SubType = "Form"
                        BuildAction = "Compile" />
```

```
      <File
         RelPath = "Form1.resx"
         DependentUpon = "Form1.vb"
         BuildAction = "EmbeddedResource" />
      </Include>
    </Files>
  </VisualBasic>
</VisualStudioProject>
```

This project definition is obvious for VB.NET and once again, although we have no actual knowledge regarding the usage of the information, it is very obvious what most, if not all, the information conveys; we have the import declarations, the source file listings and basic options identification that can be set up for a debug or release build of this application. The C# version of these project files is in fact a little simpler but conveys the same amount of information.

The technique of using XML files to describe information should by now be clear. These project files in Visual Studio .NET allow the intelligent development environment to identify many aspects of the type and nature of the currently loaded application. The final file that you can investigate is named either SimpleApp.vbproj.user or SimpleApp,csproj.user; these files hold other XML structured information allowing further configurable aspects of the development to be identified.

At this point we need to broaden this review further. In the chapter dealing with the assembly manifests it was stated that metadata is stored in XML form within each assembly and this is used by the CLR loader to ensure that code conforms to the managed code requirements etc. Unfortunately there is no direct method to review this data since it is bundled into the final assembly file, but we can, by using the ILDasm utility and dumping just the tree structure of the manifest, get a fairly good idea of the content. A typical C# manifest has the form:

```
___[MOD] C:\Documents and Settings\Administrator\My Documents\FinalVersion
of Book\Chapter8 - The Role of
XML\CSharpSoliutions\SimpleApp\bin\Debug\SimpleApp.exe
      |      M A N I F E S T
      |___[NSP] SimpleApp
      |   |___[CLS] Form1
      |   |   |      .class public auto ansi beforefieldinit
      |   |   |      extends
['System.Windows.Forms']'System.Windows.Forms'.'Form'
      |   |   |___[FLD] components : private class
['System']'System.ComponentModel'.'Container'
      |   |   |___[MET] .ctor : void()
      |   |   |___[MET] Dispose : void(bool)
```

```
|   |   |__[MET] InitializeComponent : void()
|   |   |__[STM] Main : void()
|   |
|
```

While the VB.Net version has the form:

```
___[MOD] C:\Documents and Settings\Administrator\My Documents\FinalVersion
of Book\Chapter8 - The Role of XML\VBSolutions\SimpleApp\bin\SimpleApp.exe
    |     M A N I F E S T
|___[NSP] SimpleApp
|   |__[CLS] Form1
|   |   |    .class public auto ansi
|   |   |       extends [System.Windows.Forms]System.Windows.Forms.Form
|   |   |__[FLD] components : private class
[System]System.ComponentModel.IContainer
|   |   |__[MET] .ctor : void()
|   |   |__[MET] Dispose : void(bool)
|   |   |__[MET] InitializeComponent : void()
|   |   |__[STM] Main : void()
|   |
|
```

When we investigate the XML structure of such manifests, they are virtually identical. The slight differences can be attributed to the fact that it was a slightly harder development proposition to shoehorn the original version of Visual Basic into an 'OO' environment and make it conform to the CLR requirements, than writing C# as a new 100% compliant language from scratch.

XML serialisation

The subject of serialisation techniques was investigated in Chapter 5 when we looked at the sliding block puzzle. At that time the solution derived was to create a compatible serialisation specific class and to use the binary formatter class library to stream this object to file. The disadvantage of this technique is of course flexibility. To read back the serialised data required us to have a comprehensive understanding of the structure of the class that was serialised in the first place. In the case of the simple puzzle this was not a problem since both the save and load were from within the same application. However, if we were to broaden the scope of the problem and have a producer of serialised data in one application and the consumer in another then the inflexible nature of binary streaming immediately becomes apparent.

The alternative approach is to utilise XML-based serialisation and streaming. Using this approach the data carries its own intrinsic description. It is still necessary for the consumer to understand the overall structure of the information, but it is no longer the case that exact details of the elements that form the data need to be understood. A suitable real world scenario can be drawn from the differences between knowing how to start a car as opposed to understanding the theory of the internal combustion engine. To be able to start the car you simple need to be told where to put the ignition key and how to turn it; the theory regarding fuel, ignition timing etc., which makes the engine run, is far too detailed information to perform the required task.

Standard XML serialistaion

There are in fact two basic types of XML serialisers available within the .NET class library. The reason for this is that each serialiser is aimed at a different requirement, the first XmlSerialiser will in the main produce a final XML document that conforms to the standard XML specification, with very fine control given to the developer of the application, i.e. the developer can control fairly accurately the final format of the XML document produced.

Given the definition that the XMLSerilaiser should produce a standard XML document means this mechanism has some limitations in the CLR environment. Since XML has no language specific syntax for the concept of an object's private data, any object serialised by this method will only reflect the public data and hence to recreate the object from the XML will be impossible.

SOAP-based XML serialisation

The alternative to the XMLSerialiser uses the concept of XML serialisation within the SOAP (Simple Object Access Protocol) technology; we will be looking at SOAP in more detail in the final two chapters of this book. The major advantage of this type of XML serialisation is that the entire object is considered as suitable for serialisation including all of the private data within the object. The disadvantage of this SOAP-based technology is that in its current form it is absolutely .NET Framework proprietary. Any application developed outside of the .NET environment that wishes to either produce or consume SOAP derived XML Serialisation will have problems recreating the objects unless some specific parser software is written to interpret the XML data produced.

Mapping between type systems, as we have discussed in many of the previous chapters, will always be a challenge to the designers of large distributed systems. Converting the basic CLR types into XML has its problems, as does the reverse translation, and different applications will need to do this in many different ways. The option of two completely different approaches within the .NET class framework does provide choices in the translation techniques, it is left to the system developer to make the final judgement on which to use for a particular design.

In order to give some idea of the structure of such XML serialised files we will return to the sliding block puzzle from Chapter 5 and modify the save and load options previously implemented as binary streams only. In this new design we will offer the user the option of selecting the serialisation mechanism.

The first problem encountered when looking at making this change to the design is that since we were simply performing binary serialisation, the original solution serialised an array of objects of a specific class, not a specific class containing an array of objects. In the XML solution the original solution would not map into XML serialisation since XML has no syntax mechanism to handle an array of objects of a class.

In any XML document we need a root element, when we look at serialisation this will have be a class. Without such a root element we cannot build a DOM tree. In the case of this design therefore this new root element will need to be a class that represents the playing tiles. Then we can build further child elements representing the properties of the tile elements. It was decided to use elements rather than attributes for the properties; it is left to the reader to modify the design to use attributes if they wish to.

The SerialOut class

The result of this change meant that the implementation needs to revisit the binary serialisation solution and change this to serialise the whole class rather than to serialise an array of objects:

```
[Serializable()]
public class SerialOut
{
 public SaveTile[] TileData = new SaveTile[17];
 public SerialOut() // default constructor
 {
      int i;
      TileData[0] = new SaveTile(); // not used but must be
                                      initialised
      for (i=1;i<17;i++)
```

```
                      {
            TileData[i] = new SaveTile ();
                    TileData[i].CurrentPosition =
                                    TheTiles[i].CurrentPosition ;
                    TileData[i].CurrentSize =
                                    TheTiles[i].CurrentSize;
                TileData[i].DNumber  = TheTiles[i].DNumber ;
                TileData[i].TNumber  = TheTiles[i].TNumber;
                TileData[i].TVisible = TheTiles[i].TVisible ;
                TileData[i].TEnable  = TheTiles[i].TEnable ;
                TileData[i].Empty    = MainForm.empty ;
            }
    }
    public SerialOut (int a)
    {
        int i;
        TileData[0] = new SaveTile(); // not used but must be
                                        initialised
        for (i=1;i<17;i++)
        {
        TileData[i] = new SaveTile (); // construct empty ones...
        }
    }
    public void unpack()
    {
        int i;
        for (i=1;i<17;i++)
        {
                TheTiles[i].CurrentPosition =
                                    TileData[i].CurrentPosition ;
                TheTiles[i].CurrentSize =
                                    TileData[i].CurrentSize ;
                TheTiles[i].DNumber = TileData[i].DNumber  ;
                TheTiles[i].TNumber = TileData[i].TNumber     ;
                TheTiles[i].TVisible = TileData[i].TVisible   ;
                TheTiles[i].TEnable = TileData[i].TEnable  ;
                MainForm.empty = TileData[i].Empty  ;
        }
    }
}
```

This new class is built with two constructors. The XML serialisation process requires a default constructor that is also used to copy the current game state to the local array declared within this class. The second construction is required by the reverse operation to recover the information that has been serialised. In order to recover the serialised information from the XML stream the class must create an object that mimics the original serialised object. Element zero of the array is not used in the game as the tiles are numbered 1 to 16; however, element zero must be initialised otherwise a run-time error is generated by the serialisation process. The only other public member written for this class unpack(..) is used during the deserialisation to copy back the game state from the retrieved data structure to the actual game variables.

The original SaveTile class from the solution in Chapter 5 has not been altered since it only contained the definition of the data that needed to be serialised. In the original version we also instanced the array of SaveTile within the MainForm class itself, this is of course no longer necessary since the instance is now created as a local variable in this new class.

SaveBinary(..)   The actual changes to the binary serialisation code were small, for example the save code now looks like:

```
private void saveBinary()
{
SerialOut SerialData = new SerialOut();
        IFormatter formatter = new BinaryFormatter();
        if (saveFileDialog.ShowDialog ()==DialogResult.OK)
        {
        Stream stream = new FileStream(saveFileDialog.FileName,
                FileMode.Create, FileAccess.Write, FileShare.None);
        formatter.Serialize(stream, SerialData);
        stream.Close();
        }
}
```

LoadBinary(..)   Similarly the load code had to be changed to:

```
private void loadBinary()
{
        int a = 1; // dummy variable
        SerialOut SerialData = new SerialOut(a);
        IFormatter formatter = new BinaryFormatter();
        if(openFileDialog.ShowDialog () == DialogResult.OK )
        {
          Stream stream = new FileStream(openFileDialog.FileName,
                    FileMode.Open, FileAccess.Read, FileShare.Read);
          SereialData =  (SerialOut)formatter.Deserialize(stream);
         stream.Close();
         }
SerialData.unpack ();
Invalidate();
}
```

The important point with this code is that the instance of the SerialOut class is constructed using the second constructor option, ensuring we get all the elements initialised but avoiding the specific array setup details that occur if the default constructor is used.

SaveXML(..)   The code to serialise in XML is quite similar and the save a game code has the form:

```
private void saveXML()
{
        SerialOut SerialData = new SerialOut();
        XmlSerializer serializer =
                new XmlSerializer(typeof(SerialOut));
        if (saveFileDialog.ShowDialog ()==DialogResult.OK)
                {
                        Stream stream =
                          new FileStream(saveFileDialog.FileName,
                          FileMode.Create, FileAccess.Write,
                          FileShare.None);
                        StreamWriter writer =
                          new StreamWriter(stream);
                    serializer.Serialize(writer, SerialData);
                        stream.Close();
                }
}
```

Notice the only major change is that the serialisation process is now being performed by a variable created as an instance from XmlSerializer, rather than the binary formatter used previously.

The resultant XML DOM file can be viewed by Internet Explorer to check the validity of the XML produced, the start of the file is shown in Figure 8.6.

It is clearly visible that this represents the properties of the object class and represents the state of the sliding block puzzle game at a given point in time. It is a structured XML DOM and is totally machine-readable by any application that has XML parser capability.

Recovering this file and loading it back into the application, thereby setting the game to this particular state, is quite straightforward, the code needed being:

loadXML()
```
private void loadXML()
{
        int a = 1; // dummy variable
        SerialOut SerialData = new SerialOut(a);
        XmlSerializer serializer =
                new XmlSerializer(typeof(SerialOut));
        if (openFileDialog.ShowDialog ()==DialogResult.OK)
                {
                Stream stream =
                        new FileStream(openFileDialog.FileName,
                        FileMode.Open, FileAccess.Read,
```

Figure 8.6   *The serialised XML for the sliding block puzzle*

```
                    FileShare.Read);
        SerialData =
                (SerialOut)serializer.Deserialize(stream);
        stream.Close();
        }
// now upack the data to the main arrays
SerialData.unpack ();
Invalidate();
}
```

Benefits of XML serialisation

A significant improvement in functionality is gained by offering XML serialisation, the machine and human readable characteristic of XML offers far more flexibility to this type of application than the simple and restrictive binary serialisation option.

In order to allow further investigation into the two techniques the application has gained a further menu item with two options and it is left to the reader to investigate the implementation and selection, in this case we are also using the menu attribute 'checked' and once again this investigation should lead you to conclude that the Windows Forms menu component is very powerful.

SOAP-based serialisation

In order to investigate the final serialisation option of SOAP-based XML, which allows not only the public but also the private data of an object to be serialised into an XML DOM, the sliding block puzzle has been further extended to produce a SOAP serialised form of the game status. It is beyond the scope of this book to look into the detail of SOAP packets other than to identify that in this serialisation we are actually getting the private data wrapped by some additional XML. The code to produce this serialisation is very similar to both the standard XML and binary serialisation, the .NET class library has available a standard SOAP XML formatter.

This SOAP XML serialised file will not render in Internet Explorer. The SOAP protocol elements, the header and envelope, create wrappers around the actual XML DOM structure and Internet Explorer has no parser available to interpret such a structure.

Figure 8.7   *A view of the SOAP formatted XML serialisation for the sliding block puzzle*

Summary

This chapter introduced you to the technology of XML and its integration within the .NET architecture, the examples have shown that simple parser software is quite straightforward to construct using the standard classes available within the .NET library. The discussion on the use of XML techniques within the actual .NET assemblies probably left you wondering why I bothered to include the topic. The reason is to identify that useful information can be extracted using the two technologies of system reflection and system remoting, these constitute very powerful techniques that can be used in distributed solutions but are far beyond the scope of this introductory text.

Any further discussion on these topics here would be far too complex; however, having identified what is stored in broad terms, should you wish to investigate for instance RPC (Remote Procedure Calling) within the .NET architecture, the brief overview given of the structure of the XML in the system files should form a sound foundation for exploring this advanced topic.

Finally we modified the application developed in Chapter 5 which was initially designed only to support simple binary serialisation, but now offers the options of standard XML and SOAP-based XML serialisation as well. This allows for the comparison of the techniques involved and some appreciation of the difference in the three serialisation options available within .NET For any suitable object. This last exercise will lead to some further discussion in the later chapters of the book regarding the use of SOAP techniques within web services, and the XML representation of client method access and exposed server side functionality.

Review questions

1   Using the result from the simple tree view example, modify the code to bring back the attributes for the XML elements.

2   Expand on the schemas outlined in this chapter to create a generalised schema for a multi-player game.

3   Investigate how the SOAP XML serialisation could be parsered to provide a more human-readable form of the file.

9

ADO.NET

Objective

Within the overall .NET architecture we have already seen that there is a great deal of support for distributed applications, so it not surprising that a new version of the components needed to gain programmable access to relational databases has also been included. These have been grouped under the general title ADO.NET. In this chapter we will briefly review the mechanism required to extract information programmatically from a relational database and identify the changes that have been introduced in migrating the original ADO components to the new ADO.NET components.

The primary goal for the ADO.NET components designs is to offer connectivity and data manipulation support across a broad spectrum of the most common relational database management systems, while maintaining the primary goal, total implementation language independence common to all aspects of the .NET Framework.

Introduction

The solution to the design goals for ADO.NET has been to integrate many aspects of ADO requirements into the Common Language Runtime (CLR), and to support development with a substantial set of .NET class libraries.

The question that could be asked at this point is:

What is new in this ADO.NET concept?

The answer is simple. If you ever tried to gain access to a relational database using, for instance, Visual Basic, the ADO ActiveX control provided was unique to the Visual Basic language and any skills or knowledge gained by such a development were difficult, if not impossible, to translate across to another development language such as C++.

In comparison ADO.NET, in common with the other aspects of the .NET architecture, is consistent across all of the supported languages and as indicated in the section above some of the technology required is now built into the CLR. This makes it an ideal relational database access technology for distributed application development scenarios.

Historically, ODBC (the Open Database Connectivity model) as well as the early OLEDB (Object Linking and Embedding database model) along with the more recent ActiveX controls have all at some time been the flavour of the month for distributed access to relational databases. The ADO.NET model has learnt from these technologies. It is not an emulation of any of these older technologies, it has its own unique architecture driven by the need to integrate and conform to the unambiguous virtual machine design of the CLR itself.

The interface between relational databases and the 'OO' software model has always been questionable. The idea and concepts of using an 'OO'-based database model have been investigated and refined many times, the result of such analysis has been, with very few exceptions, that the relational database model has emerged as the concept of choice.

It is nearly always felt that 'OO' works much better for software development than it does within any form of the mass data storage. The result of this continuing struggle is that a number of quite poor solutions to the integration of a relational database model with 'OO' languages have been produced. In fact, Microsoft will generally admit that they have made some poor choices in the past over the technologies for this type of integration process

The multi-tiered design model

The ADO.NET solution has evolved from the COM-based model that utilised an ODBC interface. The primary goal of the ODBC technique was to allow programming language the ability to write and issue SQL queries to a relational database management system. The solutions provided by such a technique can be viewed as a two-tier system.

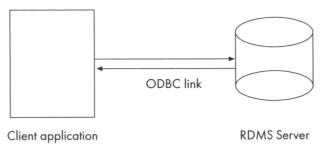

Figure 9.1   *The simplest application to RDMS connectivity model*

However, the need for a more generalised three-tier model, utilising a browser (the bottom tier) as the client interface, with a middle tier providing access to the relational database and the serialisation of the results across the network and finally a top tier, the actual relational database management system has emerged as the spread of Internet and intranet solutions to distributed applications has grown.

ODBC cannot address this three-tier solution, it has no mechanism that allows manipulated results derived algorithmically to be serialised, and subsequently sent across a network. The evolution of ADO techniques addressed many of the serialisation problems but most of the common ADO controls have very limited security. Any three-tier solution is generally designed to work across networks where security implications are paramount, so a secure ADO control working adequately behind the firewall is of little use to the designer of a three-tier system where the ADO will not have adequate security for the serialised data to pass through the firewall.

A background review of RDMS and SQL

A database is a structured collection of data; there have been a number of strategies for the organisation of data in a database, to facilitate a coherent mechanism for the creation, updating and manipulation of the data. Generally a database management system (DBMS) will exist and it is through the DBMS that any programmatic access and manipulation of the structured collection will take place. Within the Microsoft environment the two common DBMSs are 'Access' and 'SQL Sever'.

Both of these utilise a relational database model, and a Structured Query language (SQL) as the mechanism to express the criteria for extraction and manipulation of specific data. In

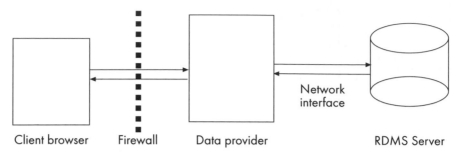

| Client browser | Firewall | Data provider | | RDMS Server |

Figure 9.2   *A more generalised three tier model*

many cases, when dealing with small single user databases it is unnecessary to consider the details of the SQL as most RDMS have an inbuilt query by example mechanism that uses visual programming-based techniques to define the requirement. However, you should never lose sight of the fact that no matter how clever these techniques may be, the final result will be the generation of SQL.

Relational model   The relational model is a logical representation of an abstract model of the data that allows the structure of the collection to be considered, without actually looking into the files themselves.

Generally a relational model has a series of tables, in each of these tables we have data fields and one or more of these fields will be linked to another table expressing some physical rule associated with the data, for instance:

■ A game can have many players.

This rule along with others would constrain the database design, for instance, of the tables holding the statistics for a multi-player computer game. From the requirement and the rules we could define two very simple tables:

Player Name	Text field
Players ID	Numeric field

Players ID	Numeric field
Level ID	Numeric field
Current Level	Text field
High Score	Numeric

Players table   *Scores table*

By linking these two tables using the field Player ID, it is possible to extract information for any player's name, about which levels they have completed, and what scores they have managed at each

Table 9.1

The major keywords in SQL

Keyword	Meaning
SELECT	Select and review fields from one or more tables
FROM	Specify tables to scan
WHERE	Criteria to apply
INNER JOIN	Join records from multiple tables to produce a single set of records in result
GROUP BY	Specify any grouping in result
ORDER BY	Specify any ordering in result
INSERT	Put data into a specific table
UPDATE	Replace data into a specific table
DELETE	Remove data from a specific table

level. The field Level ID could be used to link this table with some further descriptive data relating the levels within the game.

Structured Query Language (SQL)

It is obviously far beyond the scope of this book to look at SQL and relational algebra at anything beyond an overview. The reader is directed to the many excellent texts on the subject should you want more details. The major keywords in SQL are listed in Table 9.1.

The syntax for an SQL query has the general form:

```
SELECT * FROM table name
```

The asterisk (*) indicates the general all fields option, in most cases the (*) will be replaced by some field selectors, the table name is the indicator to the RDMS which table should be used. From our example tables, to get a list of the players this would be:

```
SELECT Players.Name FROM Players
```

This basic query can be extended to:

```
SELECT * FROM table name WHERE logical data selector
```

Now we are being selective on the records required by specifying some selector that will filter only the records we are requesting. So, for instance, this SQL will, from using our example tables, extract all the Level 1 scores for the players:

```
SELECT Players.Name, Scores.CurrentLevel, Scores.HighScore
FROM Players INNER JOIN Scores WHERE (((Scores.CurrentLevel)="1"))
```

If it is important that we order the data in some specific manner, then the query can be extended to:

```
SELECT * FROM tablename ORDER BY fieldname <ASC or DESC>
```

Here a specific field is chosen to define the resultant record order, this can be specified as either ascending or descending on this selected field's content. Obviously we could spend many more pages looking at each of the SQL keywords in detail but from the above it should be obvious that to programmatically access data collections using SQL we are going to need first to generate suitable SQL command strings and then have a mechanism to execute them. However, before we can look at creation and execution of such commands we must investigate the ADO.NET object model.

The ADO.NET model

The programmatic interfaces to the ADO.NET component object model are within the .NET class libraries System.Data.OleDb and System.Data.Sqlclient.

To illustrate the principle of accessing a relational database we can populate the simple example tables with some data and write a simple Windows Form application that will extract some specific data, and output the data to a data grid.

A simple example

Objective   To demonstrate the use of ADO.NET.

Specification   To use a simple Windows stand-alone application to access a relational database using:

■ Use of oleDbConnection object

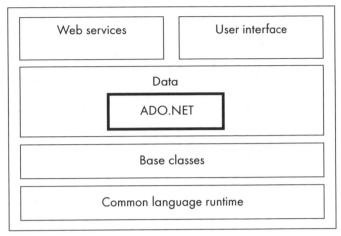

| Web services | User interface |

| Data |
| ADO.NET |

| Base classes |

| Common language runtime |

Figure 9.3 *Where ADO fits into the .NET architecture*

■ Use of an oleDbDataAdaptor object

■ Use of a DataGrid Object

The relationship of the tables can be summarised as Players, containing a primary numeric key to identify the player and the player's name and Scores contains a primary numeric key for the level (not used in this part of the example), a numeric foreign key linking back to the players table and a level indicator with a numeric field.

The design model for a Windows form application to access any database using C# follows the basic principles already identified for any stand-alone application.

The only part of the process that differs from other examples is the mechanism to obtain connectivity to the database from within Visual Studio .NET.

Visual Studio .NET allows any solution to specify the database source to use. To accomplish this; right click in the Data Connections in the Server Explorer window. Select Add Connection. In the Provider tab of the window that appears, choose the 'Microsoft Jet 4.0 OLE DB Provider' which will select a suitable access mechanism for any Access database. In the Connection tab use the (..) button to the right of the database to browse to the location and select the file, then simply click the OK button on the Add Connection window. This new connection will now be registered on the Server Explorer window's data connection list.

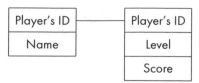

Figure 9.4   *The table relationship for the simple example*

Figure 9.5   *The Server Explorer showing a data source has been connected*

Once a path to the connection is available it is possible to select an ADO.NET OleDbDataAdapter component to the form in the design view.

■ OleDbDataAdapter.

This will cause the Configuration Wizard to start. This wizard allows you to create the necessary interface information between the selected database and your application. On the next page, the screen allows you to select the data source, one of the options listed should be the new connection just created in the Server Explorer.

You have the option to test the connection to ensure that the path specified is correct. On the next page options regarding the access mechanism to be used will be requested, leave the selection as SQL Statements and click Next.

You now have the option of building some simple SQL statements using the Query Builder. The result you are looking for is:

```
SELECT Players.Name, Scores.CurrentLevel, Scores.HighScore
FROM Players INNER JOIN Scores ON Players.PlayerID = Scores.PlayerID
            WHERE (Scores.CurrentLevel = '1')
```

In order to avoid any error messages when the query builder attempts to build the full set of SQL statements, use the advanced tab and remove the update SQL generation. An error will be generated if this is not done, because the SQL builder is unable to fully comprehend the linked nature of the tables.

Once we have the SQL generated, simply finish the wizard dialogue by clicking Next and Finish. The result will be a fully configured data adapter and the creation of an associated oleDbConnection. Once these are available all that is required is to provide some mechanism to display the resultant tables.

The next object to select is a DataSet, add this to the form in the design view. Once again you need to configure the DataSet. Select the option Untyped DataSet (no Schema), we have already briefly looked at schema concepts in the chapter on XML and in these simple examples we will avoid building any datasets with a schema requirement.

To display the DataSet created we will add a DataGrid control to our form. Finally we need to configure the database query to fill the DataSet and transfer the result to the DataGrid, the following code is added to the form constructor:

```
public MainForm()
{
    //
    // Required for Windows Form Designer support
    //
    InitializeComponent();
    // Now bind the Data base to the connection
        oleDbDataAdapter1.Fill(dataSet1,"mytable");
        dataGrid1.SetDataBinding(dataSet1, "mytable");
```

The first statement uses the Data Adapter to fill the DataSet, mytable is simply a reference name for the table in the dataset. The second line binds the data source to the DataGrid. If you have completed the above steps correctly then, when you run the application, you will get the result of the query in the data grid control. You can then experiment by populating further information into the simple database. The remainder of the code in the example solution includes the standard menu bar used throughout the examples in this book.

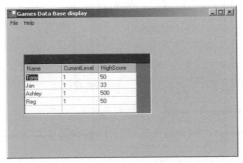

Figure 9.6   *The result of our simple query in the DataGrid*

Obviously we could once again spend a number of pages looking at how to insert, update and delete data from the database. However, this is again simply a matter of creating the correct SQL text strings and issuing the necessary commands via the oleDbDataAdapter. We can view the whole concept of using the ADO.NET components within the .NET architecture in the form shown in Figure 9.7.

Reading and writing XML Files

In the previous chapter we investigated XML documents and the basic support for XML within the .NET Framework.

A very powerful feature of ADO.NET is its ability to convert stored data from a data source to XML. Within the framework library, System.Data provides methods such as WriteXml, ReadXml and GetXml. These offer conversion of data stored in a data source into an XML document and conversely conversion of XML back into a data source format. The reasons for such conversions may not be instantly apparent but consider the situation where the application needs to transfer information to and from a data source in a three-tier application.

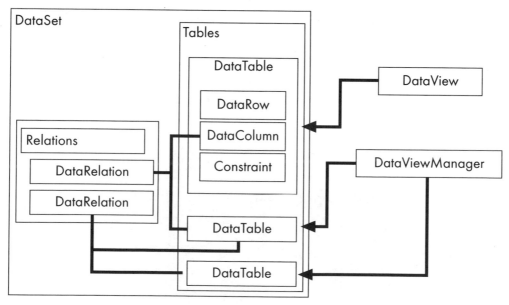

Figure 9.7   *The architecture of DataSet*

Extending the Previous Example

Objective

Using our previous simple example this example displays the XML in a text box. The XML being generated from the dataset created.

Requirement

Add a text box called XMLText to the previous form and add the extra line of code.

```
public MainForm()
{
    //
    // Required for Windows Form Designer support
    //
    InitializeComponent();
    // Now bind the Data base to the connection
    oleDbDataAdapter1.Fill(dataSet1,"mytable");
    dataGrid1.SetDataBinding(dataSet1, "mytable");
    XMLText.Text= "Writing XML \r\n" + dataSet1.GetXml() + "\r\n";
```

The method dataSet1.GetXml() retrieves and formats the dataset records into XML.

Obviously this is writing the XML to the screen, in reality most applications will want to write the XML to a file. To do this we use the WriteXml(..) method.

This brief introduction shows the close integration that the .NET architecture provides between the ADO.NET components and other technologies.

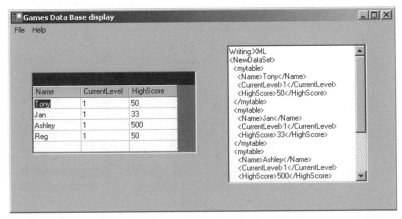

Figure 9.8   This extension showing the XML generated from the query result

Data providers – how we link to different RDMSs

Within the .NET class libraries two standard data providers are available, a third option that enables standard ODBC linkage for RDMS such as oracle has to be downloaded separately. Each of the data providers supported the following objects.

■ Connection

■ Command

■ DataReader

■ DataAdapter.

These names are generic; you will not find a unique class identifier for each name since, unfortunately even in the .NET architecture, differences exist between the various data provider classes, for instance the DataReader for SQL is called SqlDatareader, while for the OLE DB the implementation is called OleDbDataReader.

Within these four data provider objects .NET allows a client application two options for accessing the data. Both options have common connection and command structures to interact with the RDMS but they differ in the mechanism that the client can employ to look at the result of the query.

If the client needs simple row-by-row return of data then a data reader technique can be employed, whereas if the client

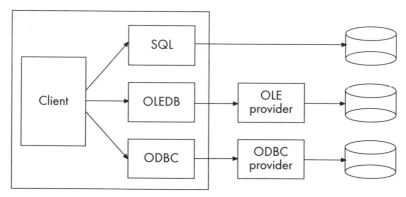

Figure 9.9   The basic architecture of the ADO.NET data providers

requires the ability to manipulate a dataset then, as in our first simple example, a data adapter approach must be used. Obviously when considering multi-tier solutions with data being sent via a network connection the data adapter approach is the obvious choice.

We have seen from the example that the data source can be a simple single user RDMS such as 'Access'. It is obvious from Figure 9.9 that SQL server is the number one choice for enterprise solutions according to the .NET architecture as it has a unique adapter and also fits into the .NET enterprise solutions model. The SQL data provider is an intrinsic part of the overall CLR.

One area that needs careful consideration concerns the creation of a single client that is able to work with multiple data sources. There is of course commonality, the fact that the .NET class library, although providing for instance two versions of the data reader SqlDataReader and OleDbReader, both these have an IDataReader interface available taking the commonality down a further level, meaning no matter which provider is being used to connect to the RDMS, the actual recovery of information is common to both.

Unfortunately this lower-level commonality is not universal across all aspects of the data providers, although it may be possible to produce a generalised client, it may mean that specific functionality for one or more of the common RDMS systems may be lost.

That's nothing new, writing portable code is time consuming and 75% portability is far better than no portability at all. Garbage collection is something we discussed in an earlier chapter, having seen that applications can pretty well ignore the problem of objects deletion, in all our examples both of Windows forms applications and component development we have done just that. However, when we are looking at a connection object, it is holding an active connection to the RDMS itself, the client application must invoke the Close(..) or Dispose(..) method on any connection object when it is no longer required.

You must not just forget about the problem and hope the automatic garbage collector will sort it out, it will not; the connection object may be out of scope for the client that created it, but it is still in scope for the RDMS it is attached to. The automatic garbage collector will not recognise the object as being ready for disposal if the connection is active. This situation is the exception to the rule that memory leaks in an application should not occur in .NET, leaving unreferenced open data provider connections creates .NET memory leaks.

Datasets

We used a dataset in our earlier example; we need to investigate more fully the functionality available within a dataset object. Any of the .NET data adapters provide the ability to hold SQL commands to:

- Select

- Insert

- Update

- Delete.

When any one of these SQL commands is executed the result of that command requires some containing object that can hold the information produced, in many cases this will be a dataset. In fact the connection to the RDMS can be closed once the result has been returned and stored in a dataset; the dataset object is completely independent of any connection to a data source.

The example showed that we could use the dataset fill(..) to bind the result of an SQL select query to a particular dataset.

Figure 9.10 identifies how the dataset, once filled, is a completely independent object within the application, data providers can share datasets, and the data tables created within a dataset are also completely independent entities.

We can view this independence by considering the following diagram in which there are two .NET data providers, each attached to their own RDMS but each is instanced from within a single client application. The resultant tables in the client's dataset are independent of the data sources they were derived from and the tables can be manipulated by the application without recourse to the originator or data source once the fill has been accomplished.

Datasets exist to let applications read and change the data they contain. The data within the dataset is grouped into one or more data tables. Since applications will need to work with such data tables in a diverse manner, various options exist to access such tables. Whichever option is used .NET Framework classes are available for:

- Data row

- Data column.

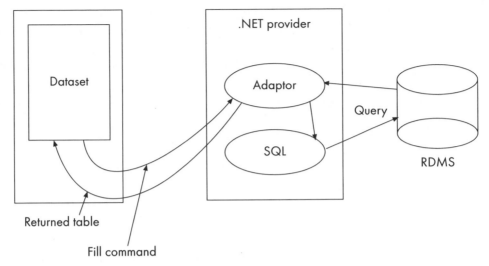

Figure 9.10   *The basic interaction associated with an ADO.NET dataset*

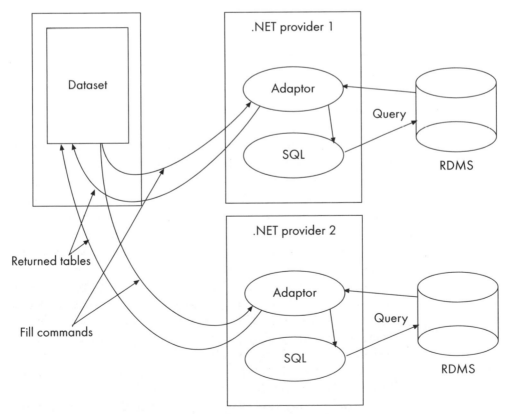

Figure 9.11   *Multiple providers filling a common dataset*

The data row represents a row or record of the table, within the dataset these rows are held as a collection. In fact the most common mechanism to access the available data is to consider the collection of data rows as a one-dimensional array of direction 'Y'. The fields within these rows are then thought of as a one-dimensional array of direction 'X'. Combining these two arrays allows any field in a table within a dataset to be directly accessed, by directly addressing the correct location in a two-dimensional array.

The data column on the other hand is considered as a collection of any one field in the table across all rows in the table. However, unlike the data rows this data column collection defines the data type of the column (field), and given this definition the whole collection defines the table's schema or design definitions of the complete data table.

In our extension to the simple example at the start of the chapter we looked at transferring the contents of a dataset to an XML document. There is a little more complexity to this mapping of datasets to XML than this simple example may have led you to believe.

Translating datasets to XML

The previous discussion has been based on the premise that some form of SQL query is needed to populate a dataset from the data source. However, a dataset can be populated from an XML document.

Having the ability to populate datasets from XML could be thought of as the long awaited rebirth of the hierarchical complex data structure. Relational modelling techniques for complex database design emerged more than two decades ago as the dominant approach. The hierarchical approach for complex structured data simply faded into oblivion. However, the 'OO' approach to complex structured data modelling resurrected the hierarchical approach, arguing that as software objects in an 'OO' design tended to have a tree structure (such trees being created by the 'OO' inheritance model), then possibly complex structured data could follow suit. This argument is flawed, the usual rational being that no single hierarchical approach could work for database designs that would be shared by multiple applications.

We have seen that XML takes a hierarchical view to structure its documents, in fact in one of the examples from the last chapter where the serialisation of an object to an XML document was being considered, the structure within the object has to be changed from serialising an array of objects, a non-hierarchical approach, to serialising an object that contained an array of information, a true hierarchical approach.

It is important therefore to understand that within the .NET environment, the class library for the ADO.NET components has been designed to accommodate the integration of the relational database approach with the needs of XML, the standard tree approach. This marriage of the two complex structured data technologies seems to work well and could offer an insight into the techniques of the future, related to enterprise-level database designs.

The obvious area that needs to be addressed is one of schemas, both XML and the relational model use totally different philosophies to describe the data in the structure. XML as we investigated in the last chapter defines its hierarchical model in terms of DTD (Data Type Definitions) or XML-schema sometimes referred to as XSD (XML Schema Definitions). In contrast the relational model uses sets of tables with groupings and relationships between common fields. Once again, as with the common language run time, we are faced with the dilemma of type mapping.

To define how the options for such mappings could be analysed would probably mean writing another complete book. Among the techniques that could be considered is the use of the DTD or XSD definitions for the XML and then to infer the relevant relationships between the data elements. The later requirement of inferred relationships being definitely a non-trivial task. Taking a very simple example XML document which contains:

```
<games>
  <player>
    <name>Reg</name>
  </player>
  <player>
    <name>Ashley</name>
    <age>22</name>

  </player>
</game>
```

If this were read by the ReadXml(..) method in a dataset, the inferred table design without any schema definition could be as shown in Table 9.1.

A single table called player with two fields, notice that even though in the first occurrence of the element player there is only one child element, in the second there are two, requiring a NULL entry in the data table field two for the first row. This translation

Table 9.1   *Inferred table design without any schema definition*

name	age
Reg	NULL
Ashley	22

has worked well but it is trivial. What if we expand the XML document to:

```
<mytable>
    <Name>Tony</Name>
    <CurrentLevel>1</CurrentLevel>
    <HighScore>50</HighScore>
</mytable>
<mytable>
    <Name>Jan</Name>
    <CurrentLevel>1</CurrentLevel>
    <HighScore>33</HighScore>
</mytable>
<mytable>
    <Name>Ashley</Name>
    <CurrentLevel>1</CurrentLevel>
    <HighScore>500</HighScore>
</mytable>
<mytable>
    <Name>Reg</Name>
    <CurrentLevel>1</CurrentLevel>
    <HighScore>50</HighScore>
</mytable>
```

This is the XML generated by the earlier example based on the SQL query of the original relational databse:

```
SELECT Players.Name, Scores.CurrentLevel, Scores.HighScore FROM Players
INNER JOIN Scores ON Players.PlayerID = Scores.PlayerID
WHERE (Scores.CurrentLevel = '1')
```

Obviously we could recreate the result table from this XML but there is no definition of the original tables at all, so we could not recreate even these rows in the original Players and Scores tables.

So the scope of XML documents to relational structure is limited, the use of suitable DTD or XSD definitions help but in a way trivialise the task. It was mentioned previously that the reason for serialising a dataset to an XML document is to assist in the process of transferring such information to a client browser within our multi-tier solution. Similarly we can wrap our serialised XML dataset within a SOAP envelope. In a later chapter we will review this more fully and identify that these SOAP envelopes may be requests to execute methods on a remote web service. Having the ability to pass a complete dataset as a parameter for the method to a remote web service constitutes a significant technological leap forward from the older ADO components working with the older ASP technologies.

One final point that should be addressed is the synchronisation issue between a dataset and the XML document that describes that dataset.

Dataset and XML synchronisation

This ability to translate tables to tree structures and vice-versa is a very powerful tool, but if both representations exist how can any application be certain that the data within the two versions is identical? In our discussion of the XML document support within .NET we briefly looked at XPath that allowed any XML document to be traversed and investigated as a hierarchical tree structure. To ensure synchronisation therefore the goal is to maintain the relational tables in the dataset as the master source and to manipulate the XML hierarchical structure by the creation of a suitable XML document that can be programmatically traversed by XPath techniques. Within the .NET Framework class, the object XmlDataDocument will create the document since it inherits from XmlDocument. This means that an XPath navigator can also be created to traverse the DOM of this XML document and programmatic access to the data via the XML route is available at the same time as programmatic assess to the source dataset itself.

Summary

ADO.NET is a key technology within the overall .NET architecture. The inclusion within the basic framework of the SQL data adapter and the availability of other data adapters from within the .NET library highlight the close integration of ADO.NET into the basic CLR. The slight variation on the mechanism for the data adapters is only to be expected when looking at the many RDMS that have support for OLE or ODBC. However, once the data is captured into a dataset then any inconsistency is removed, any supported common run-time language can manipulate the data and equally XML serialisation of the data is fully integrated into the ADO.NET philosophy.

Review question

1 Using the techniques outlined in this chapter, define a complete query application for the multi-user game's database outlined:

a. First you will need to define and expand the table definition for the levels and add some descriptive table linked using the primary key

b. Then provide a set of predefined queries and the ability to action such queries on your application

c. Experiment with both data grids and other mechanisms to display the results from a dataset.

d. Use a Windows form application template to prove your solution is correct.

10 Networking, web forms and ASP.NET

Objective

This chapter spans a number of key topics when considering the scalability of the .NET Framework from stand-alone applications to multi-tier distributed solutions:

- Client–server applications

- Web-based applications

- ASP.NET.

We will start by considering the mechanisms available for communications between applications on different machines. This will introduce the concept of socket connections and the TCP protocol.

We will then proceed to look at the techniques available within .NET that allow either the adaptation of stand-alone applications into web-based applications or, alternatively, by using the server-side techniques available within ASP.NET we can build a custom multi-tier enterprise-level solution.

Introduction

Obviously the World Wide Web (WWW) generates a great deal of excitement in both the business and computing community. However, we must not be drawn into this hype without reviewing the basic networking technologies that underpin the transfer of information via the Internet every day.

In the context of this book I could have ignored these basic networking topics and started the investigation by looking at web forms and ASP.NET, these are the technologies that enable interactive client–server systems to be built and provide the basis of any multi-tier solution. However, to do this would have ignored the fundamental networking support intrinsically built into the .NET Framework, and the importance of this basic support to the more specific topics of web applications and ASP.NET.

Any discussion on basic networking theory must focus on both sides of a client–server relationship. The client will request some action to be performed by the server, the action will take place and the response will be sent to the client.

A common form of this request–response model is demonstrated by looking at the web browser–web server interaction. In essence in this browser–server model the user places a request for a particular piece of information, the browser sends this request using a suitable protocol to a web server, the request is acknowledged and subsequently the required information is returned to the client.

To understand how this request–response model is implemented within the .NET Framework we must first look at the lowest level of the transaction, the socket structure, used by both the client and the server to route information via the network.

Sockets

The term socket refers to the Berkley Sockets Interface that was developed in the late 1970s for network programming within the UNIX operating system and has remained popular especially with C/C++ programmers ever since. Visual Basic has never had an inbuilt sockets data type, but a number of ActiveX controls which offer the same level of functionality became available in the 1990s, one of the most common being the 'WinSock' control. These controls allowed Visual Basic developers the freedom to implement the request–response model.

Within the .NET class library, sockets are implemented using a similar structure to a file stream. Using this model, a .NET application wishing to connect to another process establishes a socket stream that is available to any other .NET application,

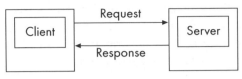

Figure 10.1   *Request–response model*

which had a similar socket stream initialised. While this connection is active, a continuous stream of data can flow across the connection. For this reason stream sockets are said to provide a stream connection-based service, the popular TCP (Transmission Control Protocol) is a good example of a protocol mechanism for controlling stream socket transmission.

As a comparison UDP (User Datagram Protocol) is an example of a packet-based communications protocol. Unlike TCP, UDP is said to be a completely connectionless service, but still using the underlying stream connection, any connectionless service implies there is no guaranteed delivery of any particular packet and the order that the packets are received may not reflect the order in which they were sent. Applications using a UDP implementation often require significantly more software to check the validity of the information than a TCP implementation.

Within our future discussions on both simple networking and subsequently on web forms, we will be using the TCP protocol model as it offers the most suitable solution for the vast majority of system solutions.

The mechanisms to establishing a simple socket connection

The server side   Typically it is the server that sits and waits for some client application to request a connection. When a request is received the server will accept the request for the connection and instigate the requirement requested by this connection.

Using the C# syntax the typical code for this creation of a connection point and awaiting an incoming request is:

```
TcpListener Listen;
Socket Ssocket;
Listen  = new TcpListener(5000);
Listen.Start();
Ssocket = Listen.Accept();
```

The first lines of the code declare two variables, a TcpListener and a Socket, the code sets up the listener structure to capture any incoming data on port 5000, this is the traditional approach on any server-side implementation.

1   The server has effectively published a standard port number

2   All clients attempt to connect to the server via this standard port.

The Start() method is known as a blocking call, any blocking call halts further execution of the code below it, until some external action occurs and the call returns. So we can define that when a blocking call returns a client will have requested a connection, the above code then accepts the connection by using the Accept() method. Using this approach serves two purposes:

1   It will cause the accept to propagate to the client indicating that the server is available

2   It allows the socket address–port combination used by the client to request the connection to be extracted and stored at the server.

It is this retrieved socket address–port combination that will be used for all subsequent information flow between the client and server for this session. In using this retrieval technique the server is free again to sit and wait for any other connection requests using its listener port.

Up to this point the term port number has been used without explanation, the original Berkley specification allows the range for port numbers as the number set – 0 to 65 535 (a 16-bit unsigned integer). The port number can be thought of as a subaddress within the main address identifying which application is attached to the physical network. We must appreciate that for any physical network IP address there may be many applications attached to different ports.

The Client Side   The structure of the implementation for the client side of a connection is similar to that discussed for the server. It of course does not set up a listener, the client sets up a socket that attempts to make a connection to a server:

```
TcpClient Csocket = new TcpClient();
Csocket.Connect (server address, server port);
```

This code snippet first declares a variable that is of type TcpClient and then uses the Connect method to request, send a connection request, to the server specified by an IP Address and Port Number.

The numeric form of IP Address has the format XXX.XXX.XXX.XXX, each field delimited by the dot is in the range 0–255. When testing locally on the same machine a loopback facility on the IP Address definition allows an address of 127.0.0.1 to loop all requests back to same machine, this feature can also be requested by using the descriptive form 'localhost'.

When the initial connection has been made both the client and server can establish a NetworkingStream that further allows the creation of the BinaryReader and BinaryWriter objects allowing actual data to be sent and received.

To illustrate the technique the following code snippets relate to the outline solution for a 'battleships' game, this is designed for a single network connection. The first instance of the game, finding no other instance running, sets up as a network listener (i.e. a server), then when a second instance starts, it attempts to connect, the listener responds and a connection is established with this second instance and we have a fairly conventional client–server configuration.

The specification for the game itself is quite primitive, once again it is the networking process that is of interest in this example not the gameplay.

The application is built inheriting from the .NET Windows Form. In Chapter 6 we developed and implemented a quite useful game board control. The GUI for this application uses two such instances of the control. The first represents the player's ships and second the attack plan on the opponent ships.

For ease of description this version randomly generates five ships on the player's board. To indicate the attack plan the player clicks on the relevant square on the opponent's board. The networking requirement is therefore to transmit the position of the move to the opponent and to receive from the opponent whether that position is a hit or a miss.

Figure 10.2 represents the first instance of the application running, and the network status is presented on a list box at the bottom.

The code snippet below is executed at startup of the application. It attempts to connect to a running server, if this is successful then the streams are created and the GameReader and GameWriter objects are instanced from this stream.

If on the other hand an exception occurs, the catch clause is activated in this case is not used directly as an error indicator, it

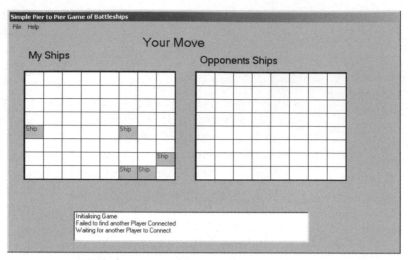

Figure 10.2   *The battleship application*

is monitoring for this exception which indicates that no server is listening.

In the catch clause the code removes the TcpClient socket and streams and instead sets up a server listener waiting for another client to start:

```
try
{
// if this works then we act as client to other players Server
      CSocket = new TcpClient ();
    CSocket.Connect ("localhost",5000);
    CStream = CSocket.GetStream ();
    GameWriter = new BinaryWriter (CStream);
    GameReader = new BinaryReader (CStream);
    Info.Items.Add ("Found another Player Connected");
    Player = 2;  // Set the player Number
    Connected = true;
}
catch
    // If we get no joy as client then set up to wait as a Server
{
    Info.Items.Add ("Failed to find another Player Connected");
    CSocket = null;  // kill the client socket...
    CStream = null;
    Server = true;
    Player = 1;
    Info.Items.Add ("Waiting for another Player to Connect");
    tcpListener.Start ();
    SSocket = tcpListener.AcceptSocket ();
    Connected = true;
    SStream = new NetworkStream (SSocket);
```

```
        GameWriter = new BinaryWriter(SStream);
        GameReader = new BinaryReader (SStream);
        Info.Items.Add ("Another Player has Connected");
        MyTurn = true;
    }
```

In placing the networking code into an application we create a further design consideration:

```
tcpListener.Start ();
```

The above call creates a blocking situation, i.e. no further execution of code below the call takes place until the call returns. In this case it will not return until a client connection is detected. This creates an unusable application if it were allowed to block forever. The user would not even be able to shut down the application if no one else wanted to play.

We must therefore investigate non-blocking techniques and the design of a multithreaded solution.

Multithreading
It would be very helpful if we could always perform one action at a time. The human body for instance performs a great many operations in parallel or in software terms concurrently: breathing, blood circulation sight, and smell to name but a few. The Windows operating system uses concurrency, it can access the hardware devices while you are typing a letter for instance.

Programming language designs will normally not have any direct data types or control structures related to the needs of concurrency. There is generally only one CPU (Central Processing Unit) on a system so concurrency has to be viewed as the ability of the operating system software to provide an environment offering pseudo concurrency, 'multiple applications or threads within an application apparently running on a single site of execution'.

It is far beyond the scope of this text to look at how such a strategy is implemented in the operating system. For the purposes of this chapter we are just going to assume that the required support is available in the operating system and that the .NET class library objects dealing with the creation of concurrent threads within an application have access to these operating system primitive structures.

Thread execution
A thread is simply a unique path of execution, so in these networking examples the setting up of a connection can be defined as a thread. This simple definition of a thread model means that any thread can be in one of the states listed in Table 10.1. Therefore if any one thread is blocked then another

Table 10.1   *Possible stages of a thread*

Status	Action
Started	Being loaded etc.
Ready	Awaiting scheduling into the CPU
Running	The active thread
Blocked	Awaiting some resource etc.
Exiting	Terminating from the application

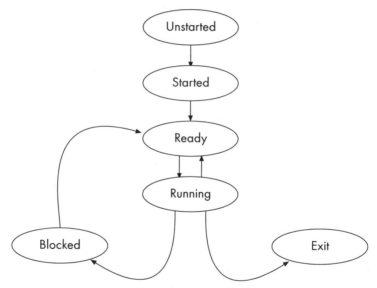

Figure 10.3   *The basic thread state model*

thread can be in the running state. In our application when the connection thread is blocked waiting for a client, any other thread can become active.

BattleShips Thread Model

To make the design simple, in the application we will have the following threads:

1   A primary thread that will start all the others and also look after the GUI form itself

2   A SetUp thread that runs once and sets up the network connection and then exits simply by the termination of the method running within that thread

3 A Play thread that loops continually and is blocked by waiting for some network messages from the other player.

To create these threads the following code is added to the constructor of the main form:

```
public Mainform()
{
 InitializeComponent();
// set up my Home Grid...
// Five ships... for this simple demo..
CreateShips();
Info.Items.Add ("Initialising Game");
StartUp = new Thread( new ThreadStart(SetUp));
Play = new Thread (new ThreadStart (PlayGame));
StartUp.Start ();
}
```

The mechanism for the declaration of a new thread, always identifies a local method that will execute as the thread starts:

```
StartUp = new Thread( new ThreadStart(SetUp));
```

This StartUp thread executes a method called SetUp(..), the code in this method resembles the previously discussed code for setting up the network connection.

The code for the thread Play is in the PlayGame(..) method, this method loops and is blocked by the call GameReader.ReadString(..), until a string message is received by the network connection:

```
private void PlayGame()
{
// thread that plays the game via the socket connection
    if (Connected==true)
    try
    {
    while (true)
        {
        ProcessMessage(GameReader.ReadString());
        }
    }
    catch( System.IO.EndOfStreamException)
    {
    MessageBox.Show("Other Player has Disconnected","Error on Socket");
    }
}
```

The method ProcessMessage() interrogates the incoming message strings and performs the appropriate action:

```
private void ProcessMessage( string Message)
{
string Value;
string HitMiss;
// now interprete the messages.
if (Message.StartsWith("Target = "))
    {
    // they are trying to hit my taget
     MoveI.Visible = !MoveI.Visible ;
     MyTurn = !MyTurn; // ensures play alternates
     Value = Message.Substring (Message.IndexOf ("=",0)+2);
     HitMiss = HomeGridPosition(int.Parse(Value));
     GameWriter.Write("Result = " +HitMiss);
    }
else
    Away.SetSqString(LastMove,Message.Substring(Message.IndexOf ("=",0)+2));
}
```

The actual code for changing a square's text and colour was fully discussed in Chapter 6 and you should review that chapter if you cannot remember how it works.

To write to a network stream is very straightforward as can be seen by the line:

```
GameWriter.Write("Result = " +HitMiss);
```

This code could be writing to any streamed device, but we assigned the object GameWriter to a stream derived for the socket connection.

Application termination in a multithreaded application is not as simple as in a non-multithreaded application. In the previous examples no special precautions have been taken regarding object references during application termination, the automatic garbage collection within the .NET Framework will tidy up such references for you. However, in a multithreaded environment when you exit the primary thread, any thread references for other active threads are left on the heap.

The following code from the Exit menu handler of the application first checks if any of the threads are active, the Abort() method for each thread is then called to terminate active threads. It is also important to clear any active socket connections, any blocked threads waiting on a network connection method cannot exit. Such active connections must be closed before the thread can terminate:

```
private void FileExit_Click(object sender, System.EventArgs e)
{
// stop the threads
```

```
if (StartUp != null)
    StartUp.Abort ();
if (Play != null)
    Play.Abort ();
if (Connected)
{
GameReader.Close();
        GameWriter.Close ();
        if (Server)
            {
            // it was a server so
                SSocket.Close ();
                SStream.Close ();
            }
        else
            {
                CSocket.Close ();
                CStream.Close ();
            }
    }
    else
        if (Server)
            tcpListener.Stop ();
Application.Exit ();
}
```

This simple example has introduced the idea of setting up a client–server application. In the next section we will be expanding on these ideas and looking at client connection to a web server.

Web pages

Having looked at general networking principles and TCP as an underlying protocol to create a stream-based connection, before going on to investigate web-based applications, we should first gain an understanding of a basic web page in terms of:

■ Content

■ Protocol to retrieve standard pages.

In this case we are only going to be dealing with the client side, we will assume that a standard Internet information server is available and provided the correctly formatted commands are issued data retrieval will take place.

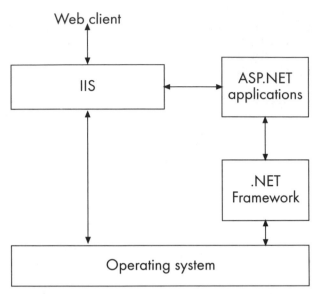

Figure 10.4   *A basic model of a web page or a web-based application in the .NET architecture*

In order to help to understand web page retrieval the following is a brief overview of the networking requirements of the web.

The HTTP protocol

In this section we will briefly look at HTTP (Hyper Text Transfer Protocol). HTTP is the protocol used to request information from a web server, the protocol comprises a set of methods and headers that allows the interaction between a client and a suitable web server. The use of a standard protocol ensures that data exchanges, (between client and server and vice versa) are performed in a uniform and predictive manner.

The concept of a standard protocol such as HTTP is to ensure that all client–server data interchanges are monitored to a common set of rules. The full description of the HTTP protocol is much too complex for this book.

Table 10.1 is a typical message sequence for the recovery of a file resource which we can view in a diagrammatic form as shown in Figure 10.5.

The content of a web page

In the discussion in the chapter dealing with XML, it was defined that the contents of any XML document can be reduced to a simple plain text file.

This is exactly the same when considering a simple web page, the markup in this case uses HTML (Hyper Text Markup

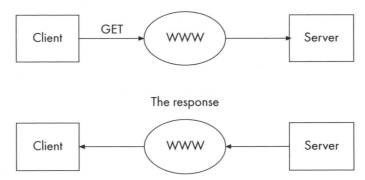

Figure 10.5   *Model of the web page or Request–Response mechanism*

Table 10.1   *A typical message sequence for the recovery of a file resource*

Client messages	*Server messages*
GET /~cm1918/book/ test.htm	
GET is an HTTP keyword to activate the get file method; this method requests that the relevant server transmits the file back to the requesting client.	
The initial response to the GET request will be either	HTTP/x.x 200 OK or HTTP/x.x 404 Not Found
	The HTTP/x.x response informs the client of the protocol and version that the server has available. The numeric and text that follow indicates the status of the request.
	The first option is a success, the resource requested is available on the server and will be transmitted back next.
	While the second option is the standard response for a resource that is not available on the server.

Language). Probably the simplest possible web pages would, in text form, have the structure:

```
<html>
    <title> A simple page </title>
    <body> <p> Some Text </p></body>
</html>
```

The initial tag <html> indicates to the client that the contents are to be rendered based on HTML markup. The <title> tag indicates the contents to be used for the client header, the <body> tag indicates the content should be rendered in the client window itself using the formatting tags associated with the text. For instance the paragraph tag <p> indicates how to format the line of text. Obviously there are many more tags within the definition of HTML, but for the purpose of this description a simple page such as this will suffice. The actual location of any HTML file requested by a client needs to be located on the WWW. This is accomplished by the use of a standard text string called a URL (Universal Resource Locator). Returning to our discussion on the HTTP protocol, assuming the server has the information (in this case the file requested) the information transfer from the server starts with header details for the client, these specify the information content in the page. The use of header information ensures that the client can present the content of the page in the same manner as it was generated. Typically for our simple example page, the header information would be:

```
Contents-type: text/html
```

This description of the content is called the MIME (Multipurpose Internet Mail Extension) type, it is an international standard used to identify possible data formats. Typical content types are:

1 text/html   web page
2 text/plain   plain ASCII no Markup
3 image/gif   an image encoded in gif format

Armed with this set of definitions the next example application is a non-rendering web client. It will request a page from a web server, and display the raw data returned in text form. We will also display the protocol message exchange, as it comes across on the network stream. The web server will be the 'localhost' on the same machine as the client and we will assume that the 'localhost' is going to be listening on the standard HTTP port of 80.

This example application, rather than rendering the web page, displays the plain text including the protocol messages.

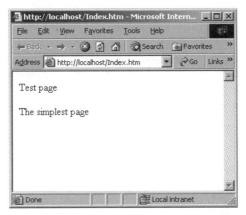

Figure 10.6   *Our test file rendered by Internet explorer from http://localhost/*
index.htm

The example demonstrates how we can use the TcpClient class to establish a client connection. In this case the client connection is made using the underlying socket class itself. This example shows that in using the .NET Framework we have not lost any flexibility, if you need to be able to manipulate the socket connect at its lowest level the supporting structure is available.

Figure 10.7   *Our test file viewed in the application from http://localhost/*
index.htm

In the example the GET command in HTTP has been constructed as a simple string:

```
StrGet = "GET /Index.htm HTTP/1.1"+ CrLf + "Host: localhost" + CrLf +
                                    "Connection : Close "+CrLf+ CrLf;
```

The event handler code for the button to send the request data is:

```
private void Cmd_Click(object sender, System.EventArgs e)
{
  Int32 bytes;
  hostadd = IPAddress.Parse("127.0.0.1");// create the correct host address
  EPhost = new IPEndPoint(hostadd, 80); // and assign the endpoint to port 80
  Received.Text = "";
  CSocket = new Socket(AddressFamily.InterNetwork, SocketType.Stream,
                                    ProtocolType.Tcp);
  CSocket.Connect(EPhost);
  if(!CSocket.Connected)
    {
    MessageBox.Show(" Unable to connect to Host ","Socket error");
    }
    else
    {
        ByteGet = ASCII.GetBytes(StrGet);
        CSocket.Send(ByteGet, ByteGet.Length, 0);
        //' Receives the page
        bytes = CSocket.Receive(RecvBytes, RecvBytes.Length, 0);
        Received.Text = ASCII.GetString(RecvBytes, 0, bytes);
    }
}
```

The response text from the 'localhost' to this request being:

```
HTTP/1.1 200 OK
Server: Microsoft-IIS/5.0
Date: Tue, 18 Nov 2003 14:47:48 GMT
Content-Type: text/html
Accept-Ranges: bytes
Last-Modified: Tue, 18 Nov 2003 12:42:48 GMT
ETag: "b0ba3779d1adc31:888"
Content-Length: 95

<html>
<header>
Test page
</header>
<body>
<p> The simplest page </p>
</body>
</html>
```

It can be seen that with a little work, this plain text file could be interpreted and displayed in a suitable rendered form. In fact there are a number of ActiveX browser controls available and as we saw in the chapter on interoperability any one of these could be built into such a .NET solution.

That completes a very brief look at the networking and protocol aspects of the .NET Framework; with all of this prefabricated structure the framework offers all of the support we will need to look at ASP.NET.

Web applications and ASP.NET

Having reviewed aspects of both networking and web client requirements we are ready to tackle the topic of web forms and ASP.NET. The minimum requirement for any web-based application would be:

■ HTML (Hyper Text Markup Language) content

■ Client-side scripting (either using a .NET supported language or java script)

■ Image and binary data on the displayed page.

When considering web applications, two distinct categories must always be considered:

■ What do we want in terms of client side processing

■ What do we want in terms of server-side processing.

In general HTML is used to construct the Graphical User Interface, (GUI) on the client side. Although an ASP.NET solution can be compared to a stand-alone Windows application development there are significant differences, these mainly manifest themselves in terms of less flexibility and availability of user controls. HTML pages constructed using this technique are sometimes referred to as 'form pages'.

Obviously the majority of the content of this page is HTML, client side scripting is of course an option when programmatic checks etc. are required. Both Java and VB as a scripting engine are available and offer the ability to ensure the validity of user input, but this may not be strictly necessary.

When we consider server-side processing there have been a number of technologies developed that enable an event generated on the client and signalled to the server to be handled effectively. Server-side activation allows far more extensive algorithmic interpretation of information to take place than could possibly be sent to, and processed by, a client browser.

With the above in mind the .NET architecture must satisfy both requirements within the one common framework. Prior to .NET one of the major technologies employed for multi-tier applications was ASP (Active Server Pages); an active server page contained the HTML to format and position the various user controls, combined with ASP scripting (on the server side), allowing programmatic manipulation and algorithmic derivation of the information that eventually would be displayed on the response HTML client page.

Within the .NET Framework ASP has evolved to ASP.NET. We are not dealing with a totally new technology, this is one of the components of the .NET Framework that has been available for a number of years, albeit in a different form. In the .NET Framework ASP.NET has standardised the format and nature of ASP to fit into the overall CLR design and has modified the programmatic aspects to allow CLR compliant languages to be used. This later change removes from ASP the interpretive (scripted) nature of its execution and replaces it with the normal .NET Framework assemblies mechanism.

Any ASP.NET page or application must contain two elements, the HTML to display and position information and controls, and the server-side application code that performs the algorithmic manipulation of the data. Probably the most important enhancement to the original ASP specification is the removal of the scripting aspects. Scripts were written in either Java or Visual Basic, both these options were interpretive, and having interpreters built into web servers generated the need for close integration and standardisation if ASP was to become universally accepted.

The need for such dependency and commonality of web servers and interpreters limited the effectiveness of an ASP solution when looking for commonality across different operating system/ hardware platforms. The dependence and commonality problems have not been totally removed by ASP.NET. The .NET Framework itself is not universally available. However, the .NET Framework is considered as a component running as a process (we discussed this in the Chapter 5), the web server is also running as a process and therefore once the .NET Framework is ported to a particular

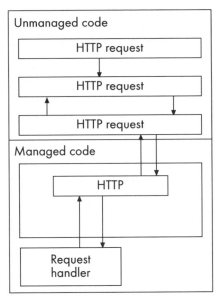

Figure 10.8   *The unmanaged code client pages to managed code server-side execution model*

operating system, the web server with .NET compatibility will have available the services of the framework.

The ultimate goal for any environment offering web based applications development must be to arrive at a situation where the flexibility offered by a comparative model removes any specific implementation language constraints and isolates any resultant application from a specific web sever/operating system/ hardware platform configuration. Possibly .NET will never fully reach this goal, but the design philosophy of ASP.NET has laid out a route map for achieving such a potential. Once again we could look at COM and CORBA and RPC, each of these technologies has attempted to offer the flexibility of componentware, but as highlighted in previous chapters these technologies have never offered the degree of flexibility required to be migrated into the web applications arena.

As we are dealing with CLR compliant languages for .NET server-side solutions, in the context of this book we will be looking at C# and VB.NET. This commonality in development languages with stand-alone application development offers, as would be expected, major advantages in respect of the learning curve. This is truly the case for transferable skills; the same skill set is required to develop distributed web based solutions as for stand-alone applications.

The overall structure of an ASP.NET, web application is slightly different to the .NET stand-alone application. The differences are minor and the reason for the changes in structure is quite obvious. If a stand-alone application is built using Windows forms, the code structure is created within one or more source files for each form. In these source files we would find the code associated with manipulation of the controls and their data as well as the event handlers for user interaction. Optionally there may be a unique external resource file associated with a form, this additional resource file identifies system or user defined special resources, specifically created for the application.

In comparison, for an ASP.NET application with its associated web forms, each web form is stored in two parts, the first with the extension '.aspx' contains the web controls etc. that are used on the client side. It will be the content of this 'aspx' file that the browser will render for the user. In addition for each '.aspx' file, a corresponding code-behind file is generated. The contents of this additional file provide the programmatic implementation for the manipulation and event handling associated with server-side controls.

It is possible to draw a simple analogy; these server-side event handlers in the code-behind file are the equivalent of the forms' event handlers in a standard Windows forms application. The structure can be therefore be visualised as shown in Figure 10.9.

The page-behind file has a very simple structure; it normally contains one basic class allowing the controls specified on the GUI to be grouped and referenced from within this class. For each of the controls on the GUI, the necessary specific event handlers can then be defined within the class. The functionality of the GUI is totally encased in the code-behind file.

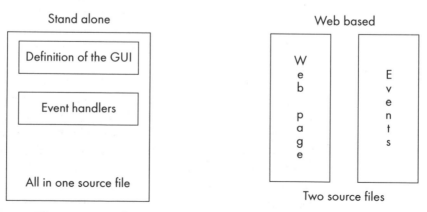

Figure 10.9   *The structure of a single form implementation*

Since any ASP.NET page can be written in either of the supported languages, both these files will either be written using C# or VB.NET, the choice being irrelevant. We have already seen in the previous examples the mapping of either of the languages to the CLR is simply a matter of syntax.

The typical web application architecture

When developing a web-based application using the .NET Framework, the flexibility offered by the technologies allows for the implementation of sophisticated multi-tier solutions (sometimes referred to as an n-tier application).

The whole concept of any multi-tiered architecture is to split the functionality of the final solution into the most logical building blocks. Within the accepted design models for such solutions the application itself is split into logical or functional grouping, the nature of these logical or functional groupings being based on the overall requirement for the system. As a reasonable definition it could be said that in any multi-tier system:

> **the overall aims of any part of this multi-tier system must be contributing to the overall system design goals.**

Splitting the design into these tiered levels does not mean distributing the system, interaction of any part of the system could be either locally within one machine or across many machine boundaries.

It is possible for all tiers in a particular solution to be running on a single machine, in fact the examples in this book have been specifically designed for such a configuration. It would be quite unreasonable to assume any student would have sufficient resources to experiment with such applications in any other manner.

Figure 10.10   *A common multi-tier system*

In Figure 10.10 the database is often called the data-tier. The RDMS associated with the structured information in the database is accessed using ADO.NET techniques (ADO.NET controls with SQL statements as we investigated in Chapter 9). In this chapter we will extend the example of the simple game database developed as a stand-alone Windows form application and allow access to that data via a web page. In Figure 10.10 the middle tier identified as the ASP.NET server controls the logical functionality of the overall application and to a lesser extent the presentation of the recovered data. This could be called the transaction process, its function is to filter and validate the requests from the client and to formulate and interpret the information flow from the data tier. The client or top tier in Figure 10.10 will be the GUI, this will interact with the user and transfer its information using standard HTTP protocols.

It would not be unreasonable to make the assumption that the top tier will always be a browser, however, as we have already identified that a number of specialist applications either in development or currently live have been extended to be HTTP aware. Such specialist designs allow this top client tier to be fully customised to a particular need.

The example

Objective   To demonstrate a simple multi tier solution

Specification   Web form based allowing a user to:

■ Log onto the system if already registered

■ Register to use the system.

Additionally this example will demonstrate the use of:

■ Server-side validation of user input

■ Forms-based authentication.

This example combines the technologies of ASP.NET and ADO.NET by providing a basic registration system for a typical multi-user game environment. The initial web form has a drop-down list of the current registered players and if the user is listed, the action to log on is to enter the correct password. If the user is not a registered player an option is available on the page to request registration as a new player. When a request for registration occurs the page is regenerated with some user controls disabled and additional entry fields active. These new fields allow the new user to enter a name and password. In the description we will also examine the server-side validation technique available as part of the .NET Framework as well as the security technique of forms-based authentication.

Database access from the Web form

After a new user registration, the user is redirected back to the log on page to complete the process. Once a player has successfully logged on they are taken to a new page that in the example does nothing. In any real game application this access page could be used as a portal to the game. A database is used for the storage of user name–password combinations; as in the previous chapter on ADO.NET this has been generated using 'Access' as the RDMS. It contains just one table, however; the technique required to access a database from a web form is the same irrespective of the complexity of the database structure itself.

Player Name	Text
Players Password	Text

No encryption has been used in this example, of course in a real application the passwords should be stored in an encrypted form.

Design considerations

In the chapter on ADO.NET where the examples accessed a database, we used the Visual Studio .NET connectivity wizard to set up the OleDbAdapter. This wizard then automatically sets an OleDbConnection and generates the SQL text strings for the oleDBCommands.

The same approach could be used here, but you have to realise that when a database is going to be accessed programmatically by a user over a WWW connection, the requirements are different to those for a stand-alone application accessing the same database.

Unfortunately the Visual Studio .NET connection wizard has no knowledge of the requirements for WWW access, students can spend many hours looking at very obscure SQL error messages that can finally be traced to incorrect connection setting, causing access permissions errors.

The Internet Anonymous User account on Windows 2000 is used by web Servers for any remote WWW access request to a server resource. Using some of the advanced features of the connection wizard, it is possible to specify this particular user account; however, failure to do this causes the access permissions on the connection string generated to default to your local development account. This automatically generated connection string will fail and as indicated the SQL error message is obscure.

In the example I have constructed the access string manually and this also meant I had to create the SQL command strings. First, let's consider the web form page load event. Based on the requirements specification I have built a drop-down list that is populated from the database, i.e. all currently register users.

```
namespace CSPasswordPage
{
public class WebForm1 : System.Web.UI.Page
{
protected string SelectQuery = "SELECT Passwords.Name FROM Passwords";
protected string InsertQuery = "";
protected OleDbCommand SelectCommand;
protected OleDbCommand InsertCommand;
protected OleDbConnection Connection;
protected OleDbDataReader DataReader;
```

Page_Load(..)
```
private void Page_Load(object sender, System.EventArgs e)
{
// Put user code to initialize the page here
SelectCommand = new OleDbCommand(SelectQuery);
InsertCommand = new OleDbCommand (InsertQuery);
Connection  = new OleDbConnection ("Provider=Microsoft.Jet.OLEDB.4.0;Data
Source=C:\\Inetpub\\wwwroot\\CSpasswordpage\\SPassword.mdb");
SelectCommand.Connection = Connection;
if (!IsPostBack)
        {
            Connection.Open ();
            DataReader = SelectCommand.ExecuteReader();
            while (DataReader.Read ())
                UserNames.Items.Add(DataReader.GetString (0));
        }
Connection.Close();
}
```

The class for this page-bchind code is inherited from System.Web.UI.Page, all web form applications should use this default inheritance.

For clarity I have removed the Visual Studio generated code for the controls set up on the page since these are very similar to the declarations seen in the previous Windows forms examples.

The protected class members declared are to enable the ADO.NET link between this web form and the database to be established. The SelectQuery string has been statically initialised, since it is constant; we only need to select the currently registered players. The InsertQuery on the other hand is initialised to null, its exact content will be dynamically generated when a new registration is requested. For clarity I have used two oleDbCommand variables, SelectCommand and InsertCommand, if you investigate the code you will see that a single variable could have been used as these two variables perform the same function and are never used concurrently.

The oleDbConnection variable Connection is built with a connection string, compared to the strings constructed by the automatic wizard. It is far simpler in many cases this simplified form of connection string is all that is required for a local database connection. It has no user account detail and so will avoid the invalid account problems identified previously. Before attempting to open a connection we set the attribute for the SelectCommand.Connect to the Connection variable.

The web form page attribute Page.IsPostback recovers a value indicating whether the page is being loaded in response to a client post back (i.e. the data values on the page have made a round trip to the server already), or if it is being loaded and accessed for the first time.

The page load event checks on this attribute to ensure that the drop-down list UserNames is only populated when the page is accessed for the first time. Failure to check for this condition results in duplicate entries being created in the list. The connection to the database is opened and the select query executed. The result of the select query is handled by an oleDbDataReader variable called DataReader. In our previous examples of ADO.NET we have used a dataset to recover the result of a select query; however, in this case we need to interrogate the information on a row-by-row basis and the DataReader is a more convenient control to use when dealing with data in this form.

The code uses a while loop to populate the list control from the result of the query. The method DataReader.GetString (o) returns the string value for the first column in a particular row (the use of a specific column number schema for the database fields requires a prior knowledge of the format of the database, this can of course be overcome as we previously investigated by the use of a XML database schema).

Once we have read all of the rows, the loop exits and the database connection is closed. The test database populates the

Figure 10.11   *The list box populated from the test database*

list box as shown in Figure 10.11. The remainder of the requirement for logging on a registered user is:

■ To obtain a password from the user

■ To compare this with the stored password in the database.

A great deal of time and effort are usually needed to write client side scripts to ensure the password boxes etc. are correctly formatted. Within ASP.NET standard validation controls on the server side eliminate this effort. Before we actually look at the password problem, let's review the available validation controls and how to use them.

Server-side validation controls

Server-side validation controls are grouped as a collection and allow the automatic validation of data to be performed server side. These validation controls also offer a standardised mechanism for error detection and message display.

Each validation control performs a specific type of data validation:

■ CompareValidator and RangeValidator.

These controls allow you validate against a specific value or a range of values:

■ CustomValidator.

You can define your own validation criteria by using this control.

As any error messages are created by the validation control, you have control where the message is displayed on the web page by placing the validation control at the desired location. You can also display a summary of the results from all validation controls on the page by using the ValidationSummary control.

Creating a validation event

By default, page validation is performed when an action control, such as Button, ImageButton, or LinkButton, is clicked. You can prevent validation from being performed when such an action control is clicked by setting the CausesValidation property of the button control to false. This property is normally set to false for a cancel or clear button to prevent validation being performed when such an action is requested.

In our particular example we need the password entry to be validated against two criteria:

1   That there is a password value in the associated TextBox

2   That the password is correct.

The first of these requires the use of a RequiredFieldValidator. To use this validation control no programmatic code needs to be written, the validation rules, error messages etc. are set in the visual designer using the properties window.

The second requirement needs a CustomValidator, the basic properties can again be set, but we must also write a validation method that will be executed on the validation request:

```
private void CustomValidator1_ServerValidate(object source,
System.Web.UI.WebControls.ServerValidateEventArgs args)
{
    // we get here to validate the pass word..
    Connection.Open ();
    SelectCommand.CommandText = "SELECT * FROM Passwords WHERE Name ='" +
                Request.Form ["UserNames"].ToString ()+ "'";
    DataReader = SelectCommand.ExecuteReader();
    DataReader.Read();
    if (args.Value == DataReader.GetString (1))
        {
            // valid password
            Password.Text = "";
            Connection.Close();
            Response.Redirect ("Logon.aspx");
        }
    else
            args.IsValid = false;
    Connection.Close();
}
```

This code constructs an SQL select statement using the selected entry in the list as the WHERE clause (this will return a single row from the database). The code then compares the first column of the result with args.Value, the parameter passed into the method that contains, in this case, the text string from the password input control attached to the validator. If these two strings match, the connection to the database is closed, the browser is redirected to the 'LogOn.aspx' page. If they do not match then the args.IsValid property is set to false. Setting the IsValid property to false indicates to the validation control that the validation failed and the error message is displayed. The web form in each of the possible scenarios is shown in Figures 10.12 and 10.13.

In both Figures 10.12 and 10.13 the error messages are in the same position, this is because a ValidationSummary control, which lists all validation error messages, has been placed on the form to group the error messages.

The remainder of this discussion will now look at dealing with a request to register a new player. The action of the New User button on the form un-hides some further text boxes and another button Control.

Note: it is very important that the **New User** button validation action is set to false, otherwise the password entry validation discussed above would attempt to validate on this action as well. Since there would be no user this would create the **error no user password** and it would be impossible to process this New User button click.

Once these new user additional text boxes become active they also require validation controls, to identify:

■ That there is a value in each text box

■ That the two versions of the password entered have the same value.

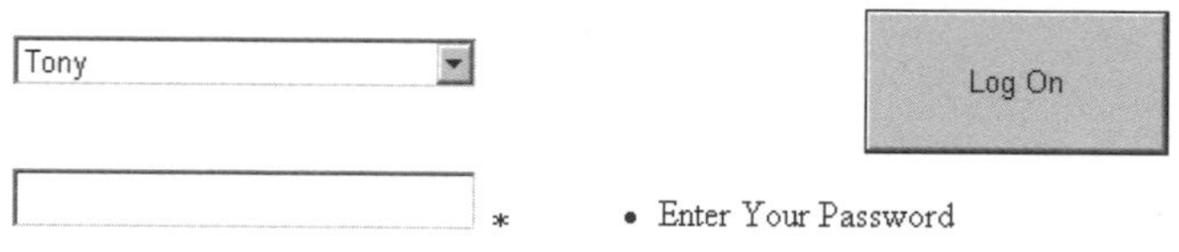

Figure 10.12   The result of no password entered

Figure 10.13   The result of an invalid password entered

The first requires a RequiredFieldValidator. A common mistake is to believe that a RequiredFieldValidator on the confirmation of password text box is also required. In fact it would be a waste, we need a CompareValidator attached instead. CompareValidators are extremely flexible, not only can they perform simple comparisons, they can also perform regular expression analysis allowing specific user input to be checked against specific format requirements; in this case we are simply looking for a match on the two password entries. With this flexibility on validation of data server side the need for specific client side checking is removed.

Is it really that simple?

There is the question of the round trip time required to run server-side validation and the effects of this on any overall system performance requirements. Client side validation may still be the only option if the round trip overhead is too great.

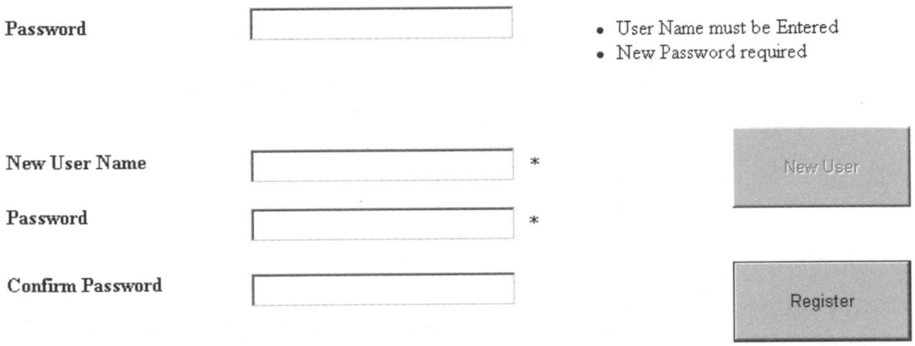

Figure 10.14   Identifying that none of the fields has been entered

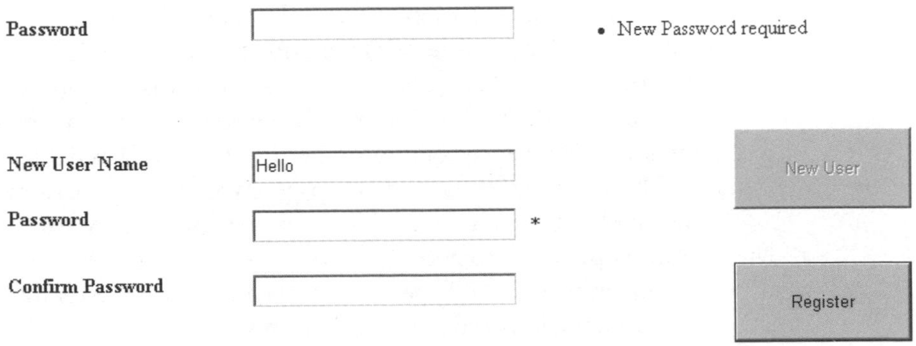

Figure 10.15   Identifying that a password must be entered

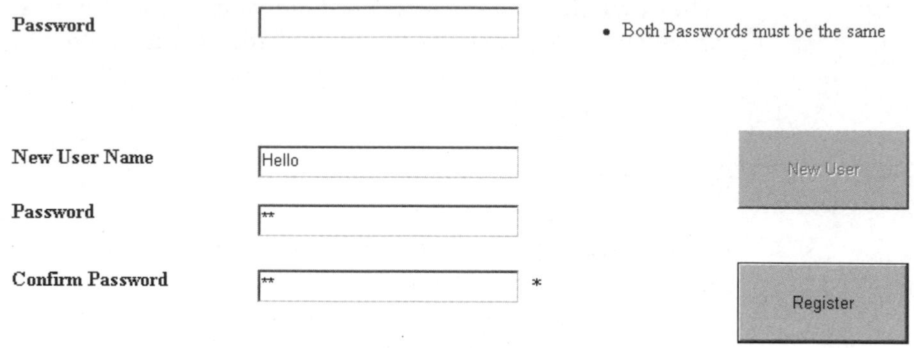

Figure 10.16   Identifying that the password entries do not match

The actual code to insert the database entry for a new player is shown below:

```
private void CmdReg_Click(object sender, System.EventArgs e)
{
// This is what happens when we get a valid set of parameters.
    Connection.Open ();
    InsertCommand.CommandText = "INSERT INTO Passwords ( Name, Pass ) VALUES
(" + "'"+NewName.Text + "','" + NewPassword.Text+"')";
    InsertCommand.Connection = Connection;
    InsertCommand.ExecuteNonQuery ();
    Connection.Close();
    Response.Redirect ("NewUser.aspx");
}
```

The usual problem with this type of SQL is to remember that the values to be inserted must be encased in single quotes. The SQL insert command string will actually look like:

```
INSERT INTO Passwords (Name , Pass) VALUES ('Hello', '123456')
```

The above means put a new row in the table passwords, the field **Name** is to have a value of Hello and the field **Pass** is to have a value of 123456. That completes the basic discussion on this example, the VB.NET solution is very similar, and once again only minor differences of syntax need to be considered.

Although it appears that the page created in this example is quite sophisticated and usable in a validation scenario, what would happen if someone on the web manages to find the LogOn.aspx page and bypasses the player logon page totally?

A mechanism is required to stop this from happening, we are going to use a Cookie, and somehow set the validation of the overall system to check that the Cookie exists on the client machine. This is accomplished by using the technique known as forms authentication, which protects a specific site, or specific pages on a site. Once protected only authenticated users can gain access.

In order to set up the authentication we are going to need to make a change to the solutions specific XML file called Web.config. There is a hierarchical structure of Web.config files within the .NET architecture, this structure is similar to the file permissions structure of a Windows NTFS, but it is far beyond the scope of this chapter to look at the interaction of the Web.config on an enterprise system. We will simply leave the higher-level files with default values and set our authentication at the solutions-level file only.

The section of the file of interest is set up with a default entry:

```
<!-- AUTHENTICATION
This section sets the authentication policies of the application. Possible
modes are "Windows", "Forms","Passport" and "None"
-->
 <authentication mode="None" />
```

The mode of authentication is set to None, any anonymous user can access any pages in this solution without being challenged.

The change we are going to make requests forms-based authentication:

```
<authentication mode="Forms">
  <forms name = "GamesCookie"
      login URL = "CSPasswordForm.aspx" protection = "Encryption"/>
</authentication>

<authentication>
  <deny users = "?"/>
</authentication>
```

These two entry changes in Web.config alter the protection mode of the whole solution, the first change sets the authentication from 'None' to 'Forms' and this specifies that all users of the solution must be validated by a specified form (in this case the password control form just developed).

Within this XML element the attribute name sets the name of a cookie that is created by the authentication form, I have called the cookie 'GamesCookie', the loginUrl attribute defines the form that will create the cookie. If any user attempts to access any page of the application without having this cookie, access will be denied.

The attribute protection also specifies the cookie is built with encryption, the cookie sent to the client machine will therefore be encrypted, anyone attempting to break into the system by creating a dummy cookie of the correct name will be thwarted. The details of the encryption technique used are beyond this introductory text.

In addition the XML authorisation element also uses the optional element deny with an attribute set to the value of '?' indicating that all anonymous users (those without the correct cookie on the machine) are denied all access rights to any page on the solution.

Having changed the Web.config file we need to go back to the password '.aspx' page and make some code adjustments to generate the correct cookie when a valid user logs on. The coding is very straightforward. The method SetAuthCookie(..) takes two parameters, and will create the encrypted authentication cookie.

SetAuthCookie(..)   `public static void SetAuthCookie(string userName,bool createPersistentCookie);`

Parameters   userName
                  The name of an authenticated user. This does not have to map to a Windows account.

                  createPersistentCookie
                  Specifies whether or not a durable cookie (one that is saved across browser sessions) should be issued.

In this case we use the username from the drop-down list, in a similar manner to that for the selection of the correct password from the database as the authentication name. The second parameter will be false, this ensures the cookie created is only valid while the user is in a session (i.e. navigating around the pages of the solution). Once a user moves out of the pages controlled by this authentication option the authentication cookie will become invalid and the whole logon process must be repeated:

```
// valid password
Password.Text = "";
Connection.Close();
FormsAuthentication.SetAuthCookie
            ( Request.Form ["UserNames"].ToString (),false);
Session.Add("name",Request.Form ["UserNames"].ToString ());
Response.Redirect ("Logon.aspx");
```

In addition to creating the cookie, I have in the above code created a session variable allowing any other pages in the solution, to identify who is the currently logged on user. This session variable can therefore be used on the 'Logon.aspx' page, typically in the page load event, to customise the greeting on the form:

```
private void Page_Load(object sender, System.EventArgs e)
{
string Username = "";
    Username = Session["name"].ToString ();
    Welcome.Text = Welcome.Text + "  " + Username;
}
```

The format for reading of a session variable is Variable = Session[key];. In this case the key value is the string we used in the authentication code to set the value. You can have multiple session variables so we could also modify the registration of new users to include session information. Let's make the necessary changes:

```
private void CmdReg_Click(object sender, System.EventArgs e)
{
    // This is what happens when we get a valid set of parameters.
    Connection.Open ();
    InsertCommand.CommandText = "INSERT INTO Passwords ( Name, Pass ) VALUES
(" + "'"+NewName.Text + "','" + NewPassword.Text+"')";
    InsertCommand.Connection = Connection;
    InsertCommand.ExecuteNonQuery ();
    Connection.Close();
    Session.Add("newuser",NewName.Text);
    Session.Add("newpass",NewPassword.Text );
    Response.Redirect ("NewUser.aspx");
}
```

Then in the 'NewUser.aspx' page load event:

```
private void Page_Load(object sender, System.EventArgs e)
{
    UserName.Text = UserName.Text + "  " + Session["newuser"].ToString ();
    Password.Text = Password.Text + "  " + Session["newpass"].ToString ();
}
```

If we test these changes by registering a new user the page does not change to the 'NewUser.aspx'.

Why?

The reason is of course that we have now set forms-based authentication and no cookie is being set in this registration code as we specified in the original design that the user needed to log on after being registered.

If you look at the user drop-down list it does contain the new registered name, this is because the authorisation attempt failed during the requested page redirection and the original page is reloaded rather than being posted back.

We need another mechanism to inform the user that the registration has been successful and that they can now log on. One alternative is to automatically log them on and create the required cookie if the database registration is successful. This would be a solution to the problem but it does mean that the authentication cookie is being created in two places and this is not good practice.

The other alternative is to create some client side indication that the registration was successful. I have so far ignored the generation of any client side scripting, this is not strictly a function of the .NET architecture as it is the browser software that actions such scripts. To solve this dilemma and to maintain our forms authentication model, dynamically creating a client script causing an alert box during page load would completely solve the problem. This can be accomplished by modifying the registration code once again, this time to set only a single session variable:

```
private void CmdReg_Click(object sender, System.EventArgs e)
{
    // This is what happens when we get a valid set of parameters.
    Connection.Open ();
    InsertCommand.CommandText = "INSERT INTO Passwords ( Name, Pass ) VALUES
(" + "'"+NewName.Text + "','" + NewPassword.Text+"')";
    InsertCommand.Connection = Connection;
    InsertCommand.ExecuteNonQuery ();
    Connection.Close();
    Session.Add("newuser",NewName.Text);
    Response.Redirect ("NewUser.aspx");
}
```

Notice I have left the redirection code pointing at a page, this ensures we get an authentication error and a subsequent reload of the password page itself. The actual '.aspx' page called is in fact never used.

To check for new registrations the load page event handler for the password page is changed to include a test for the session variable:

```
private void Page_Load(object sender, System.EventArgs e)
{
    string NewUserName = "";
    SelectCommand = new OleDbCommand(SelectQuery);
    InsertCommand = new OleDbCommand (InsertQuery);
    Connection  = new OleDbConnection ("Provider=Microsoft.Jet.OLEDB.4.0;Data
Source=C:\\Inetpub\\wwwroot\\CSpasswordpage\\SPassword.mdb");
```

```
    SelectCommand.Connection = Connection;
    try
        {
        NewUserName = Session["newuser"].ToString ();
        string message = "<SCRIPT TYPE = \"text/javascript\"> \n";
        message = message + "<!-- \n alert(\"Registration Completed For --  ";
        message = message + NewUserName+ "\");\n //-->\n</SCRIPT>";
        Response.Write (message);
        }
        catch
        {
        // no need to catch here we simple are not at the right point.
        }
if (!IsPostBack)
    {
    Connection.Open ();
    DataReader = SelectCommand.ExecuteReader();
    while (DataReader.Read ())
        UserNames.Items.Add(DataReader.GetString (0));
    }
Connection.Close();
}
```

This new code is contained in a try{}..catch{..} structure. We try to read the session variable set in a registration event, if this fails then nothing additional happens in the catch block and the remaining code executes normally, otherwise if you can read the session variable, a short Java script is created which will cause an alert on the user page as it is rendered. This is then written into the HTML file which is being returned to the client machine. This technique for writing back Java script or actual HTML content to be interpreted by the client machine is not a new feature within ASP.NET or the .NET architecture, it is a standard mechanism that has been used extensively within older ASP solutions.

Summary

This chapter looked at two major topics, networking and ASP.NET. It was never my intention in this book to teach you how to construct the HTML of a web page, that is why the example used required very little client side HTML. The purpose of the two examples in this chapter was to identify that the .NET Framework fully supports both basic networking and the requirement of WWW applications.

I hope that the two examples will give you confidence to explore more fully the features that the .NET Framework and the supplied class libraries offer in terms of both standard and custom designed distributed systems.

The BattleShip game offers a great deal of potential for improvement. The main purpose of the example was to show how elements of previous stand-alone applications could be integrated quite simply into a networked solution.

The web forms application with some of the common errors in ASP.NET identified should help you to attempt some web-based application development of your own.

In the next chapter we will be looking at programmatic access to websites in terms of web services which will naturally lead us to look at some further aspects of both networking and XML.

Review questions

1 Use a client server model to build a game of hangman. The server can create random words and the client can attempt to guess the letters in the word etc.

2 Modify the password validation web application:

a. To allow users to change their passwords

b. To have a maintenance page for an administrative user to remove entries from the database.

11 Web services

In the book so far, all aspects of the solution architecture discussed have revolved around either having a local Windows form (some of the very early examples are console based but a console application is basically a Windows form application with no GUI components), or a basic web page. In both these cases we are in an environment where the majority of the application is being driven from the interaction with a human user. If we take the example of a web development, the basic functionality for the application can be summarised as:

■ The user of the application via a browser interface will make the initial request for the relevant page – http://www.scit. wlv.ac.uk /~cm1918/somepage.aspx

■ The server that received the request is responsible for decoding the request, identifying the location of the resource and formatting a response

■ This resultant response to the browser will be decoded by the browser and then rendered onto the screen on the client machine

■ The human user will then read the information.

In this chapter we are going to move forward and look at solutions that do not directly interact with a user, we will be

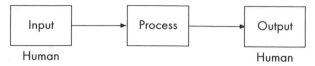

Figure 11.1   *The based process model*

investigating web services and the concept of programmatic access to functionality on a remote machine using standard connections and protocols.

Introduction

In most applications the user is the central point for the application. In the classic definition of a software solution to a problem we tend to draw the simple process diagram we looked at in an earlier chapter. The human rather than a computer program consumes the majority of the requested information.

The long-term ideal for the Internet is that it is everywhere, we can postulate that sooner or later every intelligent device will some how be connected to it. So if web servers could provide data to other computer programs running on these intelligent devices as simply as they provide web pages for browsers to render for human consumption, then the opportunity to utilise web-based communication is greatly enhanced.

This argument can be very simply demonstrated. Many users of the Internet have their email accounts with one of the major ISPs, this means that the ISP has to provide an interface to the user via a standard client browser. This is all very well but compare such User Interfaces (UI) to, for instance, Microsoft's Outlook or Outlook Express, the latter are dedicated clients that have been specifically designed to provide email functionality. Obviously the development of dedicated user interface clients does not come free, there will always be the cost of the additional development effort, but equally the performance of large complex server tasks could be greatly improved if the server did not have to format all of the client pages. Is it better for 50 client machines to do there own formatting or for a single server to format 50 pages at the same time?

There are a vast number of applications that when running on the Internet do not really need a user interface, these again would in most cases see a performance improvement if they are no longer splitting the processing time between the actual algorithmic portion of the task and web page creation. A typical example of an Internet device that does not need a user interface is the Internet telephone, here we are using voice over TCP/IP technology and there is no real need for any user interface pages to be dynamically created by the servers that offer access to such services.

The concept of all Internet access via a generic browser can be likened to many major technological breakthroughs in the past, for instance historically during the industrial revolution a single motive force (steam engine or water wheel) drove all the machines in the factory, if you did not have another power takeoff point you could not add a new machine. This evolved over time to the situation where the motive force was built into each machine and was taken for granted. Such was the impact of this that it removed many of the early limitations on the machines and provided greater flexibility and hence productivity. Today we are seeing the same scenario; new large modern applications are being designed with Internet access built directly within them. These newer applications tend not to use a generic browser technology for the client, rather they have an inbuilt dedicated client interface. The challenge is therefore to make available the technology for such developments that allow integrated Internet access without imposing any constraints.

Making such technologies available led some authors in the mid-1990s to put forward the vision that all new applications could be user configured by taking pre-built components from favoured local machine applications and gluing them together.

Producing a technology for such a concept can be investigated from two perspectives, first, it must provide the programmer with a mechanism that allows fast and effective techniques for the implementation of reusable components and second, it must have available an architecture that will allow these components to share data. The .NET architecture is not unique in offering a possible method of achieving these two goals. We can trace technology solutions back to the concepts of RPC (Remote Procedural Calling), leading to the original specification for OLE, which evolved and was enhanced into COM and subsequently DCOM (we have already discussed such componentware technologies in an earlier chapter). These technologies had one major flaw; they normally only worked transparently if all of the components involved were developed on a similar operating system. Many hundreds if not thousands of man-hours have been used to glue together and successfully integrate components developed on different systems.

Another approach that emerged was the CORBA (Common Object Request Brokerage) initiative; this comprises a set of standards that attempts to overcome vendor or hardware platform specifics. The problem with CORBA is its overall complexity and the reluctance of some suppliers to bring their own interworking technologies into line.

What is really needed is a universal solution to the programmatic access from one box on the Internet to another box on the Internet. Once such access is established the first could make use of functionality on the second and vice versa. The access must be totally independent of the programming language used to develop the component and equally important there should be no dependence on the programming language being used to integrate the components together.

In addition and equally as important as this language independence, the interoperability of the application and the components must be abstracted away from the hardware platform or the underlying operating system. This is quite a tall order when we consider interoperability, the typical user who is trying to integrate different vendors' applications on a stand-alone desktop machine may waste many hours of experimentation only to discover the two applications cannot communicate.

We have already seen that the .NET Framework offers technologies for both stand-alone applications as well as web-based solutions that implicitly meet most of these requirements.

As an example of the problem of universal programmatic access to the Internet, David Platt in his original text on the concepts of the .NET Framework uses the parallel of international air traffic control systems. He argues that the problem of obtaining the agreement from all the interested parties and then defining the necessary standards to implement such a set of protocols can be reduced to finding the lowest common denominators. In the case of the air traffic system these were defined as using designated VHF radio bands and that English would be the only language used.

Platt then goes on to identify how within the .NET solutions architecture there is a need to identify the lowest common denominators for component integration. The result put forward is that to offer universal programmatic access via a network or the web the most import items to consider are the protocol and the description of data:

■ HTTP – the Hyper Text Transfer Protocol based on its almost universal use for web browsing

■ XML – the Extensible Markup Language that as we discussed in another chapter allows the description of the information being transferred from one system to another.

Personally I would add another influential factor, the use of some universal descriptive protocol SOAP (Simple Object Access Protocol) allowing the creation of complex data object requests within simple HTTP messages. From this analysis we can draw up one conclusion – to be able to use web services using the .NET architecture we must have:

■ An understanding of the prefabricated structure of the framework.

In the previous chapters I have outlined many of the technologies that are built into the framework. Once you understand the basics, this knowledge can be used to design and extend the solutions into web services. We have seen a .NET Framework has many key aspects vital to web services built directly into its structure:

■ The framework offers a VM that has been specifically designed for the environment

■ The supported languages have been integrated fully within the framework

■ Once you are able to write applications using Windows forms, it is a simple task to expand these applications into web forms

■ The extension to any design to make a .NET component continue to follow the same basic guidelines used to develop a stand-alone application

■ ASP.NET offers a further integrated technology to make applications web based.

A web service can therefore be defined as:

Any .NET component or collection of components that can be accessed directly via the HTTP protocol.

The nature of the client accessing the web service is irrelevant, it may be a standard web browser, or alternatively it could be a custom application. The support available in the .NET Framework for a web service development is extensive, the ability to automatically hook web services to a prefabricated infrastructure that will accept incoming requests via HTTP packets and transmit data back using HTTP packets is the major contributory factor to the ease with which .NET web services can be built.

With all of this support to transform a .NET application or component into a web service makes such a development task no more difficult than developing a stand-alone solution. There are obviously differences between a standard application development and a web service development:

■ Web services are constrained by resource limitations.

We cannot take it for granted that an application can always be transformed into a web service with zero effort, but in the following examples we will take aspects of previously developed solutions and apply the necessary alterations to construct some simple demonstration of the technique.

Is it really that simple?

In theory probably yes, the dream of being able to interconnect any componentware to any other componentware using HTTP and XML as the glue has at last been achieved or so it would seem. Undoubtedly the Microsoft .NET Framework development team feel that they have taken a giant step towards the theoretical goal; however, some aspects of the practicality of such a system have to be considered.

Similar claims for both DCOM and CORBA were made but practical limitations were very soon realised. It is true to say that the .NET Framework has by its use of the CTS, removed many of the data manipulation pitfalls that these earlier componentware techniques suffered. The CTS, combined with the requirement that compliant languages are derived based on the CTS specification, has removed the dread of all developers, the variant type and its mystical powers to covert to any other data type.

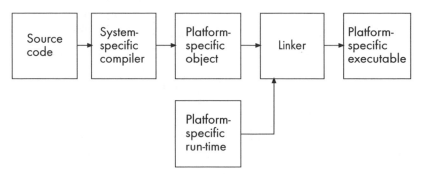

Figure 11.2　　　　The conventional development scenario

Linkage problems

One major obstacle still needs investigation, the linking of a remote client request to the correct functionality in a web service. In order to explain why this is a problem we must first review the subject of early and late binding of external functionality.

In a conventional software development environment – we looked at this in detail in an earlier chapter – the process involved in software development was described by a diagram of the form as shown in Figure 11.2.

Early binding

Figure 11.2 is the model in which all external functionality associated with a particular application's object code is linked with the definitions for external objects (components) during the initial linkage stage. In order to accomplish this we need to use platform dependent run-time support libraries. We have already discussed that the .NET architecture modifies the development process for an application to encompass JIT techniques.

Figure 11.3 shows that for any conventional stand-alone application built to execute in the .NET Framework, the application's assembly combined with the .NET class library now fully define the executable code; each method whether it is from the application assembly or the class library is JIT compiled as needed.

If the application is the client of a web service, however, this idea of full definition during the loading and subsequent JIT compilation is not possible. The component in the web service

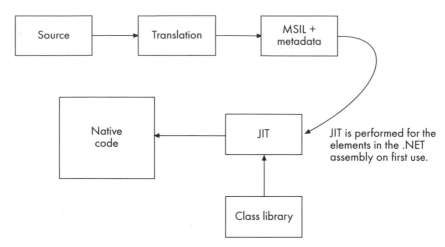

Figure 11.3   The .NET model

along with any specific run time for that component may be somewhere across the Internet.

In the conventional case where all external references are resolved during the build we call the system early bound. This second case the external service scenario, where a client application is using external functionality, requires a technique called late binding.

Late binding

In late binding the required functionality will have to finally link to the client as the client executes. This problem of late binding must be addressed during the development, a mechanism is needed that allows the build process to complete without errors (i.e. all of the external linkage must be resolved).

This requirement is not unique to componentware or web service development, standard applications that use functionality found in specialist Dynamic Link Libraries (DLLs), also require late binding. Using one of two methods generally solves the problem of late binding to a DLL:

■ The first approach is to ignore the external references altogether and use a technique whereby the application loads the library at run time.

I briefly discussed this mechanism when we looked at interoperability issues and our simple example of using the standard Windows 'cards.dll'. The concept is quite simple, the client enumerates the available functionality from the external reference and using pointer techniques selects and executes the correct method.

Such an approach in the .NET architecture would remove any concept of a managed code environment. A function pointer (or for that matter any generalised pointer) is not defined within the CTS specification. Pointer references always imply unmanaged access to any memory locations, so we are dealing with an unmanaged code environment if we pursue this approach:

■ The second approach is to resolve external references at run time using some form of a proxy stub library.

The proxy satisfies the external linkage requirement during development and can also provide type translation and data marshalling (ordering of parameter passing etc.) services to/from the external code.

In the case of a web service this proxy will construct during external requests the relevant SOAP packets and interpret the response SOAP packets to pass them back to the client. In this manner it is the proxy, which is built from within the prefabricated structure of .NET rather than the client application, that provides the ability for the solution to be HTTP aware.

In order to build and use a proxy technique, the web service must provide a description which identifies:

■ What it can do

■ The exposed methods

■ The parameters that need to be passed into or are returned by these methods.

The descriptive technique used in the .NET Framework is not unlike the type library found within componentware models such as COM. One of the major criticisms of the descriptive technique in componentware built using COM was the fact that this description needed to be locally registered on the client before the object could be used. The .NET descriptions, however, in common with all software running in the .NET Framework are built into the assembly manifest and eliminate any registration requirement.

The proxy description for a web service is stored as a structured XML DOM and uses vocabulary that conforms to the WSDL (Web Service Descriptor Language) specification. In some other texts you may find this is referred to as the contract because it lists all the things that the web service is capable of doing and identifies how a client can make use of them.

In order to explain how to create a web service we will take a simple example previously developed in an earlier chapter and using a 'localhost' web server, redevelop this functionality as a web service. Once this web service is developed we can then build two client applications:

1   The first as a standard Windows form extended to be HTTP aware

2   The other as an ASP.NET solution.

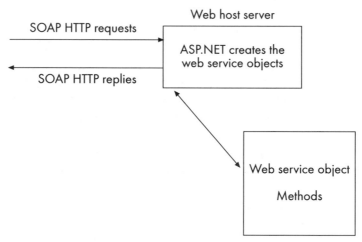

Figure 11.4   *Server side components in a web service*

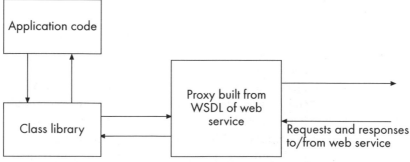

Figure 11.5   *Client-side components in a web service*

Example 309

Example

Objective

To demonstrate the design of a web service and the development of web service clients to test this web service

Specification

The web service will allow a client to connect and

■ Identify if a user is already registered and log on

■ Register a new user:

The client applications will:

■ Interface and exercise the web methods exposed by the service.

Web service design

Initially the web service will have only two methods exposed:

1   IsUser (..)   Input Parameters – Name and Password
                    Returns a Boolean

2   NewUser(..) Input Parameters – Name and Password
                    Returns a Boolean

The database will be accessed using the techniques discussed in the web forms chapter. The requirement for the database access will not be discussed again here. The following code is a typical implementation of this service in C#:

```
namespace CSPasswordService
{
[WebService(Namespace="http://TonyGrimer.com/webservices/",Description =
"Converted the Web form application to a Service")]
// Define this Service as part of my namespace.
public class CSPasswordService : System.Web.Services.WebService
{
    private OleDbCommand SelectCommand;
    private OleDbCommand InsertCommand;
    private OleDbConnection Connection;
    private OleDbDataReader DataReader;
    public CSPasswordService()
    {
    //CODEGEN: This call is required by the ASP.NET Web Services Designer
    InitializeComponent();
    }
#region Component Designer generated code
    private IContainer components = null;
    private void InitializeComponent()
```

```
    {
    }
    protected override void Dispose( bool disposing )
    {
    if(disposing && components != null)
        {
        components.Dispose();
        }
    base.Dispose(disposing);
    }
#endregion
private void MakeSelectConnection(string SQLCommand)
    {
    // this method is not exposed it makes the data base connection
    SelectCommand = new OleDbCommand(SQLCommand);
    Connection  = new OleDbConnection
    ("Provider=Microsoft.Jet.OLEDB.4.0;Data
    Source=C:\\Inetpub\\wwwroot\\CSPasswordService\\SPassword.mdb");
    SelectCommand.Connection = Connection;
    Connection.Open ();
    }
private void MakeInsertConnection(string SQLCommand)
    {
    // this method is not exposed it makes the data base connection
    InsertCommand = new OleDbCommand(SQLCommand);
    Connection  = new OleDbConnection
    ("Provider=Microsoft.Jet.OLEDB.4.0;Data
    Source=C:\\Inetpub\\wwwroot\\CSPasswordService\\SPassword.mdb");
    InsertCommand.Connection = Connection;
    Connection.Open ();
    }
[WebMethod (Description = " Method to validate a user against the DDase ")]
public bool IsUser( string Name, string Pass)
    {
    MakeSelectConnection("SELECT * FROM Passwords");
    // make the connection
    DataReader = SelectCommand.ExecuteReader();
    while (DataReader.Read ())
    {
    if ((DataReader.GetString (0) == Name)&&
                            (DataReader.GetString (1) == Pass))
        { //// both match
        Connection.Close ();
        return true;
        }
    }
    Connection.Close();
    // match Not Found
    return false;
    }
[WebMethod (Description = " Method to Insert a New user into the Data base ")]
public bool NewUser( string Name, string Pass)
```

Example   311

```
{
try
{
MakeInsertConnection("INSERT INTO Passwords ( Name, Pass ) VALUES
    (" + "'"+ Name + "','" + Pass+"')");
// make the connection
InsertCommand.ExecuteNonQuery ();
Connection.Close();
return true;
}
catch
{
return false;
}
}


}
}
```

You may be surprised just how little code is required to offer web service functionality. For clarity I have removed some of the auto generated comments from Visual Studio .NET.

The important areas within this implementation are those that identify this application as a web service.

■ Naming and defining this web service within a specific namespace URL

■ Inherit this service from System.Web.Services.WebService.

These declarations are:

```
[WebService(Namespace="http://TonyGrimer.com/webservices/",Description =
"Converted the Web form application to a Service")]
// Define this Service as part of my namespace.
public class CSPasswordService : System.Web.Services.WebService
```

Within the basic class of the service the data declarations are for the ADO.NET objects to access the database.

No additional code has been added to the class constructor in this case but you may notice that even though a web service has no visual component, the structure of the initialisation and dispose methods follow the .NET Framework requirements we have seen in all the previous examples.

The declaration of the exposed service methods:

```
[WebMethod (Description = " Method to validate a user against the DBase ")]
public bool IsUser( string Name, string Pass) {......}
```

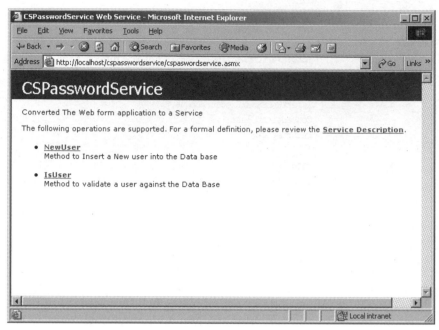

Figure 11.6   The basic description of our simple web service

This declaration identifies a web method, we have a brief description and then a typical method prototype. Investigation of the class code will show that private methods, i.e. not exposed as web methods, are also used, these perform the actual database connectivity etc. Testing a newly built web service could not be simpler; we simply request the page address from an appropriate web server:

http://localhost/cspasswordservice/cspaswordservice.asmx

The .NET Framework generates the page for the service shown in Figure 11.6 automatically. This page uses our service and method descriptions to be used to invoke and test the service itself.

In Figure 11.7 we have requested activation of the NewUser(..) method on this web service. You can see that the description has generated a page that allows us to test the functionality of the method by input of suitable parameters.

Figure 11.8 shows the reply from the service. The parameters sent are part of the URL, in this case the NewUser(..) method has returned a true response, indicating that this new user has been accepted and the parameter data has been input to the database.

Example

313

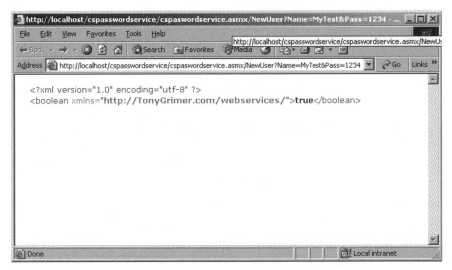

Figure 11.7   *Activation of New User Method within the browser window*

Figure 11.8   *Response from the web service to a NewUser Request*

It is important to emphasise that for such developments if you want to use remote debugging from, for instance, Visual Studio .NET, the web server must have been configured with the extensions that are part of the .NET Framework. These extensions allow the web service to execute in the .NET environment and they interpret the prefabricated infrastructure descriptions etc. This ability to interpret, execute and render useful information is a far cry from the very crude object container model that was available with a COM object for testing purposes.

It is also very important to understand that such objects (components) no longer need registry entries associated with them during the installation procedure. Using the URI and URL approach, to access web services reinforces the lowest common denominator hypothesis that we can construct the service totally within the prefabricated architecture.

In common with all software development your initial solution will probably not be the final solution, a number of iterations will be needed. Modification of such solutions in the past has been a long and in some cases tedious exercise.

In the .NET Framework maintenance or update is a simple process, the revised web service is copied over the original. The change in functionality is instant; in fact to see the effect of the change you only need to refresh the page request from the associated client. In comparison to this, if you try to upgrade a similar COM component the modified object would have needed the following:

■ To be unregistered so that previous entries are removed from the registry

■ The new version would then have needed installation

■ New entries to the registry need to be created

■ In some very extreme cases, the actual web server itself would have had to be stopped and restarted.

Self-description for web services

We have already concluded that any web services would be of little use if there were not a mechanism for remote clients to obtain a working knowledge of the functionality within the service. The technique outlined above of trying out the service using a browser could be used, but this only gives an overview, it is often quite slow and offers no automation to the process.

Realistically, therefore, this is not an option when a new client is being developed. A far more logical approach is for the web service to provide a mechanism for obtaining a detailed description.

Obviously, this could be a simple text document explaining the functionality, but a standard format which is both human- and machine-readable offers a far more reasonable degree of flexibility. The WSDL (Web Service Descriptor Language) is such a standard format, the client of a web service can read the WSDL in order to identify the methods the service exposes, the parameters these require, and the protocols that are supported. In fact that is how in the previous example the browser is interpreting the information. As already identified the WDSL is a very similar technique to the IDL used to create the type library used by COM components.

WSDL is based on the XML DOM using a defined standard vocabulary, resulting in the descriptions being both human- and machine-readable. Most modern software development environments can now be described as 'intelligent', they read and write additional files that describe the project or solution currently under development.

Having this intelligence, coupled with the WSDL description of the web service, will assist most development environments to extract the WSDL from the service and use the information gained, to simplify the implementation of the clients. It is a simple matter to get the WSDL file from a particular web service using our example above, simply modify the URL to:

http://localhost/cspasswordservice/cspaswordservice.asmx?WSDL

The full WSDL file for this service is quite complex and daunting, an extract is shown in Figure 11.9. It is really not important to understand the WSDL, you only need to be aware that it is available and can be used. Although any client of the web service could deal with the raw WSDL file, it is far more appropriate to make use of any available tools to create the proxy to the service. Once the proxy is available clients can reference the proxy and avoid any direct reference to WSDL.

In the .NET SDK command line tool kit, the utility, 'wsdl.exe' is available to create a proxy, but the command line tool is quite difficult to use. Fortunately an alternative approach exists within Visual Studio .NET, you can specify a web reference to the service you wish to use and provided the development machine has access to the resource it will generate a complete proxy directly into the project under development.

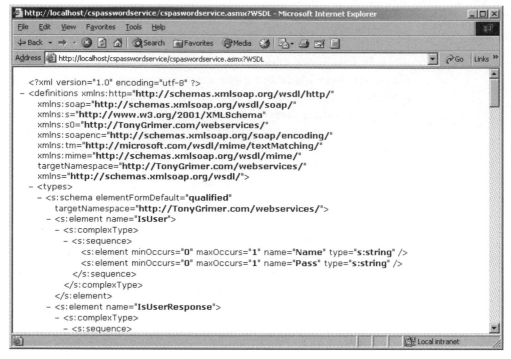

Figure 11.9   The WSDL for our simple example

Using VS.NET to create the proxy

To create the proxy, start a Windows forms application development project (this will be the client), and in this case I have selected VB.NET as the language. In the solutions explorer window where in previous examples we added component references this time we add a web reference, the form in Figure 11.10 in the request dialogue we direct the reference to built service.

Once the service has been selected VS.NET will display the automatically generated page we saw in the last section. Clicking on Add Reference creates the new entry in the solutions explorer as shown in Figure 11.11.

This new entry in the solutions explorer defines the WSDL etc., and the proxy files for the service under the general heading 'localhost' (i.e. in this case the web server is on the local machine). If you are interested explore the project directory and find the actual VB.NET Files that are auto generated by this reference (the actual definition of the proxy methods). In this case

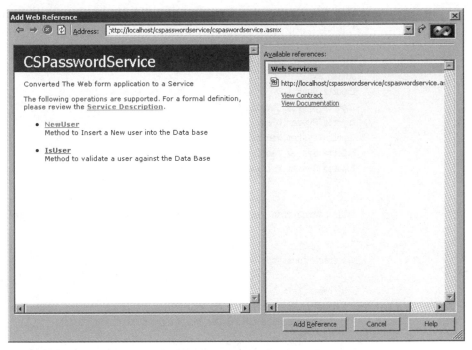

Figure 11.10   *Selecting a service in the service reference dialogue*

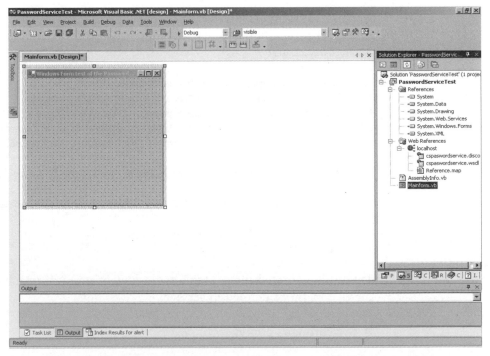

Figure 11.11   *The new reference to the web service in the solutions explorer*

this file is called reference.vb. Its contents are fairly standard VB.NET code, an extract is shown below:

```
Option Strict Off
Option Explicit On
Imports System
Imports System.ComponentModel
Imports System.Diagnostics
Imports System.Web.Services
Imports System.Web.Services.Protocols
Imports System.Xml.Serialization


'
'This source code was auto-generated by Microsoft.VSDesigner, Version
1.0.3705.0.
'
Namespace localhost

    '<remarks/>
    <System.Diagnostics.DebuggerStepThroughAttribute(),  _
     System.ComponentModel.DesignerCategoryAttribute("code"),  _

System.Web.Services.WebServiceBindingAttribute(Name:="CSPasswordServiceSoap"
, [Namespace]:="http://TonyGrimer.com/webservices/")>  _
    Public Class CSPasswordService
        Inherits System.Web.Services.Protocols.SoapHttpClientProtocol
        Public Sub New()
            MyBase.New
            Me.Url = "http://localhost/cspasswordservice/
cspaswordservice.asmx"
        End Sub
<System.Web.Services.Protocols.SoapDocumentMethodAttribute _
("http://TonyGrimer.com/webservices/IsUser", RequestNamespace:="http://
TonyGrimer.com/webservices/", ResponseNamespace:="http://TonyGrimer.com/
webservices/", Use:=System.Web.Services.Description.SoapBindingUse.Literal,
ParameterStyle:=System.Web.Services.Protocols.SoapParameterStyle.Wrapped)>
 _
        Public Function IsUser(ByVal Name As String, ByVal Pass As String) As
Boolean
            Dim results() As Object = Me.Invoke("IsUser", New Object() {Name,
Pass})
            Return CType(results(0),Boolean)
        End Function
```

The auto-generated file contains two types of proxy for each of the web methods defined in service:

■ Synchronous proxys

■ Asynchronous proxys.

The first synchronous proxy allows requests to be sent by the client, the client will then wait for a reply. Obviously, if we are accessing the service across the WWW large delays could occur.

The alternatively asynchronous proxy provides two methods for each web method:

■ The first is the request method that returns immediately

■ The second is the recover method to obtain the result for a particular request.

Asynchronous operation requires the use of a multi-threaded design for the client, the requirement is very similar to our example in a previous chapter for the battleships game. It is beyond the scope of this material to look any further into the multi-thread design requirement for asynchronous service clients.

Windows client design

Continuing with the VB.NET Windows Client design the simplest choice is to use synchronous proxy options. The implementation of this client application has few specialist areas, the majority of the code is common to all the examples previously investigated.

In order to access the web service we only need to import the namespace, declare a variable and initialise the service for use:

```
Imports PasswordServiceTest.localhost
Public Class mainform
    Inherits System.Windows.Forms.Form
    Private PassWordService As CSPasswordService
#Region " Windows Form Designer generated code "
    Public Sub New()
        MyBase.New()
        InitializeComponent()
        PassWordService = New CSPasswordService()
```

It is important that in the case of a web service you call the constructor to initialise the service, without making this call no reference will be created between the client and the service. The two web methods in the service are called from the event handlers for the buttons on the form. Below is a call to IsUser(..) with a name and a password extracted from the text boxes on the form:

```
If (PassWordService.IsUser(user.Text, UserPassword.Text)) Then
    MessageBox.Show(" User Verified", "Log On")
```

Notice we are implying the need for a true response, the web service you may recall is written in C# in this case, but the code is looking at a true response within VB.NET. Once again this identifies the importance to the .NET Framework of the CTS, we do not need to concern ourselves with the definition of the Boolean true, because in both cases C# and VB.NET we are manipulating the same core CTS data type.

The other web method NewUser is called in exactly the same manner:

```
If (PassWordService.NewUser(user.Text, UserPassword.Text)) Then
    MessageBox.Show("New User Added Please Log On", "New User")
```

The remainder of this test application has the menu system implemented as standard for all examples within this book. The only other code in this example is some rather crude data validation routines to ensure we do not pass over invalid fields to the service.

Having tested the web service with a standalone application we can now investigate using the web service from a web application. Once again we already have a web application written in the previous chapter. This interacted with a database, so the redevelopment of this, uses much of the previous code and seems an obvious approach in this case.

Web client design

We will need to create a web reference in our web application project, this is accomplished in exactly the same manner as for the Windows application. A new reference appears in the solution explorer and if we look at the auto-generated file, in this case 'reference.cs', in the project directory we have proxy methods, generated in this case in C#:

```
namespace CSTestPassService.localhost {
    using System.Diagnostics;
    using System.Xml.Serialization;
    using System;
    using System.Web.Services.Protocols;
    using System.ComponentModel;
    using System.Web.Services;

    [System.Diagnostics.DebuggerStepThroughAttribute()]
    [System.ComponentModel.DesignerCategoryAttribute("code")]

[System.Web.Services.WebServiceBindingAttribute(Name="CSPasswordServiceSoap"
```

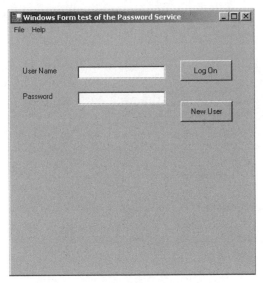

Figure 11.12   *A Windows-based client for the web service*

```
, Namespace="http://TonyGrimer.com/webservices/")]
    public class CSPasswordService :
System.Web.Services.Protocols.SoapHttpClientProtocol {

        public CSPasswordService() {
            this.Url = "http://localhost/cspasswordservice/
cspaswordservice.asmx";
        }
    [System.Web.Services.Protocols.SoapDocumentMethodAttribute("http://
TonyGrimer.com/webservices/IsUser", RequestNamespace="http://TonyGrimer.com/
webservices/", ResponseNamespace="http://TonyGrimer.com/webservices/",
Use=System.Web.Services.Description.SoapBindingUse.Literal,
ParameterStyle=System.Web.Services.Protocols.SoapParameterStyle.Wrapped)]
        public bool IsUser(string Name, string Pass) {
            object[] results = this.Invoke("IsUser", new object[] {
                    Name,
                    Pass});
            return ((bool)(results[0]));
        }
    }
```

A simple comparison of this proxy code with the previous auto-generated proxy code for a Windows form application shows full compatibility. This similarity strengthens the premise that building web services within a prefabricated framework ensures compliance:

**using the lowest common denominators of
SOAP, HTTP and XML it is possible to build**

WWW services, applications and specialist clients that seamlessly integrate with each other.

The use of the web service from within the web application is again similar to web service use from a stand-alone application. For instance to call the web method IsUser(..) from the web application the code in C# is:

```
if (PasswordService.IsUser (UserNames.Text, Password.Text))
        {
        // valid password
```

Similarly to call the NewUser web method we use the code:

```
PasswordService.NewUser (NewName.Text,NewPassword.Text);
```

Summary

In this chapter we have introduced probably one of the most important aspects of the .NET Framework, the web services. With such a powerful set of facilities the whole debate on scalability of such frameworks is encapsulated in a nutshell. We have investigated the framework infrastructure, and shown that the framework allows the integration of previously complex tasks such as web-based components usage to be no more complicated than stand-alone application development.

As a definition a web service can be viewed as a .NET class, stored on some remote machine, with the ability to be accessed using Remote Procedure Call techniques. The use of SOAP and the associated XML definition of the functionality available on the remote site, coupled with the use of HTTP as a transport protocol, opens the way for very large-scale system design incorporating web services.

In order to identify how the web service methods are accessed the whole service can be described or indexed using the WSDL (Web Service Description Language), which is a fixed vocabulary XML structured document.

Intelligent development environments such as Visual Studio .NET utilise this WSDL to develop a proxy technique ensuring external clients have the ability to access the functionality within the service. The proxy can in fact serve two purposes: first, it ensures that the client programs can satisfy all references during the development phase when the service may not be fully available and second, it is the prefabricated structure that translates the outgoing and incoming SOAP packets to a suitable data form for both the client and the web service.

Development of any web service requires access to a local or remote web server, in the examples I used a 'local host' installed on a Windows 2000 platform. Appendix A shows a possible alternative, the WebMatrix product, which avoids the complication of setting up the Internet information server on your local machine.

A benefit of using Visual Studio, is the option to display in Internet Explorer the WSDL descriptions of any web service. This facilitates the very quick check on the functionality of web methods via a simple browser interface.

In the next chapter we will be taking all the investigated technologies of the .NET Framework and applying them to a multi-tier solution. The case study presented shows how, by using the knowledge gained, it is possible within the .NET Framework to develop a non-trivial solution to a distributed system-based requirement.

Review questions

1 One aspect of the whole topic of web services not looked at in this chapter is UDDI (Universal Description, Discovery and Integration) and disco (Discovery) files. When you look at the solution for any of the examples these files are available, research what they offer.

2 Answer the following questions:

a. Why are messages to/from the web service created as SOAP packets?

b. Why is HTTP the most common Internet protocol?

c. Could FTP be used as the transfer protocol for web service messages and what, if any, would be the advantages?

3 Write a simple web service to throw a dice. Any client should be able to request how many dice to throw, and then throw the dice and be told the total. Use the browser technique to debug and test the methods and prove it is working.

4 Extend the solution of Question 3 and write a simple client application to display the result of the dice throws.

12 The case study

Objective

In the previous chapters each technology built into the .NET architecture has been viewed as a unique entity with suitable examples to illustrate the use of the technologies. At this point you may remember that most of the examples have been leading towards this final case study; this was outlined in the discussions in the first chapter. All of the previous examples were intentionally designed to allow them to be executed as a complete solution; however, they have also been designed to be functional parts of much bigger solutions if required. In the first chapter an attempt was made to define a unique description covering all aspects of the technologies found within the .NET architecture, this case study brings such a description to life.

Microsoft's assertion is that the .NET architecture is a solutions framework, a framework that can span from simple stand-alone desktop application development right up to enterprise-level multi-tiered distributed systems. This case study shows that this is probably a realistic definition. The case study will take aspects of the previous examples, in which we identified how the .NET architecture solved specific problems, and expands on the functionality as needed, with the overall goal of building a complete tiered distributed system. The final solution allows a simple multi-player game to execute as a web service identifying the potential of such an architecture across a network or even the WWW.

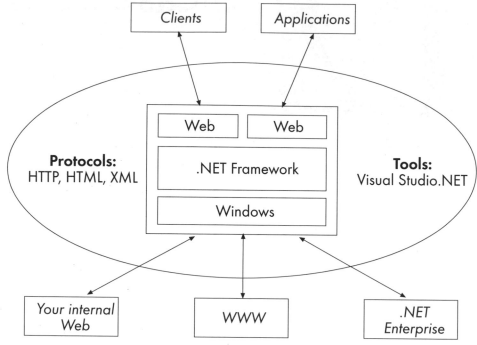

Figure 12.1   The .NET architecture

Introduction

In the context of the previous chapters, it has been necessary to explain a vast amount of new concepts. The layout of these chapters is such that I have tried to look in a logical order at the interesting technologies that fit into the jigsaw which as a whole is the prefabricated framework. Using this framework-based architecture allows the development of anything from a stand-alone application to a distributed system using a common set of components.

You may feel I have not covered some aspects as fully as others or equally I spent too much time on a particular point. To redress this balance, this case study is going to develop a fairly comprehensive solution to what would initially seem a non-trivial problem.

It is based on a distributed multi-tier system using a simple 'Access' database linked into a web service, with a specifically designed client application. A .NET component developed in an earlier chapter is integrated into the web service, and the interoperability component from another of the earlier chapters is used in the client application. This design highlights the ability to reuse .NET software in such a manner and the benefits of building within a prefabricated structure.

The actual web service has deliberately been kept simple. Its design offers a great deal of potential for further development in the future, meaning that you can experiment with a tiered solution in a limited resource environment.

The client for the service has also been kept relatively simple, again offering the potential for further work, but equally the simplified design, for instance of the GUI, ensures that there is no design distraction from the important aspects of a scalable solution.

To avoid any bias on the implementation, each part of the three-tier solution is presented in both VB.NET and C#. In fact the two components identified above and developed in the earlier chapters have already been implemented using both languages enabling you to mix and match a complete range of final solutions.

This is of course a very simplified distributed system. However, in designing and describing the solution, the pieces of a much more complex jigsaw are being fitted together.

The problem

The choice of a card game allows you to relate to the final solution and offers the ability to experiment with such ideas. Traditionally multi-tier systems examples are very complex. In the main the physical resource requirements are large, using, for instance, an e-commerce system to demonstrate the key aspects offers little scope for any student to experiment with the implementation.

In contrast, I am sure most of you have played the game of 'Pontoon' at some time. Its rules are simple, the aim is to get your hand of cards closer to the value 21 than the dealer. In the USA the game has slightly modified rules and is called Blackjack, while in Europe there is a variant of the game played in the casinos called Baccarat. First let's review a basic requirement specification.

Specification

Create and shuffle a deck of playing cards

- The dealer can always be defined as the computer player

- Deal two cards to each player including the dealer

■ Allow the players to request a further card be added to their hand

■ Calculate the totals held by each player using the rules

■ Picture cards (Jack, Queen or King) have a value of 10

■ Face cards have the value they show

■ Any Ace can be counted as a 1 or a 10

■ Once all players have finished and declared they are 'sticking'. Calculate the winners

■ If a player has the same total as the dealer, the dealer beats the player.

These are the most basic requirements but they will suffice for our design study. Other rules, if implemented, could make the game more interesting and to give you the opportunity to experiment could include:

Additional features

■ 'Pontoon' is a face card and an ace and can only be beaten by a dealer's 'Pontoon'

■ Five cards with a total of less than 21 is a 'five card trick' and can only be beaten by a 'pontoon'

■ If a player is dealt two identical cards initially these can be 'split' and the player has the option to play them as two separate hands

■ Getting to a total of 21 by having three face cards each with the value seven is an unbeatable hand.

Similarly gambling rules could also be considered, these offer you the ability to write a further .NET component to integrate into the final web service. The following are some basic guidelines that you may wish to consider:

Optional features

■ Each player is given an initial stake

■ For each hand of cards the player must select an amount to gamble (the stake) before each hand is dealt

■ If the player loses the stake is lost.

■ The player will win from the dealer the value of his stake unless the winning hand is 'pontoon', 'a five card trick', or the unbeatable 'three sevens hand' when the player wins twice his stake

■ Each player can elect to 'buy' another card rather than simply to 'twist'; to 'buy' another card the player must increase his stake.

The above enhancements are worth considering. Once the basic implementation discussed for this development has been understood, such modifications will give you the opportunity to investigate the framework more fully and will naturally require changes to the design of all three aspects of the multi-tier solution.

'Pontoon' the web service

This web service design has been based on the key requirements outlined above. It allows multiple clients to connect and play in a single game of 'Pontoon'. This concept of all connected clients playing in a single game brings with it some further design considerations which identify other aspects of the prefabricated structure of the .NET Framework.

The design will obviously utilise the lowest common denominators rule for any web service discussed in previous chapters, the functionality will be described using XML, and SOAP formatted requests will be made by the client to the service using the HTTP protocol.

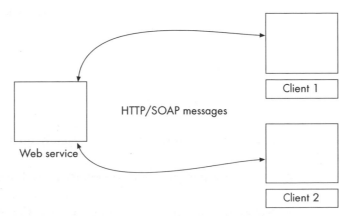

Figure 12.2   *An outline overall structure of the case study*

Allowing external programmatic access to any application is an intrinsic part of the .NET Framework and it is only necessary to specify the functionality to be exposed by the web service and to create the necessary proxy information once the basic algorithmic solution is completed. The result will be the generation of a web service that any client can reference and use.

We can extract from the examples in other chapters of the book some aspects of the required functionality:

- Card Game control – used within the actual service:

  ❏ The card game control offers the creation, shuffling and maintaining of the status of dealt hands of playing cards

- Card Display control – used by the client:

  ❏ The display control used the interoperability with WIN32 API services to gain access to the inbuilt 'cards.dll' for displaying playing cards.

- ADO.NET – used by the web service:

  ❏ ADO.NET looked at accessing a database and the concepts of forms based authentication.

It is now possible to redefine our basic 'pontoon' game as a web service in the follolwing terms:

- Create a unique pack of cards

- Shuffle the cards, monitor for all 52 cards dealt and recreate a shuffled new pack for the game to continue

- Deal cards initially in pairs to the players

- Deal a single card to a specific player on request

- Maintain a count of the value of each hand as it is played

- Apply the 'pontoon' counting rules to each hand on request.

As we are running this as a web service and the HTTP protocol is stateless (i.e. no history of any transaction or communication is available once the client–server interaction has completed), this adds a further complication to the design.

A mechanism is required to identify which clients are playing and the status of each of these clients relative to each other. A possible approach would be to use session variables. In the previous discussion on session variables we saw that using session variables and cookies ensures that any web service can uniquely identify its clients.

The cookie approach would solve the common pack of cards for each unique client access problem, but a session variable would not allow the sharing of information across sessions. This web service design requires that as clients join the game they must join the current game session and not be isolated within there own session. A technique does exist – it modifies the session variable technique to global application variables.

Global application variables

Using global application variables brings with it added complications. As with any global-based system care must be taken to ensure mutual exclusion on any write access, otherwise resource conflicts can occur. With this design we will need to hold global application variables for the lifetime of the service (i.e. from the time the first client connects until the last client disconnects). These global variables will identify the deck of cards being used, the current status of the game and the players' current status.

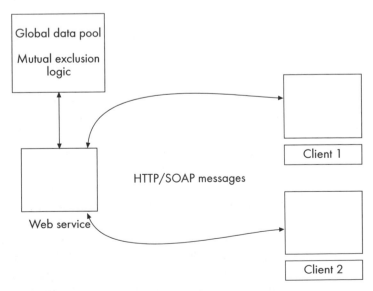

Figure 12.3   *A modified overview*

The design for a multi-player game implies that we can identify the players. This means that within the web service a data source will be used to maintain both users and historical statistics for the users. In a previous chapter the technology of OLE/ODBC linkage from within the .NET Framework to databases has been discussed, with examples linking a database to a stand-alone desktop application.

The techniques used can be extended to link a database to a web service. The design of the database itself is minimal, but the opportunity exists for the database design to be expanded with any amount of additional information related either to the overall game or individual players.

The typical player to password table will have the form:

Player Name	Text
Players Password	Text

The historic information is not being implemented in the demonstration solution but a further table linked to the above can be specified based on a one to many relationship:

■ Any client may play in many games:

Player Name	Text
Date of Game	Date
Number of Hands	Number
Number of Wins	Number

It is left to the reader to extend the database to encompass this table and modify the web service to make use of this additional information. With this final element added to the design we can visualise the overall solution as shown in Figure 12.4.

Figure 12.4 completes our basic definitions of the web service and the data server. It would be possible to commence on the development of the server side aspects of this solution based on these requirements. However, it would be foolish to design and implement the server side aspects without any consideration of the client design. For the purpose of this case study the detail of the actual Graphical User Interface (GUI) of the client is being ignored. The client will be used only for testing functionality; no consideration will be given to the aesthetics or usability of the client interface itself.

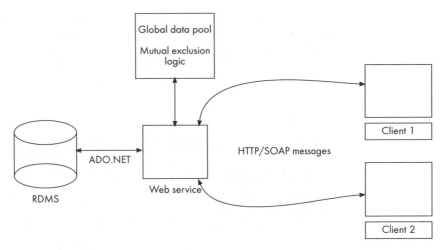

Figure 12.4   *Adding the data source*

'Pontoon' the Windows Client

The client is based on a Windows forms stand-alone application running in the .NET Framework. It will use the various synchronous proxy interfaces created by the WSDL of the web service, thereby having HTTP cxtensions available to programmatically access the exposed functionality of the web service itself. Obviously another extension that the reader could consider is to use the available asynchronous interfaces in a multi-threaded client design; such an enhancement would greatly improve the overall performance of the system. This overall design is solely for explanation of this type of solution and when tested its performance was quite poor.

In a previous chapter when looking at the interoperability of .NET with other technologies, one of the examples developed was a 'Display Playing Card' component created by wrapping an existing Windows dynamic link library. The component, you will recall used the available 'cards.dll' (shipped will all versions of Windows since Windows 3.1.1), which allows playing cards to be displayed using the same face and back designs as those found in the standard Windows games. Multiple instances of this component are the obvious choice for this client to display the playing cards to the user.

In the introduction to the case study, the requirement implied the client would always be a player, never the dealer for the game. The web service must therefore always be the dealer; we need to look at a technique to synchronise the client players to the dealer. The dealer will have to make the decision on who has won.

This requires that the clients gain access to the overall game status, the solution is based on a client–server configuration. HTTP is stateless so we need some form of polling mechanism, allowing the client to poll the web service and wait until all other clients are at the same overall game status.

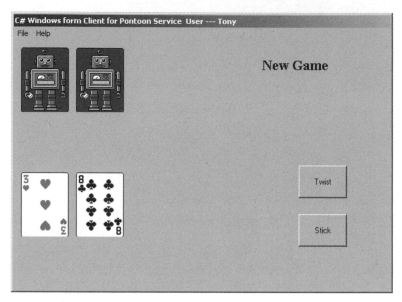

Figure 12.5   The prototype client window

Implementation of the 'Pontoon' web service

The actual implementation code listing for the web service is quite extensive; in order to make this description manageable various aspects of the implementation have been selected for discussion.

First, we can look at the exposed web methods using Internet Explorer to display the descriptions.

1 LogOn – An ADO.NET interfaced method allowing players to gain access to the game

2 Deal – This creates the hand of cards for each player logged on

3 DealToPlayer – Deals a single additional card to a player the equivalent of a twist

4 Stick – Indicates the player wants to hold these cards and await a result

5 GetStatus – The synchronisation method waiting for all players to complete an action

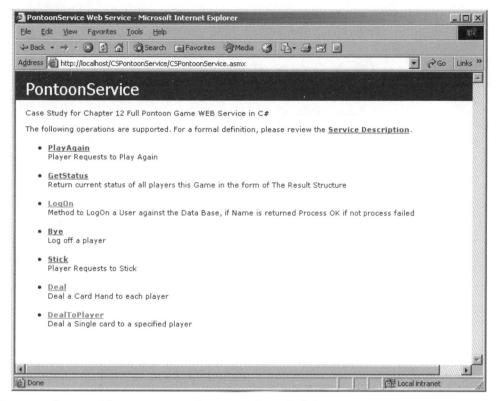

Figure 12.6   *The pontoon service exposed method descriptions*

6   PlayAgain – Another synchronisation point to start a new hand of the game

7   Bye – indicating that a player is leaving the game.

The implementation of the service uses three classes declared as:

```
public class Aplayer
public class TheResult
public class PontoonService : System.Web.Services.WebService
```

The first two classes are used by various web methods to define the return values to the client.

The final class, the web service itself, inherits its functionality from System.Web.Services.WebService, it is this inheritance that makes available the HTTP and SOAP programmatic access to the application.

Looking first at the detail of the implementation of the web service global storage mechanism, the following code extract from the service constructor runs each time a web method is remotely requested:

```
// now check for a current game in progress only need to see if one of these
// is null, if so create defaults as application entries
// if not null load the values back.
if ((GameOfCardsCntrl.GameOfCards)Application["CardDeck"] == null)
{
// yes its null so store the deafults as this is a start up
CardDeck.NewHand (); // This is the first service attachment so deal a Hand
    lock(this)
        {
        Application["CardDeck"] = CardDeck;
        Application["Players"] = Players;
        Application["PlayersStatus"] = PlayersStatus;
        Application["NoPlayers"] = NumberOfPlayers;
        }
}
else
{
    CardDeck = (GameOfCardsCntrl.GameOfCards)Application["CardDeck"];
    Players = (string[])Application["Players"];
    NumberOfPlayers = (int)Application["NoPlayers"];
    PlayersStatus = (int[])Application["PlayersStatus"];
}
```

The code identifies key requirements that need to be considered when any application uses global storage techniques:

■ If there is no initialisation then global objects will be null in C# or nothing in VB.NET

■ As one or more instances of the service may be active the global objects must be protected by mutual exclusion on all write accesses to avoid conflicts

■ When reading a global object to the service variable a psuedo casting of the global object to the local object type is required.

Using a lock on the instance of the service naturally creates mutual exclusion. Mutual exclusion will ensure that until the global write has completed, no other instance of the service can gain write access to the variables and create inconsistency in the stored values.

In Figure 12.7 without mutual exclusion instance 2 of the service can interrupt any write access to a global object from instance 1. The result of such an interruption would be

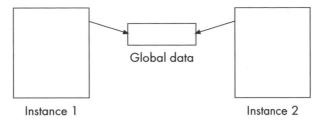

Instance 1   *Instance 2*

Figure 12.7   *A simple mutual exclusion lock on global objects*

indeterminate. No mutual exclusion is required on read access of global objects as no inconsistency can be created by multiple read requests.

Next we consider the information required by the client and look at the two classes created in the web service that satisfy that need. In many instances the client will need to be aware of the status of all the players currently logged into the game.

APlayer class

```
namespace CSPontoonService
{
public class APlayer
    {
        public int PlayerNo;
        public int HandValue;
        public string PlayerInfo;
        public string PlayersHands;
        public string PlayerDisplayHand;
        public int Status;
        public APlayer()
        {
            PlayersHands = " ";
            PlayerDisplayHand ="";
            PlayerNo = -1;
            PlayerInfo = "";
            HandValue = 0;
            Status = 0;
        }
    }
}
```

This class only has a constructor and holds six variables:

■ PlayersHands – is a string human-readable form of the card hand for a player, in fact this variable is not used in our test client, it was put into the class purely to help with the debug process

- PlayerDisplayHand – is again a string but in this case it formats the card hand in a manner suited to the Display Playing card control used by the client

- PlayerNo – is a numeric field identifying the player

- PlayerInfo – this string was again put in for debug purposes initially but proved useful for sending over status strings related to this player

- HandValue – numeric calculation of the hand value, the value is calculated based on the basic rules of pontoon

- Status – identifies the status of this player.

The possible status codes for the game have been defined as:

Code	Meaning
0	No player
1	Logged on and cards dealt
2	Hand improved by at least one twist
3	Hand < 21 player requested a stick
4	Hand > 21 player bust
5	Request by player to play next hand

TheResult class

```
namespace CSPontoonService
{
    /// <summary>
    /// Summary description for Result.
    /// </summary>
    public class TheResult
    {
        public APlayer[] Player;
        public TheResult()
        {
            // default constructor
            int i;
            Player = new APlayer[4];
            for (i=0;i<5;i++)
                Player[i] = new APlayer();
        }
    }
}
```

This is simply an array of APlayer class instances allowing the status of the whole game to be returned by a single web method call; you will notice from the array declaration that the number of players has been limited, this is purely for the demonstration version of the service, if you investigate the original specification of the web service no physical limits were implied. The size of a pack of cards needs consideration if we do not limit the number of players joining the game. Why is this the case?

To illustrate the use of the returned class structure look at an extract of the reply message following a programmatic invoke of the Deal (..) web method.

Figure 12.8 shows that only two XML sets of data are valid, the first player called Computer and the second player called Tony. The XML descriptions for each of the valid players identifies the current hand held along with the information needed for the card display control and the current card hand values.

Notice that for **Tony** the service has applied the highest value rule to an ace making the total 13 rather than three.

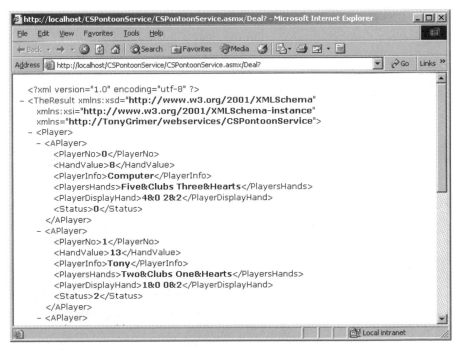

Figure 12.8   *Response to a deal request to the web service*

Once again it must be emphasised that the client will not have to interpret this information. As we saw in the previous chapters, the web service uses a serialisation of XML and proxy marshalling so the client is presented with a programmatic representation of the above data locally without any knowledge of its origin or the XML used to transfer it from the service to the client.

It would be extremely boring to look at and discuss all of the web methods in detail the complete set of source files, in both C# and VB.NET, are available with the support material for this book.

I have chosen to investigate fully the web method invoked if a client wants to stick (i.e. play the cards held and wait until the dealer attempts to get close to 21).

```
[WebMethod (EnableSession=true, Description = "Player Requests to Stick")]
public void Stick(string Name)
{
    SetAPlayersStatus(findplayer(Name),3);
    // Now check if anyone is still playing
    if (StillPlaying(3))
        return;
    else
        {
        // Sort out the dealers hand..
        while(GetLocalPlayersHandValue(findplayername(0))<17)
                CardDeck.DealACard (0); // cards to dealer
            if (GetLocalPlayersHandValue(findplayername(0))>21)
                SetAPlayersStatus(0,4); //Dealer Bust
            else
                SetAPlayersStatus(0,3); // Dealer Sticks
            return; //
        }
}
```

This method is invoked with the client providing the player's name as the parameter:

- The first action is to set the player's status to three, notice the use of some local private methods within the class to translate the name to a numeric value and vice versa

- The next action is to check is to see if all the clients attached to this game are at status three or greater. This is a private method within the class

- If other players are still active the method returns

- The client would then need to set a period activation of some method to call the GetStatus(..) to monitor when all players have finished either by busting or sticking

- The logic of the method is that the last player to stick will run the else clause of this method.

The else clause simply creates a dealer's hand:

- Fixed rule that the dealer must have 17 or more before the dealer can stick. There is no real logic to this approach, it was a simple expedient to get the example finished

- The process then goes on to check the dealer's hand for bust and to set the dealer's status to either busted or stuck

- Any other client's polling software will pick up this dealer status change and can look at the card hands they are holding for a win or lose situation.

The request–response model used in this solution clearly shows this type of game design is not suited to a web service platform. However, it has allowed us to investigate the design and implementation of the web service without the physical constraints and resource requirements normally associated with web service investigation that are generally far beyond the means of a student. I strongly advise that you experiment further with this model; areas to investigate are:

- Other possible synchronisation techniques

- Expand the solution based on the requirements outlined in the introduction.

The fact that this solution technique is slow and reliant on periodic polling by the client is of little consequence, valuable knowledge can be gained by experimentation.

Windows Client   It is possible to complete more than 85% of the web service design, implementation and testing without starting on the actual client. This would not be a very sensible approach and as you can see, I have left debug information, useful for testing, in the web service returned data structures so a suitable client could be developed in parallel.

Initially you could design a client that used the string values rather than the display control to identify player hands, testing the relevant web methods completely before commencing on any graphical design. The basic implementation only requires an interface with the web service and some event handlers to request and recover information from the web service.

So far in the examples we have in the main used one project one solution. In this case, as with the component development, we will need multiple projects in a single solution, this is a very powerful concept. This client development provides an idea opportunity to take another look at using such a configuration in VS.NET.

If we are dealing with a multi-tier or even a simple client–server configuration we must view the whole system as one solution, with the constituent parts considered as separate projects within the solution. In taking this approach we will have the solution within one integrated design environment at the same time.

Once we have this development structure, it is possible to define the relationship between the projects, i.e. any dependence that will include both code and build order.

Assuming you have built the web service as a single element solution then to expand it to this philosophy requires only a minor change. While viewing the web service solution start a new project using the menu option.

In Figure 12.10 you can see that rather than starting a new solution the client is being created within the current solution space.

Figure 12.9 looks at the solution explorer; it now contains two projects, the web service and the Windows Client, I have also added the web reference from the first to the second. No circular referencing problems are created by this configuration because the web service, although directly relating to the first project, only interacts with the second project using SOAP messages carried by HTTP protocol; there is no direct coding interaction.

There is a drawback to this technique of multiple projects in a single solution, when dealing with web services. Modification to the web service may change the exposed methods, and such changes will cause the client application to need to update the web reference. The technique to update the reference is very straightforward but easily forgotten causing some most obscure error messages.

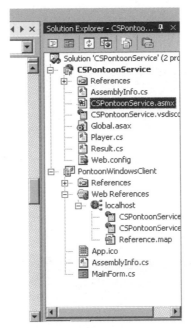

Figure 12.9   *The solution explorer clearly shows both projects and the web service reference in the client project*

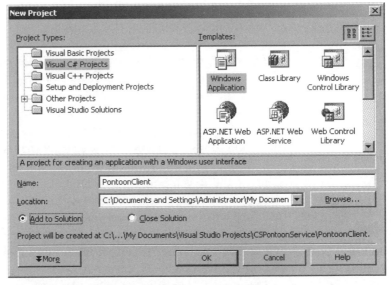

Figure 12.10   *Starting the client project in the same solution space as the pontoon service*

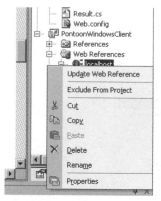

Figure 12.11   *Updating a web reference*

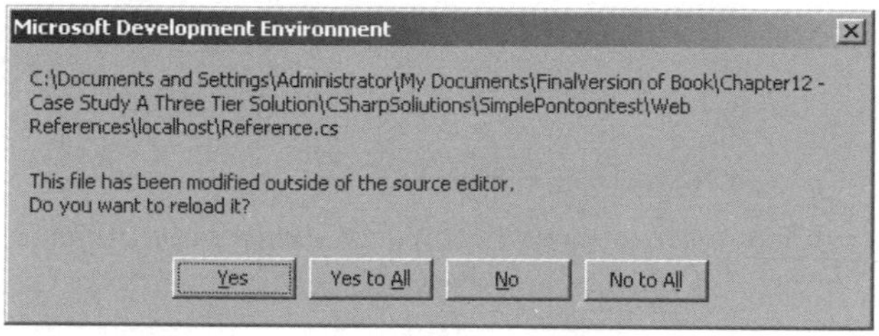

Figure 12.12   *Possible dialogue following an update request*

Figure 12.11 shows how by a right click on the web service reference, in this case localhost, followed by selecting Update Web Reference completes the required synchronisation of the proxies.

The dialogue box shown in Figure 12.12 may appear during an update dependent on the degree of modification you have made to the web service. The dialogue is informing you that the reference file in the client is not a copy of the reference file generated by the web service itself, generally accepting the Yes to All option to resynchronise the files is all that is required.

Before leaving the topic of web service interaction with the client in the development environment, it is worth noting that Visual Studio .NET creates a modification to the project directory structure when you add a web reference.

A new folder is added to the client project directory after a web services reference is added, in fact its contents reflect a local copy of the web service information.

These four files fully describe the web service to the client allowing the client to construct suitable proxy and marshalling code. In more advanced use of web services, far beyond the scope

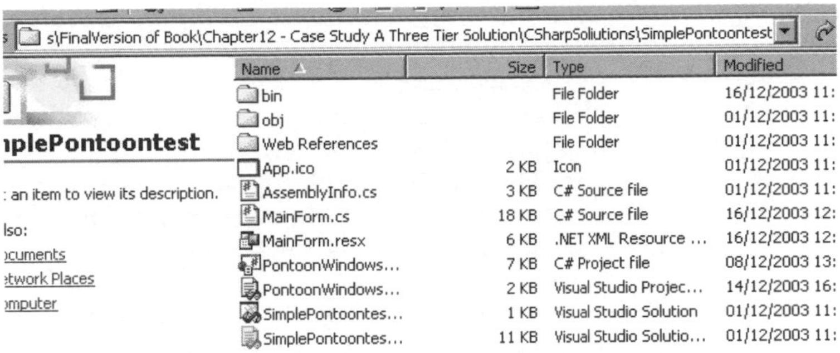

Figure 12.13   A *new folder in the project file for the client – Web References*

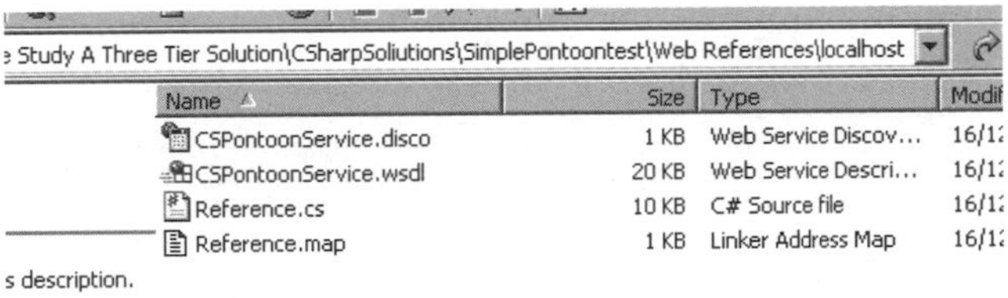

Figure 12.14   *The files in the folder – Web References*

of this book, the contents of these files can become important programmatically to the client side development.

Client development

Client development in this case follows the same guidelines used for a windows application throughout the examples in the book. To create the service within the main class the following declaration is used:

```
private localhost.PontoonService PService;
```

This creates the variable PService which will be used to gain access to the pontoon service. In the form constructor the web service constructor is invoked by:

```
PService = new localhost.PontoonService();
```

You may wish to review at this time the discussion from the previous sections dealing with action in the web service constructor and the allocation and maintenance of the global objects.

The remainder of the code within the application deals with the interaction with the web service, handling the event clicks from the buttons and some simple logic related to the periodic synchronisation of the client.

LogOn(..)

```
private void CmdLog_Click(object sender, System.EventArgs e)
{
    // attempt a Log On..
      localhost.APlayer Reply;
    Reply = new localhost.APlayer ();
    if ((UserName.Text.Length > 0) && (Password.Text.Length >0))
    Reply = PService.LogOn (UserName.Text,Password.Text );
    if (Reply.PlayerInfo == UserName.Text)
    {
    // debug to get confirnation uncomment below.
    //MessageBox.Show("You are Now Logged In","Pontoon LogOn");
        UserName.Visible = false;
        UserLabel.Visible = false;
        Password.Visible = false;
        PassLabel.Visible = false;
        CmdLog.Visible = false;
        user = UserName.Text;
        this.Text = this.Text+ "  User --- " + user;
        SetUpGame();
    }
    else
    MessageBox.Show("You failed to Log In Because .. "+ Reply.PlayerInfo,
    "Pontoon LogOn");
}
```

This event handler shows how to create local variables based on web service classes, then how to invoke a method on the web service and use created local variables to interrogate the result of the web service method.

The next section of code is the periodic timer used to see if all players have either bust or stuck by looking at player zero who from out specification of the web service design is always dealer.

Synchronisation

```
private void ResultT_Elapsed(object sender, System.Timers.ElapsedEventArgs e)
    {
    localhost.TheResult Result;
        Result = new localhost.TheResult ();
        // This is enabled when we stick or bust
        Result = PService.GetStatus ();
        DisplayCards("Deal",Result.Player[0].PlayerDisplayHand );
        if (Result.Player[0].Status ==4)
            // dealer has bust
        {
            ResultT.Enabled = false;
            StatusText.Visible = true;
            if (!Busted)
                StatusText.Text = " Dealer Bust You Win";
            else
                StatusText.Text = " New Hand you are Bust! ";
```

```
        }
        else
            if (Result.Player[0].Status == 3)
                // Dealer has stuck
            {
                ResultT.Enabled = false;
                StatusText.Visible = true;
                if (MyTotal > Result.Player[0].HandValue )
                    StatusText.Text = " You Win";
                else
                    StatusText.Text = " You Lost";
            }
            CmdPlayAgain.Visible = true;
    }
```

Once again this code shows the use of classes defined in the web service being used to instance local variables. Although all of the above discussion has looked at the C# solution the VB.NET solution is identical apart from the normal syntax differences.

Summary

It is hoped that in taking this approach to the design of a tiered solution has enabled you, the reader, to appreciate how the various aspects of the .NET architecture are structured. We have only used some relatively basic concepts to link the various technologies together within the .NET Framework but the final solution is relatively complex although in using such a simple real world problem further experimentation is possible.

I have not built a web service game previously using componentware techniques, but I have tried to create fairly complex components in COM and DCOM.

After completing this basic implementation using the .NET Framework there is no comparison, the prefabricated nature of the .NET architecture allows a staged development technique to be used effectively, it also had the advantage that it was accomplished without too many late nights and endless cups of coffee which typified the COM, DCOM route. The source files used for all aspects of the solution are available in both C# and VB.NET. I prefer C# but this is probably because when I was developing commercial software, it was mainly using C/C++ and I find C# a more natural environment. The VB.NET solution was no more difficult. VB.NET has the features required and a similar interface to the .NET Framework as C#.

Review questions

1 Could the display component used on the client be transferred and become part of the web service?

2 In the case study we did not actually use the WSDL of the web service, is this true and if not where was it used?

3 How did this overall application use the SOAP protocol?

4 Are web methods actually shared when a second client connects?

5 Could another client access the session object used to track the state of a session created by another client.

6 There are a great number of modifications and enhancements that you could attempt based on the extensions outlined for the game in the earlier part of the chapter. Such extensions will require changes to both the web service and to the associated client, modify the implementation and review how these changes affect performance.

7 The solution presented uses the data server to hold the basic player statistics; another technique would be to use either a local or central XML file. Try to develop an XML streaming technique on the service to store game statistics.

8 Cookies could offer another mechanism for tracking the client connections, using the discussion in the previous chapters on cookies and some further research, can you find a better way of monitoring users joining and leaving the game?

9 An alternative technology to a pure .NET web service would be to look at .NET remoting. This is a more advanced topic that we have not covered in this book but could provide a useful tool to investigatate if you want to look at server-side games.

Appendix A

The purpose of these brief notes is to help you. They should guide you through your first .NET project if you are unfamiliar with Visual Studio.NET. Although the screen shots are from VS.NET 2002, the operation of later versions is very similar.

Windows standard application

This example describes the creation of a C# project building for a simple Windows application, the process is identical for VB.NET. In this case we are selecting from the left pane in Figure A.1 Visual C# Projects; to create a VB.NET version select a Visual Basic Project instead.

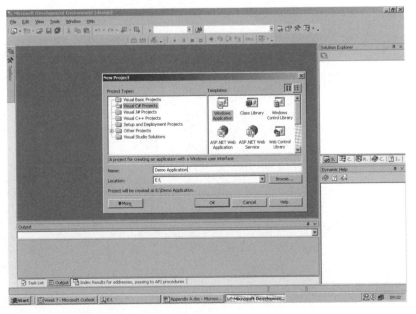

Figure A.1   *Setting up the project*

Start the Visual Studio .NET application by selecting Menu>
File>New. Select the Visual C# Projects option in the left pane
and select the Windows Application in the right pane as
illustrated in Figure A.1. Using the two text boxes select a name
and a location for the project files:

■ In this case the project is called Demo Application

■ The Location has been set to E:\.

This will result in the files for this project being located at
E:\Demo Application. When you click on OK the screen shown in
Figure A.2 will be displayed.

This simple application will mimic the initial example in
Chapter 5, it will have a text box and a button only.

From the toolbar drag a text box and a button onto the form.
Once you have positioned them on the form you should have the
screen illustrated in Figure A.3. The name and properties of these
controls can now be set up in the properties pane.

■ For the Form:
    ❏ Text – Demo Application.

■ For the Text Box:
    ❏ Name – Output
    ❏ Text – Clear the default text.

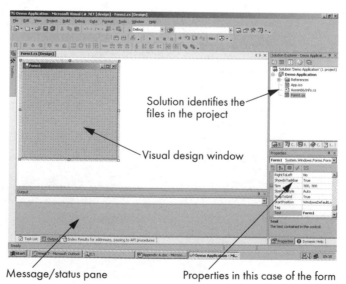

Message/status pane   Properties in this case of the form

Figure A.2   *The new project screen*

■ For the Button:
  ❏ Name – CmdOK
  ❏ Text – OK.

The effect of these changes will be shown in the designer window as in Figure A.4.

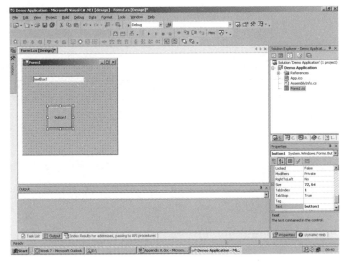

Figure A.3   *The project with a text box and button*

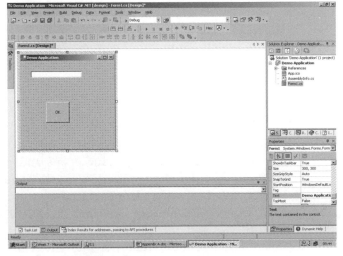

Figure A.4   *The form with properties changed*

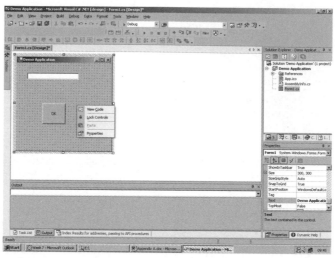

Figure A.5   Menu shown after right-click on form

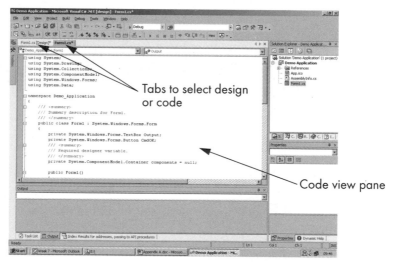

Figure A.6   The code file pane

To access the code file for this form right click on the form, when the menu appears select View Code, as shown in Figures A.5 and A.6. The code file pane opens and we have the auto-generated code for this application, notice it is using an XML tree view so we can if we wish open and close sections of the code.

To insert code you can now simply select the correct location in the file and type in your code. In our example the functionality will be when the user clicks the button, the Text Box will display Welcome to VS.NET.

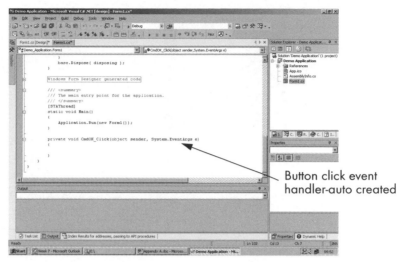

Figure A.7   *Adding the click event code*

To accomplish this:

■ Select design Tab:

■ Double click on the button on the form.

This will cause the code view to be shown again but in this case a new event handler has been created for the button click event. This is very similar to the legacy Visual Basic (VB6) design environment; VS.NET is monitoring the event handler code to resource tracking for you (i.e. the designer does not have to identify this code snippet to the button click event, the VS.NET design mode manages these resources). In this event handler we type the following line of code:

```
private void CmdOK_Click(object sender, System.EventArgs e)
    {
        Output.Text = " Welcome To VS.Net";
    }
```

This is the C# code required to change the text attribute of the Text Box called Output programmatically when this event handler executes. To build the project we can either use Menu > Build > Build Solution or the build icon on the build toolbar.

The result of the build is reported in the message/status pane. If you do get an error; clicking on the error message will take you to the line that has the error you may also notice that the VS.NET

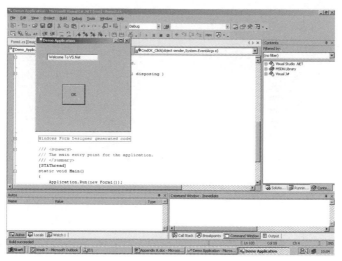

Figure A.8   Running the application

environment is constantly checking syntax etc. if you mistype the result pane will have error messages even before you attempt to build the solution.

To run the project we can either use Menu > Debug > Start its short-cut function key F5 or the run icon on the debug tool bar.

Running the application and clicking on the button will cause the screen illustrated in Figure A.8.

Obviously the VS.NET environment has far more functionality than this; however, to learn about its functionality you need to be able to get a project started and this simple example has done just that.

Web or web service application

The scenario for applications that are destined to run on a web server is somewhat different to the basic application as shown above.

The major problem is that the development code for such applications will not be stored on a local folder, the VS.NET system stores these development files on the remote web server itself.

Option 1   The first option is to install a copy of the Microsoft Internet Information Server (IIS) on your development machine. If you follow this route you will need to configure the IIS and ensure that you have the server extensions installed. The IIS will then become your 'localhost', this will mean that you will now be able to access web-based systems by using an address of the form:

http://localhost/xxxx.xxx

in a local browser. The only disadvantage is that IIS will open port 80 by default, and could be visible if your machine is connecting externally to the Internet creating a potential security problem if incorrectly configured.

To use IIS you also need to ensure that the VS.NET is correctly configured to allow remote debug server side. The instructions related to this process are available both on the VS.NET distribution disk one and as recommendations for remote debugging in the VS.NET help system.

Option 2

As an alternative you can use the WEB Matrix environment also developed by Microsoft. This is not as powerful an environment as VS.NET and certainly does not offer the same amount of debug flexibility.

It is free to download from www.asp.net and offers a stable web application or web service development platform. I have agreed with Microsoft that I will make available on the support site for this book a link to the free download of WEB Matrix.

Again you select your language and type of project and specify the location as shown in Figure A.10.

As you start the project the options are to select a graphical design view, HTML view or a code view:

- In this case the project is called web Demo Application

- The location has been set to E:\

- The view is set to graphical design

- Then drag and drop a button and a text box onto the form from the tool bar

- Add the following code:

```
void CmdButton_Click(object sender, EventArgs e)
{
 Output.Text = "Hello Windows";
}
```

- Run the application.

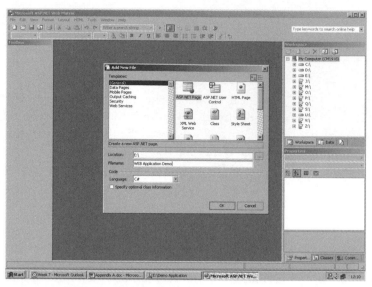

Figure A.9   *Starting a WEB matrix project*

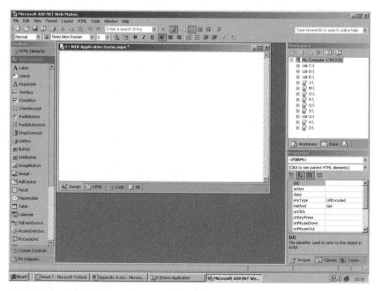

Figure A.10   *WEB Matrix basic project view*

The result is shown in Figure A.11 and simply informs you that the special WEB Matrix, web server is being started.

WEB Matrix offers far more than this in terms of functionality but once again the purpose of this short walk was to show that there is an alternative to VS.NET for web applications or web service development.

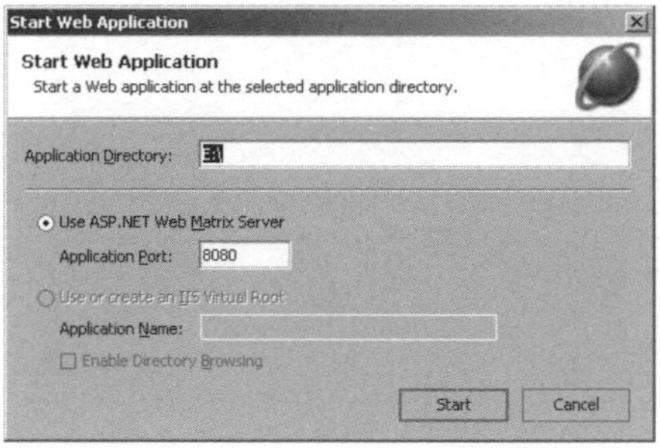

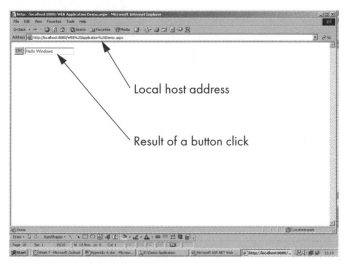

Figure A.11   *WEB Matrix 'local host' server start*

Figure A.12   *The application running in IE*

B

Appendix B

Web resources

The following web resources should assist you to further enhance your knowledge of .NET. The list represents only a small portion of the available sites, using any one as a starting point will allow you to investigate further, generally about the .NET architecture and framework or more specifically about one of its technologies.

■ www.microsoft.com – This is the main portal into Microsoft's Web site. It contains extensive resources on all topics related to the .NET architecture.

■ http://www.worldofdotnet.net – A good general site on .NET.

■ www.msdn.microft.com/downloads/samles/Internet/xml – One of specific portals into Microsoft developers network specifically for XML offering sample code in C++, VB.NET and C# for XML validation etc.

■ www.asp.net – Microsoft's specific overview site for ASP.NET, includes various quite large samples and a link to the download area for the WEB Matrix development system discussed in Appendix A.

■ www.w3.org – The World Wide Web Consortium (W3C) is the organisation that oversees the development of technologies on the Internet and World Wide Web. There are many interesting links from this site to technology discussions and FAQs (frequently asked questions) regarding technologies.

■ www.w3.org/xml – The XML pages look at the latest developments in XML.

- www.w3.org/TR – This contains technical reports and links to the latest working drafts.

- www.cyber-matrix.com – Links to various programming language tutorials, books, tips and hints.

- http://www.c-sharpcorner.com – A good site for C# information, there are also sections on VB.NET and ASP.NET.

- www.gotdotnet.com/team/clr/about_clr.aspx – An overview on the Common Language Specification.

- www.csharphelp.com/archives3/archive525.html – An overview of the CTS.

- www.c2.com/cgi/wiki?CommonLanguageInfrastructure – A set of links looking at the definitions for the CLI.

- wwww.msdn.microsoft.com/library/default.asp?url=/library/en-us/dndotnet/html/win32map.asp – A unique set of lists that map the .NET class library to the actual WIN32 API structure.

- msdn.microsoft.com/library/default.asp?url=/library/en-us/cpgenref/html/cpconrelationshiptocommontypesystemcommonlanguagespecification.asp – The Microsoft view of the CTS to CLR relationship.

- www.samgentile.com/cts.htm – A third party view of the relationship between the CTS and CLR.

- www.xml.org – This is a good source of reference for DTD, schemas and namespaces.

- www.xml.com – Provides links to XML web resources.

- www.aspfree.com – Free demos and source files for ASP.NET.

- www.aspnetfaq.com – FAQ site for all matters related to ASP.NET.

Index

Index